Microsoft Dynamics AX 2012 R3 Reporting Cookbook

Over 90 recipes to help you resolve your new SSRS Reporting woes in Dynamics AX 2012 R3

Deepak Agarwal

Chhavi Aggarwal

Kamalakannan Elangovan

[PACKT] enterprise

PUBLISHING

professional expertise distilled

BIRMINGHAM - MUMBAI

Microsoft Dynamics AX 2012 R3 Reporting Cookbook

First published: September 2013

Second edition: March 2015

Production reference: 1240315

Published by Packt Publishing Ltd.
Livery Place
35 Livery Street
Birmingham B3 2PB, UK.

ISBN 978-1-78439-538-4

www.packtpub.com

Credits

Authors

Deepak Agarwal

Chhavi Aggarwal

Kamalakannan Elangovan

Reviewers

Parag Gunwant Chapre

Muhammad Anas Khan

Henrik Marx Larsen

Commissioning Editor

Usha Iyer

Acquisition Editor

Neha Nagwekar

Content Development Editor

Natasha DSouza

Technical Editor

Ankur Ghiye

Copy Editors

Puja Lalwani

Adithi Shetty

Alpha Singh

Trishla Singh

Project Coordinator

Rashi Khivansara

Proofreaders

Simran Bhogal

Maria Gould

Bernadette Watkins

Indexer

Monica Ajmera Mehta

Production Coordinator

Komal Ramchandani

Cover Work

Komal Ramchandani

About the Authors

Deepak Agarwal (Microsoft MVP) is a Microsoft Certified Professional and has been working professionally on Dynamics AX since 2011. He has worked with different versions of Axapta, such as AX 2009, AX 2012, R2, and R3. He has had a wide range of development, consulting, and leading roles, while always maintaining a significant role as a business application developer. Though his strengths are rooted in X++ development, he is a highly regarded developer and has knowledge of technical aspects of Dynamics AX development and customization. He has also worked on base product development with the Microsoft team.

He was awarded the Most Valuable Professional (MVP) on Dynamics AX in 2013 and 2014 by Microsoft.

He has also contributed to the following books:

- *Microsoft Dynamics AX 2012 Reporting Cookbook*
- *Microsoft Dynamics AX 2012 Programming*
- *Microsoft System Centre Configuration Manager*

Deepak shares his experience with Dynamics AX on his blog at `http://theaxapta.blogspot.in/`.

Sincere thanks to my friend, Himashu, for his motivation and support.

I would also like to thank Mr. Kamalakannan Elangovan, the author of *Microsoft Dynamics AX 2012 Reporting Cookbook, Packt Publishing*, the earlier version of this book. Thanks to the Packt Publishing team for this great opportunity. It's a privilege to work with you all.

Also, thanks to all the reviewers who invested their time and provided useful feedback, which helped us a lot to make this book more effective and useful.

Chhavi Aggarwal started working on Dynamics AX in 2012. She is a Microsoft Certified Professional and has worked on both the 2009 and 2012 versions of Dynamics AX. She is an expert in SSRS reports and has also done a lot of customization and development in Dynamics AX R2/R3 through X++. She has a very deep knowledge of the technical aspects related to Dynamics AX R2/R3, as well as sound technical and logical skills in customization and development. She has also worked with the Microsoft team for standard base development.

I am grateful to my loving parents for motivating and supporting me through thick and thin. Sincere thanks to Mr. Puneet Agarwal (elder brother) and Mrs. Ankita Agarwal (sister-in-law), in addition to my dearly youngest brother Ankit Aggarwal for being the strongest pillars in my most difficult times.

I offer my immense reverence to the honorable Mr. Kamalakannan Elangovan, the author of the previous version of *Microsoft Dynamics AX 2012 Reporting Cookbook*, who has always been a great source of inspiration. Also, a special thanks to the Packt Publishing team, who always stood beside us throughout this entire journey.

I am overwhelmed by the invaluable role played by the reviewers for their helpful comments and suggestions.

Kamalakannan Elangovan has over 8 years of development experience in Dynamics AX. He shares a passion for product development and has pioneered multiple ISV solutions on Dynamics AX. In the past, he has worked with Innovites to create the first multidimensional ISV solution for cable industries called "InnoVites for cable". Building the solution from scratch, he gained great insights into building, selling, and promoting a product among customers and partners in the Microsoft Ecosystem. You can find out more about him at `http://about.me/casperkamal`

Kamal is enthusiastic about sharing his learnings with the community, which led him to create one of the first few blogs for AX in 2006. It is currently available at `http://kamalblogs.wordpress.com`. He is active on Twitter and is very well known in the community by his pseudonym, "Casperkamal".

First of all, I would like to thank my wife, Sangeetha, and my little daughter, Anu, for their considerable support during the long hours I put into this book. I also want to apologize for the time I stole from them to invest in this book.

Thanks to Dhangar Naveen who spent a considerable number of hours working along with me in making the examples involved in each recipe.

Special thanks to the wonderful team at Packt Publishing who have patiently guided and supported me in making this book a reality.

Also, a big thanks to the readers of my blog, my fellow bloggers, and the Dynamics AX community, who have directly and indirectly inspired me to create this book.

About the Reviewers

Parag Gunwant Chapre is currently working with Tieto Software Technologies Limited as a senior technical consultant. He completed his BE in CSE from Nagpur University in the year 2008 with first a division. He has over 6 years of experience in MS Dynamics AX 2009/2012 and ASP.NET/C#.NET.

Parag has worked with top MS Dynamics AX companies, such as Systems Advisers Group (SAG Global), Tectura Corporation at Noida, and Tata Consultancy Services in Pune. He has worked on different versions of Axapta, such as AX 2009, AX 2012 R2, and R3.

His work experience includes Windows and web applications, SSRS development, Microsoft Dynamics AX 2009/2012, Application Integration Framework (AIF), Microsoft Dynamics Connector, and MS Dynamics CRM.

He completed his certification in Windows and web application (.NET), Installation and Configuration, Introduction development, and MorphX Solution Development in MS Dynamics AX 2009/2012.

He has received much appreciation from various clients for developing SSRS reports and MS dynamics AX Integration with MS Dynamics CRM.

I would like to thank my parents and sister for their continuous support, guidance, and encouragement.

Special thanks to Rashi and the Packt Publishing team, who provided me with a chance to review this book.

Muhammad Anas Khan is a Microsoft Certified Professional, working as a technical consultant for Microsoft Dynamics AX at MazikGlobal, where he is responsible for delivering consultancy for Dynamics AX implementation projects. His technical expertise includes Application Integration Framework (AIF), forms, SSRS and SSAS reporting, Batch Framework, Role-based Security and custom workflow development.

He has more than 6 years of experience in the software industry, where he held various engineering positions to develop global enterprise systems. His career vision is to frame the right problems and find efficient solutions that deliver value to customers, partners, and shareholders. He has a master's degree in computer science from IBA University and lives with his family in Karachi.

You can find him on LinkedIn at https://www.linkedin.com/in/muhammadanaskhan, and read his Dynamics AX blog at http://dynamicsaxinsight.wordpress.com/.

> I would like to thank my family for their continuous support especially my brother, Sohaib Khan, for guiding me well throughout my career.
>
> Special thanks to Rashi and the whole Packt Publishing team for giving me the opportunity to review this book.

Henrik Marx Larsen has been implementing ERP across a number of industries, including wholesales, manufacturing, and financial services since 1994. In 1998, He started working with Microsoft Dynamics AX (formerly known as Damgaard Axapta) as a developer and helped deliver many projects across Europe. In recent years, Henrik Marx Larsen has worked as a Solution Architect on a number of enterprise projects and today is heading international jewelry giant PANDORA's global implementation of Microsoft Dynamics AX. He holds a BSc (Hons) in Computer Science from De Montfort University.

www.PacktPub.com

Support files, eBooks, discount offers, and more

For support files and downloads related to your book, please visit www.PacktPub.com.

Did you know that Packt offers eBook versions of every book published, with PDF and ePub files available? You can upgrade to the eBook version at www.PacktPub.com and as a print book customer, you are entitled to a discount on the eBook copy. Get in touch with us at service@packtpub.com for more details.

At www.PacktPub.com, you can also read a collection of free technical articles, sign up for a range of free newsletters and receive exclusive discounts and offers on Packt books and eBooks.

https://www2.packtpub.com/books/subscription/packtlib

Do you need instant solutions to your IT questions? PacktLib is Packt's online digital book library. Here, you can search, access, and read Packt's entire library of books.

Why subscribe?

- ▸ Fully searchable across every book published by Packt
- ▸ Copy and paste, print, and bookmark content
- ▸ On demand and accessible via a web browser

Free access for Packt account holders

If you have an account with Packt at www.PacktPub.com, you can use this to access PacktLib today and view 9 entirely free books. Simply use your login credentials for immediate access.

Instant updates on new Packt books

Get notified! Find out when new books are published by following @PacktEnterprise on Twitter or the *Packt Enterprise* Facebook page.

I would like to dedicate this book to my parents, who never let me down in the toughest times of my life, and to my nephew Shivansh Agarwal.

–Deepak Agarwal

This book is dedicated to Dick De Jong who selflessly mentored and trained me in the art of software development.

–Kamalakannan

Table of Contents

Preface

Reporting provides consolidated, factual, and up-to date information about any area of business in an organization. This will help the organization member to take the right decision for their business. It acts as a treasure trove of reliable information for long-term planning and decision making.

In Microsoft Dynamics R2, AX provides the tool to build the SSRS reports but in Microsoft Dynamics R3, the tool to build the SSRS reports in a more simple and efficient way. This book will give over 90 more recipes for beginners to understand the SSRS reports in Microsoft Dynamics AX R3 faster and in a simplified manner.

What this book covers

Chapter 1, *Understanding and Creating Simple SSRS Reports*, helps you to walk through the basis of SSRS reports and create a simple report using queries. This chapter will also help you understand the basic characteristics of reports.

Chapter 2, *Enhancing Your Report – Visualization and Interaction*, covers how to enhance the visualization and interaction of reports through parameters, creating data regions and charts, and formatting the reports.

Chapter 3, *A Report Programming Model*, helps you build the SSRS reports programmatically inside Dynamics AX and add the validations programmatically.

Chapter 4, *Report Programming Model – RDP*, helps you to develop the advanced reports using the data provider framework. In this chapter, we will create a report using RDP classes.

Chapter 5, *Integrating External Datasources*, covers how the SSRS reports can be extended to include other data sources or through the integration framework.

Chapter 6, *Beyond Tabular Reports*, helps you understand the other formats of reports such as using matrices and charts. This book also covers the interesting components of reports such as gauges, rectangles, and lists.

Chapter 7, Upgrading and Analyzing Reports, discusses the approaches for moving the MorphX-based reports into SSRS reports and also covers the patterns of reports.

Chapter 8, Troubleshooting and Other Advanced Recipes, dives into the performance and troubleshooting of SSRS reports. This will also introduce the log viewer through which you can analyze the report usage and its log.

Chapter 9, Developing Reports with Complex Databases, discusses developing the SSRS reports that have complex data and how to drive that data into reports using maps, views, and queries.

Chapter 10, Unit Test Class and Best Practices Used for Reports, helps you create the unit test classes for a report, which will help you test the business logic being written to develop reports. It will also tell you best practices to be followed when developing the reports.

What you need for this book

To practice the content in this book, you need the following software:

- Microsoft Dynamics AX 2012 R3
- SQL Server Reporting Services
- SQL Server Analysis Services
- Microsoft Visual Studio 2010
- Microsoft Visual Studio 2013 in case of CU8

Alternatively, you can use the Virtual Image available for Microsoft Dynamics AX 2012 R3 through the Microsoft Learning download center.

Who this book is for

This book is aimed at IT administrators looking to develop their own reports for their internal demands and for X++ developers who want to deepen their understanding of SSRS reports.

This book requires some basic knowledge of the SQL server reporting system, Microsoft Dynamics AX 2012, X++, and MorphX. Some examples are based on C#.NET; however, it is not a must to read this book.

Sections

In this book, you will find several headings that appear frequently (Getting ready, How to do it, How it works, There's more, and See also).

To give clear instructions on how to complete a recipe, we use these sections as follows:

Getting ready

This section tells you what to expect in the recipe, and describes how to set up any software or preliminary settings required for the recipe.

How to do it...

This section contains the steps required to follow the recipe.

How it works...

This section usually consists of a detailed explanation of what happened in the previous section.

There's more...

This section consists of additional information about the recipe in order to make the reader more knowledgeable about the recipe.

See also

This section provides helpful links to other useful information for the recipe.

Conventions

In this book, you will find a number of text styles that distinguish between different kinds of information. Here are some examples of these styles and an explanation of their meaning.

Code words in text, database table names, folder names, filenames, file extensions, pathnames, dummy URLs, user input, and Twitter handles are shown as follows: "Add a new report to this project and name it PKTWarehouseMobileDeviceDetails."

A block of code is set as follows:

```
=drillVoucher(!Parameters.AX_ReportContext.Value,
              !Fields.ItemTrans.VoucherNum.value,
              !Fields.ItemTrans.TrandDate.value,
              !Parameters.AX_CompanyName.Value);
```

Any command-line input or output is written as follows:

```
$>rs.exe -i C:\timeout.rss -s
  http://[SSSRSServerName]:80/Reports -v timeout="72000" -l 0
```

New terms and **important words** are shown in bold. Words that you see on the screen, for example, in menus or dialog boxes, appear in the text like this: "Right-click on the **Dataset** node and select the **New Dataset** option."

Warnings or important notes appear in a box like this.

Tips and tricks appear like this.

Reader feedback

Feedback from our readers is always welcome. Let us know what you think about this book—what you liked or disliked. Reader feedback is important for us as it helps us develop titles that you will really get the most out of.

To send us general feedback, simply e-mail feedback@packtpub.com, and mention the book's title in the subject of your message.

If there is a topic that you have expertise in and you are interested in either writing or contributing to a book, see our author guide at www.packtpub.com/authors.

Customer support

Now that you are the proud owner of a Packt book, we have a number of things to help you to get the most from your purchase.

Errata

Although we have taken every care to ensure the accuracy of our content, mistakes do happen. If you find a mistake in one of our books—maybe a mistake in the text or the code—we would be grateful if you could report this to us. By doing so, you can save other readers from frustration and help us improve subsequent versions of this book. If you find any errata, please report them by visiting http://www.packtpub.com/submit-errata, selecting your book, clicking on the **Errata Submission Form** link, and entering the details of your errata. Once your errata are verified, your submission will be accepted and the errata will be uploaded to our website or added to any list of existing errata under the Errata section of that title.

To view the previously submitted errata, go to https://www.packtpub.com/books/content/support and enter the name of the book in the search field. The required information will appear under the **Errata** section.

Piracy

Piracy of copyrighted material on the Internet is an ongoing problem across all media. At Packt, we take the protection of our copyright and licenses very seriously. If you come across any illegal copies of our works in any form on the Internet, please provide us with the location address or website name immediately so that we can pursue a remedy.

Please contact us at `copyright@packtpub.com` with a link to the suspected pirated material.

We appreciate your help in protecting our authors and our ability to bring you valuable content.

Questions

If you have a problem with any aspect of this book, you can contact us at `questions@packtpub.com`, and we will do our best to address the problem.

1

Understanding and Creating Simple SSRS Reports

This chapter will cover the following topics:

- ▶ Using a query as a data source in a report
- ▶ Creating auto designs from datasets
- ▶ Grouping in reports
- ▶ Adding ranges to the report
- ▶ Deploying a report
- ▶ Creating a menu item for a report
- ▶ Creating a report using a query in Warehouse Management

Introduction

Reports are a basic necessity for any business process, as they aid in making critical decisions by analyzing all the data together in a customized manner. Reports can be fetched in many types, such as ad-hoc, analytical, transactional, general statements, and many more by using images, pie charts, and many other graphical representations. These reports help the user to undertake required actions. Microsoft SQL Reporting Services (SSRS) is the basic primary reporting tool of Dynamics AX 2012 R2 and R3.

This chapter will help you to understand the development of SSRS reports in AX 2012 R3 by developing and designing reports using simple steps. These steps have further been detailed into simpler and smaller recipes. In this chapter, you will design a report using queries with simple formatting, and then deploy the report to the reporting server to make it available for the user. This is made easily accessible inside the rich client.

Reporting overview

Microsoft SQL Server Reporting Services (SSRS) is the most important feature of Dynamics AX 2012 R2 and R3 reporting. It is the best way to generate analytical, high user scale, transactional, and cost-effective reports. SSRS reports offer ease of customization of reports so that you can get what you want to see. SSRS provides a complete reporting platform that enables the development, design, deployment, and delivery of interactive reports. SSRS reports use Visual Studio (VS) to design and customize reports. They have extensive reporting capabilities and can easily be exported to Excel, Word, and PDF formats.

Dynamics AX 2012 has extensive reporting capabilities like Excel, Word, Power Pivot, Management Reporter, and most importantly, SSRS reports. While there are many methodologies to generate reports, SSRS remains the prominent way to generate analytical and transactional reports. SSRS reports were first seen integrated in AX 2009, and today, they have replaced the legacy reporting system in AX 2012.

SSRS reports can be developed using classes and queries. In this chapter, we will discuss query-based reports. Reports using classes will be discussed in later chapters.

In query-based reports, a query is used as the data source to fetch the data from Dynamics AX 2012 R3. We add the grouping and ranges in the query to filter the data. We use the **auto design** reporting feature to create a report, which is then deployed to the reporting server. After deploying the report, a menu item is attached to the report in Dynamics AX R3 so that the user can display the report from AX R3.

Through the recipes in this chapter, we will build a vendor master report. This report will list all the vendors under each vendor group. It will use the query data source to fetch data from Dynamics AX and subsequently create an auto design-based report. So that this report can be accessed from a rich client, it will then be deployed to the reporting servicer and attached to a menu item in AX.

Here are some important links to get started with this chapter:

> ▸ Install Reporting Services extensions from `https://technet.microsoft.com/en-us/library/dd362088.aspx`.
>
> ▸ Install Visual Studio Tools from `https://technet.microsoft.com/en-us/library/dd309576.aspx`.

▸ Connect Microsoft Dynamics AX to the new Reporting Services instance by visiting `https://technet.microsoft.com/en-us/library/hh389773.aspx`.

 Before you install the Reporting Services extensions see `https://technet.microsoft.com/en-us/library/ee355041.aspx`.

Using a query as a data source in a report

Queries offer the simplest and easiest way to retrieve data for SSRS reports in Dynamics AX R3. They are very advantageous as they are reusable, and the same query can be used as the data source of another SSRS report in Dynamics AX R3. They are also very easy to design.

We can create queries in two ways: either by using the query class, or under the **Queries** node in **Application Object Tree** (**AOT**). In this recipe, we will create a query under the **Queries** node in AOT and use it as a data source in SSRS reports. Later on, we will guide you on how to add the query as a data source through Visual Studio.

Getting ready

To work through this recipe, you will require AX 2012 R2 or AX 2012 R3 rich clients with developer permission.

How to do it...

Create a new query named `PKTVendorDetails` under the **Queries** node in AOT, and add some fields in the query. Create a new SSRS report in Visual Studio 2010 and add the **PKTVendorDetails** query into that report as a data source.

1. Open the AX Development Workspace (*Ctrl + D*).
2. Go to **AOT** | **Queries** and add a new query.
3. Rename the query to `PKTVendorDetails`.
4. Go to query's data source node and add the new data source.
5. Rename the data source to `VendTable` and set property table to `VendTable`.
6. There are two steps to select fields from `VendTable`. You can use any of these:

    ❑ Go to the **Fields** node under the **VendTable** data source and set **Dynamic Property** to `Yes`. This will automatically add all the fields in the **VendTable** to the query.

❏ Drag and drop the required field directly from the table. Drag **VendGroup**, **AccountNum**, **InvoiceAccount**, and **Blocked** from **VendTable** as shown in the following screenshot. This is the best way to optimize the query and, consequently, reduce the fetch time, so we will go for this option in our recipes.

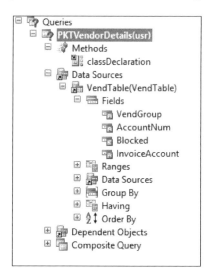

7. Save the query.

8. Now open Visual Studio.

9. Navigate to **File** | **New** | **Project**.

10. In the new project dialog, select **Microsoft Dynamics AX**, and then **Report Model**.

11. Set the name as `PKTVendorDetailsReport`.

12. Now, right-click on project in **Solution Explorer** and **Add** a new **Report** to the **PKTVendDetailReport** project as shown in the following screenshot:

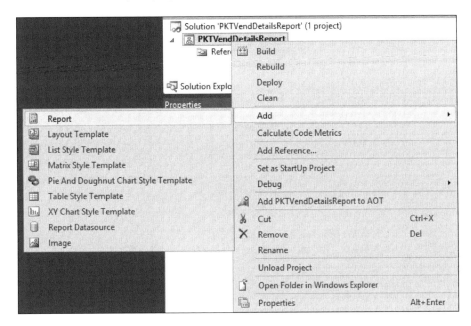

13. Rename the report as `PKTVendorDetailsReport`.

14. Now open the report by double-clicking on it in **Solution Explorer**.

15. Right-click on the **Dataset** node and select the **New Dataset** option.

16. Rename the dataset as `VendorMaster`.

17. Now, right-click on the **VendorMaster** dataset and select **Properties**.

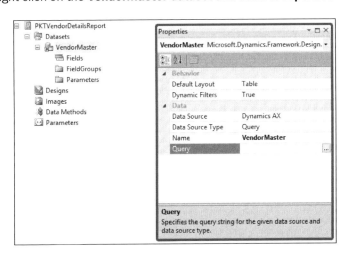

18. Click on the ellipsis (...) button 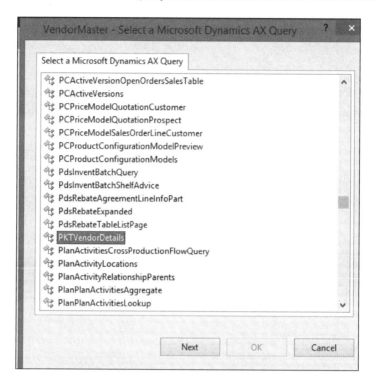 in **Query**.

19. Select the **PKTVendorDetail** query from the list and click on the **Next** button.

20. Select **All Fields** since we dropped all the unwanted fields during the creation of the query. From the **All Display Methods** node, select **Name**. Click on the **OK** button.

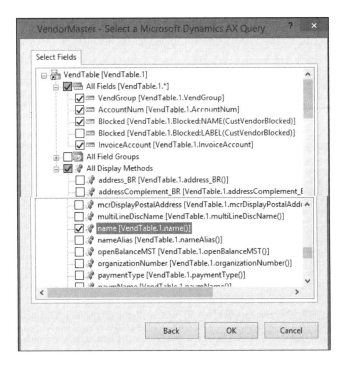

This will generate the fields list for the dataset. This completes the addition of a dataset to a report.

How it works...

In this receipe we have used queries as a datasource in SSRS report in Dynamics AX R3 as queries are reusable and can help to add the ranges in a report.

Connecting VS to AX

When creating a new report project in Visual Studio, if there is no option such as Microsoft Dynamics AX, then ensure that you have your reporting extensions installed. When you have multiple instances of Dynamics AX installed, Visual Studio identifies the instance to connect to from the client configuration. The active client configuration is used to establish the connection. The layer in which the report must be created is also fetched from the client configuration.

Retrieving metadata and data

With AX 2012, **Windows Communication Foundation** (**WCF**) based system services have been introduced. This includes the metadata service, query service, and user session service. The SSRS reporting extension uses the query and metadata services. The metadata service helps the report designer in Visual Studio to retrieve the metadata information of Queries, Tables, and **Extended Data Types** (**EDT**). The query service is used to fetch the data.

Verify the query

In the case of a complex query, a better approach would be validating the query before it is included in the report. Write a job in Dynamics AX that will use the query to retrieve the data and print the values to the infolog. This will help in identifying the problem when there is an issue with the report.

No joins

The report supports multiple datasets, but as in AX forms these datasets cannot be joined and they remain independent.

Creating auto designs from datasets

There are two ways to design an SSRS report in Visual Studio:

- ▶ **Precision design**: This is for advanced structured design
- ▶ **Auto design**: This is for general tabular design

In this recipe, we will create a simple auto design report by using the dataset added in the previous recipe, which will fetch the data and show it in the report.

In auto design, there are layouts that are already built in, and we can choose one in which we want to show the data, based on our preferences.

Getting ready

To develop reports in Dynamics AX 2012 R3, you need Visual Studio, through which you can design, develop, and deploy the reports. SQL Reporting Services must be properly installed and configured. You must also have access to the reporting manager to manage and see the reports present in AX 2012 R3.

How to do it...

In this recipe, we will add an auto design under the **Design** node of the report. We will then assign its layout properties to **ReportLayoutStyleTemplate** and print the report.

There are some standard report templates in AX. You can choose any of them for pre-designed layouts.

1. Right-click on the **Designs** node, select **Add**, and then select **Auto Design**. This will create a new auto design under the **Design** node. Rename it as `VendorMaster`.

2. In the **VendorMaster** properties, set the **LayoutTemplate** property to **ReportLayoutStyleTemplate** and set the **Name** property to **VendorMaster**.

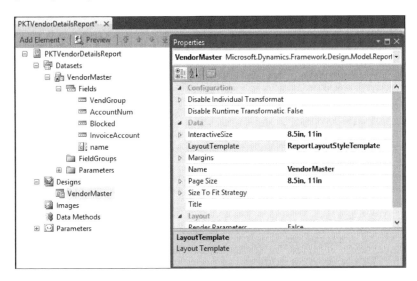

3. Under the new auto design node, right-click on **VendorMaster** and select **Add | Table**. Set the properties for this table as shown in the following screenshot:

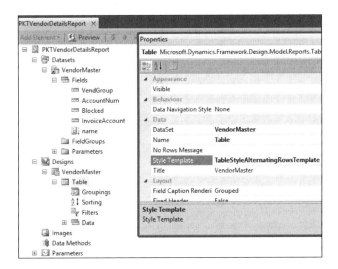

4. Notice that the fields are added to the table design automatically.

5. Right-click on **Auto design (VendorMaster)** and select **Preview**. This will show a preview of the report.

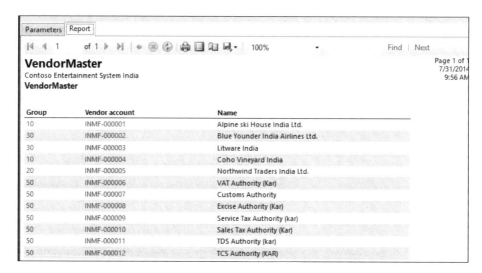

6. To rearrange the fields as per the user requirement, go to the **Data** node under the **Table** node. You can move fields in two ways, by:

    ❑   Using the right-click menu options, such as **Move to Top**, **Move Up**, **Move Down**, **Move to Bottom**

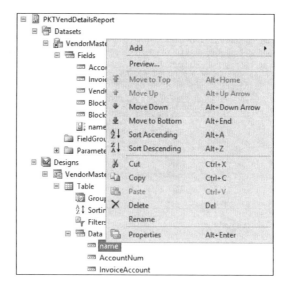

    ❑   Using shortcuts, like *Alt* + Up/Down arrow

The new format will look like the following screenshot:

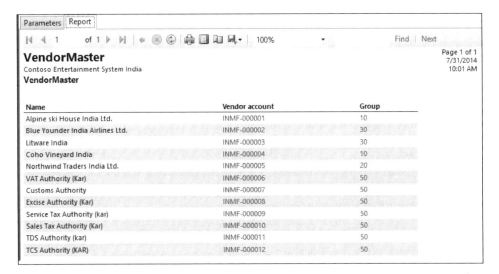

How it works...

Auto design is much easier to design and develop when compared to precision design. The default type (table/chart) for auto design is defined in the properties of the dataset. The default type determines what kind of control is added when the dataset is dragged and dropped into the auto design node.

Templates: Templates are responsible for printing the header, footer, and company name on a report. They also manage the font and colors. Currently, AX does not support printing the company image in the header through auto design.

Report preview: This accesses the default company in AX to show a report preview. So, ensure that the default company in AX has data, otherwise you may not find data in the preview.

Standard SSRS reporting doesn't have the concept of auto design. This is only available in the AX SSRS implementation.

Grouping in reports

Grouping means putting things into groups. In the previous recipe, all the data shown in the report was listed sequentially. Grouping data simplifies the structure of the report and makes it more readable. It also helps you to find details, if required.

We can group the data in the query as well as in the auto design node in Visual Studio. In this recipe, we will structure the report by grouping the **VendorMaster** report based on the **VendorGroup** to make the report more readable.

How to do it...

In this recipe, we will add fields under the grouping node of the dataset created earlier in Visual Studio. The fields that have been added in the grouping node will be added and shown automatically in the SSRS report.

1. Go to **Dataset** and select the **VendGroup** field.
2. Drag and drop it to the **Groupings** node under the **VendorMaster** auto design.

    This will automatically create a new grouping node and add the **VendGroup** field to the group. Each grouping has a header row where even fields that don't belong to the group but need to be displayed in the grouped node can be added.

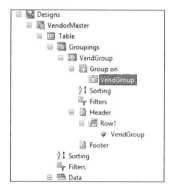

This groups the record and also acts like a header, as seen in the following screenshot:

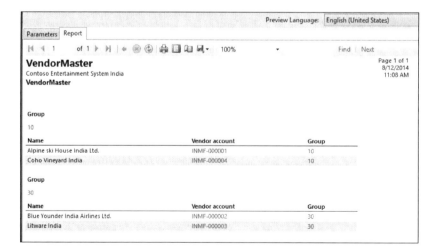

How it works...

Grouping can also be done based on multiple fields. Use the row header to specify the fields that must be displayed in the header. A grouping can be added manually but dragging and dropping prevents a lot of tasks such as setting the row header.

Adding ranges to the report

Ranges are very important and useful while developing an SSRS report in AX 2012 R3. They help to show only limited data, which is filtered based on given ranges, in the report.

The user can filter the data in a report on the basis of the field added as a range. The range must be specified in the query. In this recipe, we will show how we can filter the data and use a query field as a range.

How to do it...

In this recipe, we will add the field under the **Ranges** node in the query that we made in the previous recipe. By adding the field as a range, you can now filter the data on the basis of **VendGroup** and show only the limited data in the report.

1. Open the **PKTVendorDetails** query in AOT.

2. Drag the **VendGroup** and **Blocked** fields to the **Ranges** node in AOT and save your query.

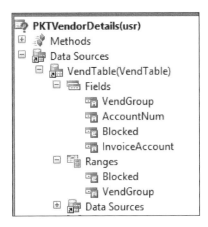

3. In the Visual Studio project, right-click on **Datasets** and select **Refresh**.

4. Under the parameter node, **VendorMaster_DynamicParameter** collectively represents any parameter that will be added dynamically through the ranges. This parameter must be set to true to make additional ranges available during runtime. This adds a **Select** button to the report dialog, which the user can use to specify additional ranges other than what is added.

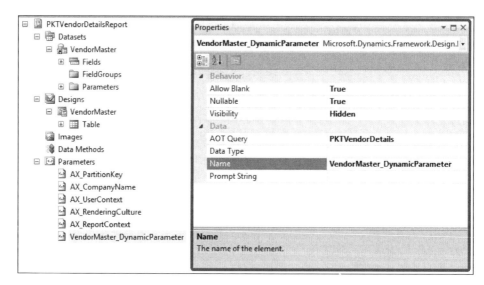

5. Right-click on the **VendorMaster** auto design and select **Preview**. The preview should display the range that was added in the query. Click on the **Select** button and set the **VendGroup** value to 10. Click on the **OK** button, and then select the **Report** tab, as shown in the following screenshot:

6. Save your changes and rebuild the report from **Solution Explorer**. Then, deploy the solution.

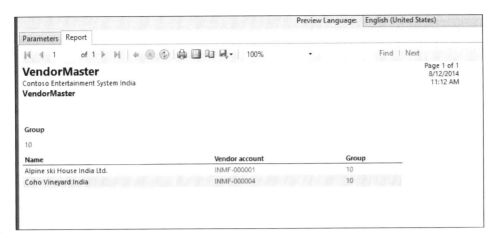

How it works...

The report dialog uses the query service UI builder (that we will cover in later chapters) to translate the ranges and to expose additional ranges through the query.

Dynamic parameter: The dynamic parameter unanimously represents all the parameters that are added at runtime. It adds the **Select** button to the dialog from where the user can invoke an advanced query filter window. From this filter window, more ranges and sorting can be added. The dynamic parameter is available per dataset and can be enabled or disabled by setting up the **Dynamic Filters** property to **True** or **False**.

> The Report Wizard in AX 2012 still uses **MorphX** reports to auto-create reports using the wizard. The auto report option is available on every form that uses a new AX SSRS report.

Deploying a report

SSRS, being a server side solution, needs to deploy reports in Dynamics AX 2012 R3. Until the reports are deployed, the user will not be able to see them or the changes made in them, neither from Visual Studio nor from the Dynamics AX rich client.

Reports can be deployed in multiple ways and the developer must make this decision. In this recipe, we will show you how we can deploy reports using the following:

- ▶ Microsoft Dynamics AX R3
- ▶ Microsoft Visual Studio
- ▶ Microsoft PowerShell

Getting ready

In order to deploy reports, you must have the permission and rights to deploy them to SQL Reporting Services. You must also have the permission to access the reporting manager configuration.

Before deploying reports using Microsoft PowerShell, you must ensure that Windows PowerShell 2.0 is installed.

How to do it...

Microsoft Dynamics AX R3 supports the following ways to deploy SSRS reports.

Location of deployment

For each of the following deployment locations, let's have a look at the steps that need to be followed:

1. Microsoft Dynamics AX R3:

    1. Reports can be deployed individually from a developer workspace in Microsoft Dynamics AX.

    2. SSRS reports can be deployed by using the developer client in Microsoft Dynamics AX R3.

    3. In AOT, expand the **SSRS Reports** node, expand the **Reports** node, select the particular report that needs to be deployed, expand the selected report node, right-click on the report, and then select and click on **Deploy Element**.

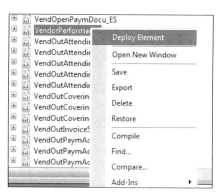

    4. The developer can deploy as many reports as need to be deployed, but individually.

5. Reports can be deployed for all the translated languages.

2. Microsoft Visual Studio:

   1. Individual reports can be deployed using Visual Studio.

   2. Open Visual Studio. In **Solution Explorer**, right-click on the reporting project that contains the report that you want to deploy, and click on **Deploy**.

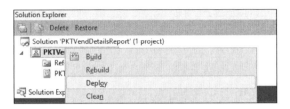

   3. The reports are deployed for the neutral (invariant) language only.

3. Microsoft PowerShell:

   1. This is used to deploy the default reports that exist within Microsoft Dynamics AX R3.

   2. Open Windows PowerShell and by using this, you can deploy multiple reports at the same time.

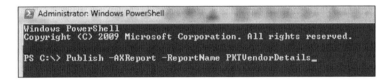

   3. Visit http://msdn.microsoft.com/en-us/library/dd309703.aspx for details on how to deploy reports using PowerShell.

4. To verify whether a report has been deployed, open the report manager in the browser and open the **Dynamics AX** folder. The **PKTVendorDetails** report should be found in the list of reports.

> You can find the report manager URL from **System administration | Setup | Business intelligence | Reporting Services | Report servers**.

5. The report can be previewed from **Reporting Services** also. Open **Reporting Services** and click on the name of the report to preview it.

How it works

Report deployment is the process of actually moving all the information related to a report to a central location, which is the server, from where it can be made available to the end user. The following list indicates the typical set of actions performed during deployment:

1. The RDL file is copied to the server.

2. The business logic is placed in the server location in the format of a DLL.

   Deployment ensures that the RDL and business logic are cross-referenced to each other.

 The MorphX IDE from AX 2009 is still available. Any custom reports that are designed can be imported. This support is only for the purpose of backward compatibility. In AX 2012 R3, there is no concept of MorphX reports.

Creating a menu item for a report

The final step of developing a report in AX 2012 R3 is creating a menu item inside AX to make it available for users to open from the UI end.

This recipe will tell you how to create a new menu item for a report and set the major properties for it. Also, it will teach you to add this menu item to a module to make it available for business users to access this report.

How to do it...

You can create the new menu item under the **Menu Item** node in AOT. In this recipe, the output menu item is created and linked with the menu item with SSRS report.

1. Go to **AOT | Menu Items | Output**, right-click and select **New Menu Item**. Name it **PKTVendorMasterDetails** and set the properties as highlighted in the following screenshot:

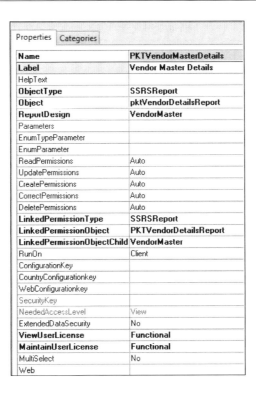

2. Open the **Menu Item** to run the report. A dialog appears with the **Vendor hold** and **Group** ranges added to the query, followed by a **Select** button. The **Select** button is similar to the MorphX reports option where the user can specify additional conditions. To disable the **Select** option, go to the **Dynamic Filter** property in the dataset of the query and set it to **False**.

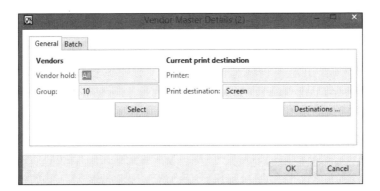

The report output should appear as seen in the following screenshot:

VendorMaster		
Contoso Entertainment System India		
VendorMaster		
Group		
10		
Name	**Vendor account**	**Group**
Alpine ski House India Ltd.	INMF-000001	10
Coho Vineyard India	INMF-000004	10
Group		
30		
Name	**Vendor account**	**Group**
Blue Younder India Airlines Ltd.	INMF-000002	30
Litware India	INMF-000003	30
Group		
20		
Name	**Vendor account**	**Group**
Northwind Traders India Ltd.	INMF-000005	20
Group		
50		
Name	**Vendor account**	**Group**
VAT Authority (Kar)	INMF-000006	50
Customs Authority	INMF-000007	50
Excise Authority (Kar)	INMF-000008	50
Service Tax Authority (kar)	INMF-000009	50

How it works...

The report viewer in Dynamics AX is actually a form with an embedded browser control. The browser constructs the report URL at runtime and navigates to the reports URL. Unlike in AX 2009, when the report is rendering, the data it doesn't hold up using AX. Instead, the user can use the other parts of the application while the report is rendering. This is particularly beneficial for the end users as they can proceed with other tasks as the report executes.

The permission setup is important as it helps in controlling the access to a report. However, SSRS reports inherit user permission from the AX setup itself.

Creating a report using a query in Warehouse Management

In Dynamics AX 2012 R3, Warehouse Management is a new module. In the earlier version of AX (2012 or R2), there was a single module for Inventory and Warehouse Management. However, in AX R3, there is a separate module.

AX queries are the simplest and fastest way to create SSRS reports in Microsoft Dynamics AX R3. In this recipe, we will develop an SSRS report on Warehouse Management.

In AX R3, Warehouse Management is integrated with bar-coding devices such as RF-SMART, which supports purchase and receiving processes: picking, packing and shipping, transferring and stock counts, issuing materials for production orders, and reporting production as well. AX R3 also supports the workflow for the Warehouse Management module, which is used to optimize picking, packing, and loading of goods for delivery to customers.

Getting ready

To work through this recipe, Visual Studio must be installed on your system to design and deploy the report. You must have the permission to access all the rights of the reporting server, and reporting extensions must be installed.

How to do it...

Similar to other modules, Warehouse Management also has its tables with the "WHS" prefix. We start the recipe by creating a query, which consists of **WHSRFMenuTable** and **WHSRFMenuLine** as the data source. We will provide a range of **Menus** in the query. After creating a query, we will create an SSRS report in Visual Studio and use that query as the data source and will generate the report on warehouse management.

Open AOT, add a new query, and name it `PKTWarehouseMobileDeviceMenuDetails`.

1. Add a **WHSRFMenuTable** table.

2. Go to Fields and set the **Dynamics** property to **Yes**.

3. Add a **WHSRFMenuLine** table and set the **Relation** property to **Yes**. This will create an auto relation that will inherit from table relation node.

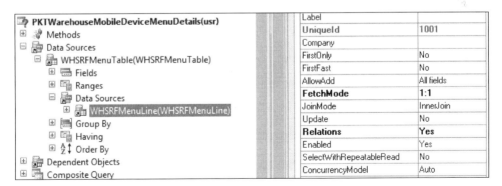

4. Go to **Fields** and set the **Dynamics** property to **Yes**.

5. Now open Visual Studio and add a new Dynamics AX report model project. Name it `PKTWarehouseMobileDeviceMenuDetails`.

6. Add a new report to this project and name it `PKTWarehouseMobileDeviceDetails`.

7. Add a new dataset and name it `MobileDeviceDetails`.

8. Select the **PKTWarehouseMobileDeviceMenuDetails** query in the **Dataset** property.

9. Select all fields from both tables. Click on **OK**.

10. Now drag and drop this dataset in the design node. It will automatically create an auto design. Rename it `MobileMenuDetails`.

11. In the properties, set the layout property to **ReportLayoutStyleTemplate**.

12. Now preview your report.

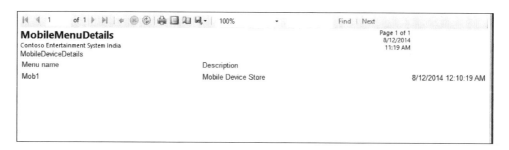

How it works

When we start creating an SSRS report, VS must be connected with Microsoft Dynamics AX R3. If the Microsoft Dynamics AX option is visible in Visual Studio while creating the new project, then the reporting extensions are installed. Otherwise, we need to install the reporting extensions properly.

2
Enhancing Your Report – Visualization and Interaction

We will look at the following recipes in this chapter:

- Creating multiple data regions and charts in reports
- Creating a chart data region
- Creating a new layout template
- Expression in reports
- Aggregation in reports
- Adding an image in auto design
- Formatting reports
- Adding unbounded parameters in reports
- Adding filters to data regions
- Adding document map navigation to reports
- Creating drill-up/drill-down actions in reports

Introduction

In every industry report, presentation plays an important role. Hence, every report development process places huge focus on the presentation and visualization of the report. This chapter offers you the knowledge of different available options that can be used to enhance visualization in reports through sample implementation. The chapter focuses on enhancing visualization and the interactivity in a report using Visual Studio's inbuilt tools. A report case is picked up and passed through several transformations to make it visually appealing. The flow is such that the concept and the practice are put side by side, so by the time the chapter is finished you will be familiar with the features.

Creating multiple data regions and charts in reports

This recipe will show how different data regions can be used to render data. Usually, a data region, in simple terms, is isolated small reports that share the parameter and datasets. This and the next recipe will help you understand how multiple regions can be created in SSRS. The first of the two data regions will display detailed customer transactions, while the second data region will show a pie chart that shows the total value of the transactions against each customer group.

Getting Ready

This and the other recipes in the chapter will extend the report built in this section. Working through *Chapter 1, Understanding and Creating Simple SSRS Reports*, should make it easier to create SSRS reports. So, following the guidelines from the previous chapter, create a simple SSRS report.

In the following recipe, we will create a customer account statement, which shows the transactions of different customers, by using multiple data regions:

1. Create a **PktCustTransList** query that includes the **CustTable** and **CustTrans** tables. Remove the unwanted fields and retain only the fields that are shown in the following screenshot. It's good from the performance perspective to use only fields and methods that are actually used in the report. This can be easily achieved by the drag and drop functionality.

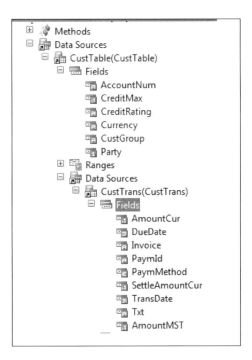

2. Open Visual Studio and create a new report model project called **PktCustTransReport**. Create a dataset that refers to the **PktCustTransList** query.

3. When selecting the fields in the query window, select all the fields and the **name** data method from **CustTable**.

How to do it...

1. Drag the **CustTrans** dataset to the auto design node. This will create a table design layout.

2. The grouping ability of data regions helps present data effectively by ordering and organizing it.

3. Drag the **CustGroup** field to the **Group on** node. Also drag the **AccountNum** field from the dataset to the **Group on** node.

4. Expand the **Group on** node and navigate to the **Row1** property. Drag the field's **Currency** and **Party_Name** to the **AccountNum** group node.

5. The grouping helps render the data in a summarized view. The order of the grouping property determines the order in which the data is summarized. In this case, it is first by the customer group followed by customer.

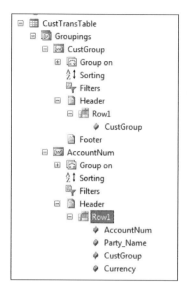

6. Preview the report and see the multiple groupings in action as shown in the following screenshot:

Customer group				
10				

	Customer account	Name	Customer group	Currency
	1102	Sunset Wholesales	10	USD

Invoice	Due date	⇕ Date		Amount	Description
100009	3/16/2012	1/16/2012		15,614.16	Sales invoice 100009
100035	3/1/2012	1/1/2012		125,059.83	Sales invoice 100035
100037	3/30/2012	1/30/2012		9,703.48	Sales invoice 100037

How it works...

The Dynamics AX 2012 R3 SSRS reporting system differs from the legacy reporting system. If you have been working with the legacy reporting system, that is, MorphX reports, your mind might tune in to find two records: one for the customer table and the other for customer transactions. Here in Dynamics AX 2012 R3, it works differently with SSRS, where the data is completely flattened. This means if the customer table has c1 and c2 records and the transactions table has t11, t12, t21 and t22 records, then the flattened dataset of an SSRS report will have four records where each line will hold c1 t11, c1 t12, c2 t21 and c2 t22.

The benefit of grouping on a flattened dataset is to recreate the data structure. So here, the grouping helps classify the transactions by customer and, in turn, acts as the header record.

Creating a chart data region

We will incorporate our second data region through this recipe. The same report has two sections that summarize the same data in alternate ways.

In this recipe, we will create a chart data region. This chart data region will show the total value of transactions against each customer group. The report will show a summary through the chart, followed by details of the transactions. Creating charts was not possible in the legacy system; however, with the new framework, it is just a matter of a few clicks and setups, as you will see in this recipe.

You can create and modify report definitions (.rdl) in the report builder and report designer in SQL Server Data Tools. Each authoring environment provides different ways to create, open, and save reports and related items.

For more details, visit http://technet.microsoft.com/en-us/library/dd207141(v=sql.110).aspx.

Getting ready

This recipe is in continuation of the previously developed report in the *Creating multiple data regions and charts in reports* recipe in this chapter.

How to do it...

1. Right-click on the **Designs | TransactionDetail** node and select **Add | Pie or Doughnut Chart**.

2. Name it CustTransPie.

3. From the dataset, drag the **AmountMst** field and drop it in the **Data** node under the chart.

4. Set the following properties for the **AmountMST** control:

Property	Value
Caption	=SUM(Fields!AmountMST.Value)
Expression	=SUM(Fields!AmountMST.Value)
Point label	="Group =" + Fields!CustGroup.Value

5. From the dataset, drag the **CustGroup** field and drop it in the **Series** node under the chart.

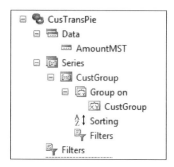

6. Start the preview. The preview will show the chart followed by the table. (The order is based on the position of data regions under auto design.)

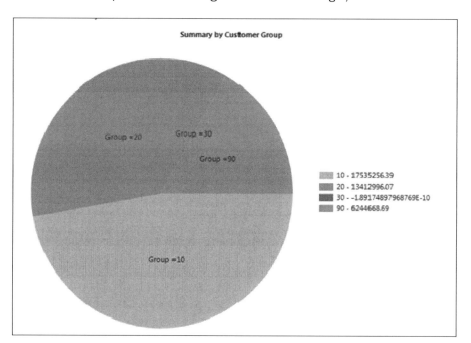

How it works...

Multiple data regions present the capability to offer different representations of data. A data region creates smaller slices of the report to present related information in an isolated region. Each data region is attached to a dataset, and they are mutually exclusive except for the parameters. Parameters are shared between data regions and there is no ability to define parameters per data region.

SSRS supports the following different visualizations for data regions through auto design, and a broader list through precision design, as discussed in *Chapter 6, Beyond Tabular Reports*:

▶ List data regions

▶ Table data regions

▶ Matrix data regions

▶ Chart data regions

 You can also use views as data sources. Just add a view to the query and it is ready to be used as a data source. Due to huge data normalization done in AX 2012 with DirpartyTable, Financial Dimensions, and more, using views can make it easier and accurate to retrieve data.

Creating a new layout template

In *Chapter 1, Understanding and Creating Simple SSRS Reports*, we discussed how to use templates to standardize a report. There are several predefined layout and style templates that you can use for your reports. These templates are standard templates for Microsoft Dynamics AX reports and provide consistent layout and style settings.

The following table lists the predefined templates that are available, and describes what each template can be applied to:

Template name	What each template can be applied to
BarChartStyleTemplate	Bar chart data regions
ColumnChartStyleTemplate	Column chart data regions
LineChartStyleTemplate	Line chart data regions
ListStyleTemplate	List data regions (top-down list or horizontal list data regions)
MatrixStyleTemplate	Matrix data regions
PieAndDoughnutStyleTemlate	Pie or doughnut chart data regions
ReportLayoutStyleTemplate	Reports (company information is displayed in the report header)
ReportLayoutStyleTemplateNoCompany	Reports (company information is not displayed in the report header)
RoleCenterReportLayoutStyleTemplate	Reports that display in a role center
TableStyleTemplate	Table data regions

Apart from using standard layouts, we have also the option to add a new template. Each style template is specific to a data region type and contains the layout and style setting for that data region, which is displayed in the body of report. This recipe will show how to create custom layout templates that can be used to standardize report aesthetics, such as font, size, color, and so on.

How to do it...

1. Open Visual Studio and select **View | Application Explorer**. This displays the entire AOT as in the AX environment in Visual Studio.

2. Navigate to the **Sharedlibrary** project under **Visual Studio Projects | Dynamics AX Model Projects**. Right-click and select **Edit**.

3. This project contains all the predefined templates. Right-click on the project and go to **Add | Table style template**. (Choose the template based on the data region, such as table, list, and so on.)

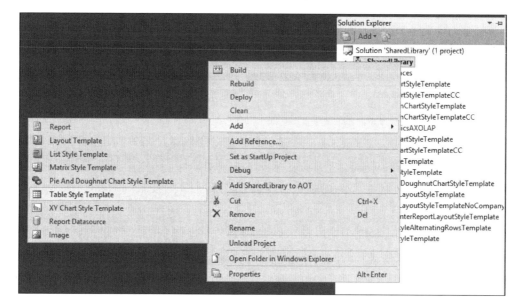

There is no inheritance concept among templates. Each template is independent and must define the entire formatting.

4. Double-click the template to open it in the editor, and rename it `PktTableStyleFancyTemplate`.

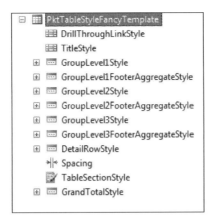

5. In the current report design, there are two levels of groupings defined: **CustGroup** followed by **AccountNum**.

6. To set the fonts for both the levels, the **GroupLevel1Style** and **GroupLevel2Style** nodes must be modified.

7. Expand **GroupLevel1Style** and double-click on **FieldCaptionStyle** to open the form shown in the following screenshot (alternatively, open the properties window):

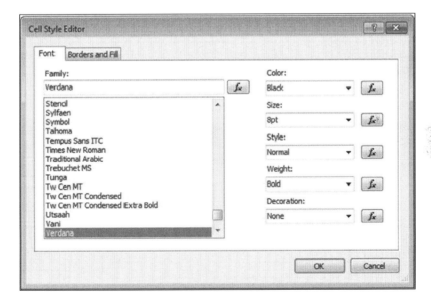

8. Set the following properties for both the nodes:

Property	Value
Font | Family	Verdana
Font | Size	8pt
Borders and Fill | Style	Dashed

Repeat the same procedure for the **FieldValueStyle** node and set the properties except for the last one, which is not needed.

1. The template is set for the groupings; the next step is to set the template for the detailed rows.

2. Navigate to **DetailRowStyle | FieldCaptionStyle** and set the following properties:

Property	Value
Font | Family	Verdana
Font | Size	8 pt

3. Repeat the same for **DetailRowStyle | FieldValueStyle**.

4. Templates don't need deployment and they are available once they are created. Switch to the report node and select the **CustTransTable** table data region.

5. The dropdown will have the new template that was added. Set it as the template for the current report.

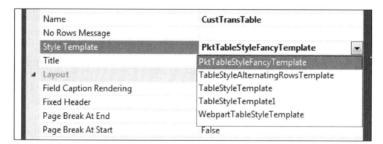

6. Right-click and preview to see that the fonts are different and the group nodes have a dashed line.

How it works...

Layout templates define the general layout settings, such as company name, date, page number, and formatting for a report. Style templates are applicable to data regions, and depending on the data region the type of template also varies. AX offers a set of predefined report layout and style templates.

These templates provide the ability to present a uniform look and feel across reports. The elements in a template are fixed depending on the type; so elements cannot be added or removed but only have different formatting. Templates are useful only in the case of auto design and are not used in the case of precision design.

 Layout and style templates are used in auto design reports and not accessed for precision design reports. If you want your reports to have the same look and feel as standard reports you must use the predefined layout and style templates.

Expression in reports

Expression is a very interesting property in SSRS reports. It is mostly used to do customizations at runtime. Expressions are basically used to change report appearances and report content at runtime. Microsoft Visual Studio has some built-in functions that can be used in expressions. In this recipe, we will implement the most important feature of printing the alternate line in different colors.

How to do it...

1. In the template, select the **DetailRowStyle | FieldValueStyle** node.

2. For the **Background Color** property, choose the **<Expression...>** list:

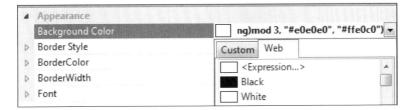

3. The **Edit Expression** window will pop up.

4. Type the following expression in the **Edit Expression** window, as shown in the screenshot:

```
=iif(RowNumber(Nothing)mod 3, "#e0e0e0", "#ffe0c0")
```

5. Save the template and go back to the **PktCustTransList** report for a preview.

6. The report should now appear with a different color on every third line when previewed, as seen in the following screenshot:

How it works...

Expressions are a powerful means through which you can manipulate the content and the formatting style of the report data. These are widely used across the report model to retrieve, calculate, display, group, sort, filter, parameterize, and format data. They are not just limited to the ones listed but apply to many other properties. A precise definition would be that anywhere in the report if a dropdown list displays **<Expression...>**, then expressions can be applied. Expressions start with the equals sign (=).

Expressions create a wide scope for manipulation by providing access to standard functions, data methods, fields, labels, and more. This can be compared to an Excel cell where a formula is evaluated to produce data. Expressions are evaluated when the report is run, so the results can be seen through the preview.

Here are a few sample expressions:

Sample expression	Purpose
`=Fields!FirstName.Value`	Displays the value of the `FirstName` field

`=IIF(Fields!Amount > 100,`
`Fields!LineAmount * 3,`
`Fields!LineAmount * 2`
	Evaluates if amount is greater than `100`, then line amount multiplies by `3`; otherwise, multiplies by `2`
	
	`IIF` conditions check the condition and return `true` or `false` based on the condition

`=Year(Fields!OrderDate.` `Value)`	Displays the year from a date field
`=Day(Fields!JoiningDate.` `value)`	Displays the day from the date field

`=Sum(IIF(Fields!Quantity.`
`Value > 0,Fields!Amount.`
`Value , 0))`
	Conditionally sums the value of the amount field

`=RowNumber(Nothing)`	Starts counting from the outermost data region

The expression syntax is based on Visual Basic, and any syntax error is highlighted by a red color in the Expression window.

 For more details on expressions, visit `https://technet.microsoft.com/en-us/library/hh535216.aspx`.

Understanding prefix symbols in simple expressions

In the AX 2012 R3 SSRS reporting system, we use simple expression symbols to indicate whether the reference is to a field, a parameter, a built-in collection, or the `ReportItems` collection. The following table shows examples of display and expression:

Item	Display text example	Expression text example
Dataset fields	**[Sales]**	`=Fields!Sales.Value`
	[SUM(Sales)]	`=Sum(Fields!Sales.Value)`
	[FIRST(Store)]	`=First(Fields!Store.Value)`
Report parameters	**[@Param]**	`=Parameters!Param.Value`
	[@Param.Label]	`=Parameters!Param.Label`
Built-in fields	**[&ReportName]**	`=Globals!ReportName.Value`
Literal characters used for display text	**\[Sales\]**	`[Sales]`

Many invoice report designers tend to use the IIF() function to test the parameter expression for a true or false result and then explicitly return a true or false result from the function. Since all expressions can return Boolean results, and although this technique will work, it's redundant to use the IIF() function for this purpose. For example, the following expression could be used in place of the previous example:

```
=IIF(Parameters!ShowQuantity.Value = True, False,
True)
```

The following example would be used to test the result of a non-Boolean value:

```
=(Parameters!ReportView.Label="Retail")
```

By wrapping an expression containing a comparison operator in parentheses, the expression returns a Boolean result.

Aggregation in reports

Aggregate functions are very useful in SSRS reports in AX R3 to calculate the aggregate values that show the numeric data. Totals are an obvious need in all reports. For example, the sum aggregate function calculates the total of transaction amounts. SSRS provides easy and powerful aggregation capabilities. This recipe will discuss a couple of aggregation methods and how they can be applied at different levels.

How to do it...

In this recipe two aggregations will be implemented:

▸ Total value of transactions per customer

▸ Count of the total number of transactions per customer

To define the total value of transactions implement the following steps:

1. Navigate to the **Data | AmountMst** node.

2. Set the **Aggregation Function** property to **Sum**.

To display the count of records implement the following steps:

1. Go to the **Groupings | AccountNum** node in the table data region as shown in the following screenshot:

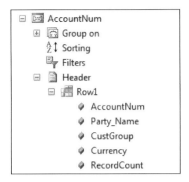

2. Right-click and go to **Add** | **Field**.

3. Set the following properties:

Property	Value
Caption	Transactions
Expression	=CountRows()
Name	RecordCount
Text Align	Left

4. Preview the report and notice the aggregated values appear with the customer details. The transactions column indicates the number of records while the other is the total value of the transaction.

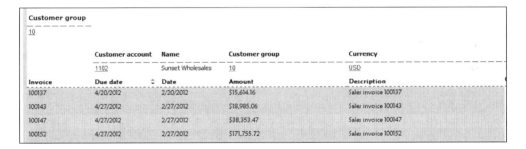

How it works...

Aggregation provides the ability to calculate data based on various functions, such as Count, Sum, Avg, Min, and Max. These are applicable to a data region or dataset. The results of aggregation can be displayed based on the data region.

Here are some aggregate functions:

Aggregate functions	Syntax	Purpose
sum	Select sum(fieldname) from table_name	Returns sum of all transactions
min	Select min(fieldname) from table_name	Returns minimum value of the data
max	Select max(fieldname) from table_name	Returns maximum value of the data
avg	Select avg(fieldname) from table_name	Returns average value of the data
count	Select count(fieldname) from table_name	Returns the number of non-null items

 To use aggregate functions in AX 2012 R3, you should use integer/real dataType/values.

When a certain field is to be displayed aggregated in the entire report, then the aggregation can be configured in the properties of the field in the dataset. Each field has a property called **Aggregate Function** that must be configured in this case. If the aggregation is only for the specific data region, then it must be defined in the report control in the data region.

Aggregate function results can be displayed as a summary in the header/footer of table and list data regions. In a matrix report, the columns and rows can be aggregated to display a grand total.

Adding an image in auto design

Images can easily be displayed in SSRS reports along with data in Dynamics AX R3. We can control the images dynamically at runtime by using expressions. This recipe will help you learn about using images in a report and using expressions to choose the images dynamically. A new column will be added to the report that indicates whether the transaction date was before or after the due date.We will use a tick image to show whether the transaction date was before the due date and a cross image for transactions that are after the due date. A visual expression is easier to identify than just having a Boolean type value.

How to do it...

1. Identify the images that are going to be used and set them with right resolutions. (Syncfusion® Metrostudio has been used to generate these images.)

2. On the **Images** node, right-click and add a new image.

3. Locate the path of the image in the **ImageSource** property of the **Images** node.

4. The image is imported and a thumbnail becomes visible. The system identifies the nature of the file automatically.

5. Repeat the same steps to add the second image.

6. In the **CustTransTable** table data region, expand the **Data** node and add a new image type field.

7. Set the following properties:

Property	Value
Caption	`"On Time"`
Source	`"Embedded"`
MEME type	`"image/png"`
Expression	`=IIF(Fields!DueDate.Value<>Fields!TransDate.Value, "Wrong", "Right")`

8. The report is ready to display images. Start a preview to see the expression getting evaluated to display the appropriate image.

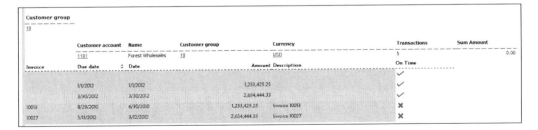

How it works...

Images are used in scenarios to display a company logo or a product image. There are several ways to reference an image in a report: embedded images, external images, and database images. The following tabular overview details the reference type and their usage:

Reference type	Applicable to	Description
Embedded	Auto/Precision design	The image is part of the report or shared components
Database	Auto/Precision design	The image is stored as binary data in a table field such as product image
External	Precision design	The image is referenced through a URL or location

 Adding a company logo is a common scenario, but at the moment only precision design supports it. Auto design cannot reference the company image in the report header.

See also

▶ The *Adding headers and displaying company images* recipe in *Chapter 4, Report Programming Model – RDP*

Formatting reports

Formatting is very useful in SSRS reports to organize all the data. If you look carefully, the amount values in the previous report output recipes are not properly aligned.

In this recipe, we will make some formatting changes and align amount values as well as text fields.

How to do it...

1. To set the alignment, modify the **Text Align** property to **Left** and set the **Format String** property to **Currency**.

2. For the **AmountMST** field in the table data region, modify the **Format String** property and set it as **Currency**. The revised report will appear as shown in the following screenshot:

	Customer account	Name	Customer group	Currency		Transactions	Sum Amount
	1101	Forest Wholesales	10	USD		5	$0.00
Invoice	Due date	Date	Amount	Description		On Time	
	1/1/2012	1/1/2012	($1,233,425.25)			✓	
	3/30/2012	3/30/2012	($2,654,444.33)			✓	
						✓	
10013	8/29/2010	6/30/2010	$1,233,425.25	Invoice 10013		✗	
10027	5/11/2012	3/12/2012	$2,654,444.33	Invoice 10027		✗	

How it works...

The format string property has a set of predefined formats that can be applied to a specific field, such as `Date`, `Number`, and so on.

> If you have set up custom values on different properties and want to set the original value, then just right-click on the property window and then click on **Reset**. This will reset the selected property to its default value.

Adding unbounded parameters in reports

Parameters bring in interactivity to reports. In the previous chapter, we discussed how a new parameter can be added to a dataset through a query. There can be scenarios where we may have wanted to have a parameter that is not linked to dataset but needed it for the purpose of reporting. These parameters are referred to as unbound parameters. In this and the following recipe, we will discuss how to add a parameter and how to use it in the report. The *How it works* section of this recipe should also help you understand reports in more depth.

In this recipe, we will add two parameters, one of type Boolean and the other String type. The following recipe will show how they will be put to use.

How to do it...

1. Go to the **Parameter** node in the report and right–click on it. Go to **Add | New Parameter**.
2. In the new parameter, set the following properties:

Property	Value
Name	ShowPieChart
Prompt string	Show Pie Chart
Data Type	Boolean
Default Value	True
Nullable	True
AllowBlank	True

3. Follow the same procedure and add a second parameter to the **Parameter** node. Set the following properties:

Property	Value
Name	CustGroup
Prompt string	Customer Group
Data Type	String

4. Previewing the report should show two new parameters in the report dialog, but filling these values will not have any influence as these have not been linked to the report.

How it works...

Parameters are the means to get user input in reports. The parameters of an SSRS report can be found under the **Parameters** node in the report.

There are two kinds of parameters here:

▸ **System parameter**: These are parameters that start with AX_ and are defined by the system for internal purposes. However, they can be made visible to the user based on the requirement, except for the AX_UserContext parameter.

▸ **User-defined parameter**: These are parameters that are defined in the dataset and any other parameters that are added are referred to as user-defined parameters.

System parameter

System parameters are hidden by default and have a default value, which is defined through an expression. For example, the AX_CompanyName parameter has the following expression filled in by default:

```
=Microsoft.Dynamics.Framework.Reports.BuiltInMethods.
GetUserCompany(Parameters!AX_UserContext.Value)
```

System parameters consist of the following:

Parameter	Function	User modification
AX_CompanyName	Indicates the company from which the data is to be fetched	Allowed
AX_RenderingCulture	Language in which the report is rendered; for example, English	Allowed
AX_ReportContext	Indicates whether the report is running in EP or client	Allowed
AX_UserContext	User who runs the report	Not recommended
AX_PartitionKey	Defines the active partition for the report	Not allowed

User-defined parameters

There are two more types under user-defined parameters: bounded and unbounded parameters.

Bounded parameters

Parameters that are connected to a dataset are identified as bounded parameters. If a dataset is linked to a query, then the parameters are automatically created from the fields that are added to the **Ranges** node in the AOT query.

Unbounded parameters

These are parameters that are added manually and may or may not be connected to a dataset. These are used for the purpose of formatting, calculations, and so on.

Parameters and data source types

As seen in the previous chapter, AX SSRS supports different types of data sources, such as Query, RDP, OLAP, and external data sources. The parameters that are defined depend on the linked data source. This section will detail query-based parameters.

Query parameters

When a query is added as a dataset, the ranges defined for the query are automatically added to the **Parameters** node of the dataset and the report. The dataset parameters can be seen under the parameter node in dataset. Fields cannot be added manually in dataset parameters. Each parameter in the dataset refers to a report parameter, which can be seen through the **Report parameter** property:

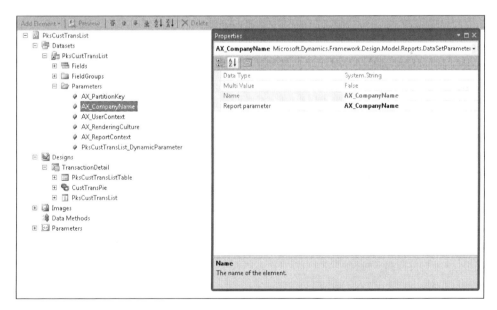

If multiple datasets are added and they refer to the same type of field as parameter (for example, `ItemId`), then both the dataset parameters are added to the report parameter. This results in a redundant report parameter for the same field type. In this case, delete one of the two report parameters and then modify the dataset pointer to point to the same report parameter.

Dynamic filters

In line with the legacy system (AX 2009), it is possible to allow more parameters to be added by the user through the query framework. To enable this, set the **Dynamic filters** property to **Yes** in the data source node.

 If you delete the dynamic parameter from the report parameter node by mistake, then you can retrieve it by right-clicking on the dataset and selecting **Refresh**.

See also

▸ The *Adding Ranges to the Report* recipe in *Chapter 1, Understanding and Creating Simple SSRS Reports*

Adding filters to data regions

This recipe will use the parameters added in the previous recipe and influence the report. From the two parameters added, the Boolean type will be used to show or hide the chart data region while the string type will be used to restrict the data shown in the table data region.

How to do it...

1. Select the **CustTransPie** chart data region and open its properties.
2. In the visible property, key in the following expression. This links the first parameter to control the visibility of the data region:

   ```
   =IIF(Parameters!ShowPieChart.Value, True, False)
   ```

3. Navigate to the **Filters** node of **CustTransTable** and create a new filter.

4. In the new filter node, set the following properties:

Property	Value
Name	`CustGroup`
Value	`=1`
Expression	`=IIF((Parameters!CustGroup.Value=Fields!CustGroup.Value),1,0)`

5. The data region displays only the data for which the expression evaluates to 1.

6. Now that the report is finally over, select **Preview** and activate the **Parameters** tab. The parameters that were added will be visible along with the standard parameters. Verify the parameters through the report preview.

   The report is now ready to be deployed. The deployed report dialog should appear as shown in the following screenshot:

7. The deployed report will be displayed as shown in the following screenshot:

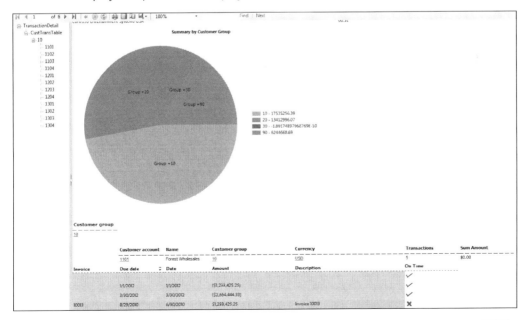

How it works...

Filters are present in the data region and are used to apply a filter to a specific data region. A filter works on the client side and operates on flattened data. It is used in cases where the data needs to be restricted only to a certain data region and not the entire dataset. As you can see, the chart data summarizes the data for the entire report, but the table data region shows the data only for the selected customer group.

Filters must be used cautiously and must not be considered as alternatives for query ranges. The reason is that the system fetches the whole data from the data source, after which it applies the filter. Check the property of the **CustGroup** field in filters as shown in the following screenshot:

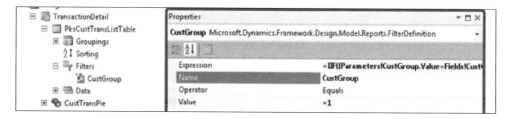

Adding document map navigation to reports

A document map helps to navigate to report items. The user can click on the navigational link to jump to the report items that need to be displayed. It is similar to a table of contents. Whenever the user clicks on the navigational link, it refreshes the report. A navigational link can be added by setting the `DocumentMapLabel` property of the SSRS report.

In this simple recipe, we will see how we can create a powerful navigation system for a report. Document map navigation is an easy-to-use navigation style for reports.

How to do it...

1. The table data region already has the relevant table groupings based on **CustGroup** followed by **Account num**.
2. Select the **CustTransTable** table data region and set the **Data Navigation Style** property to **DocumentMap**.
3. Now preview the report.

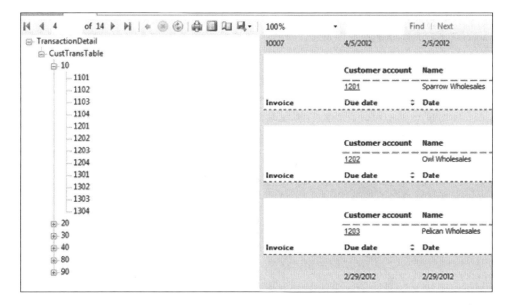

4. The navigation on the right-hand side is generated through the document map. This gives a summarized view and enables easy navigation to the right customer account without searching through a number of pages.

How it works...

The document map is an interesting design addition that offers an easier way to navigate through the report. This can be compared to a table of contents generated in a word document. To apply a document map to a data region, it is necessary to have grouping implemented.

Creating drill-up/drill-down actions in reports

Data in an SSRS report can be organized by adding drill-up/down-actions to it. The user can reveal details by clicking and can hide other details. Drill-down actions provide the plus and minus sign on a textbox, through which a user can reveal or hide the data accordingly.

Drill-down actions make the SSRS report in AX 2012 R3 very interactive and creative. By using the tables, a user can hide or reveal the rows and columns.

In this recipe, we will get introduced to another navigation style for reports. This is used to collapse or expand data. Additionally, we will learn about the list type data region.

How to do it...

1. In order to get a feel for this navigation style, hide the previous design. Go to the **CustTransTable** table data region and set the **Visible** property to **false**.

2. Right-click on the **Auto design** node, and go to **Add | List** data region.

3. On the new data region **CustTransList** list drag the same set of fields as in the table data region.

4. Similarly, add two levels of groupings, **CustGroup** followed by **AccountNum**.

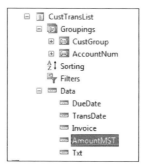

5. Select the **CustTransList** data region and set the **Data Navigation Style** property to **DrillDown**.

6. Now your report should appear with collapsible groups in the preview as shown in the following screenshot:

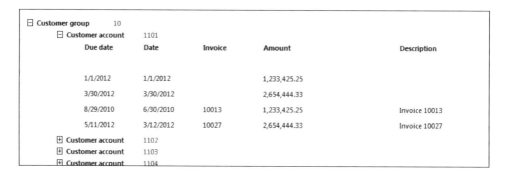

How it works...

This is another navigation method like the document map. It displays collapsible groups in reports that can be expanded and closed by the user. This can be applied to Table, List and Matrix types of reports. The user can display the data in table, matrix which is nested inside the table or matrix. Data can also be displayed in a sub-report, which is contained within the main report.

3
Report Programming Model

We will look at the following recipes in this chapter:

- Opening a report through a controller
- Modifying the report query in controller
- Opening a report with a dialog
- Creating a report using the UI builder class
- Adding a lookup on a report dialog using the UI Builder class
- Connecting the UI builder class with a contract class
- Adding ranges from unbound parameters to a query
- Modifying the UI by caller
- Turning off a report dialog
- Setting up security for reports
- Adding up the report menu items into privilege
- Calling multiple reports from a controller
- Calling multiple reports simultaneously using a single controller
- Debugging a report model
- Adding data methods in business logic
- Adding a URL drill through action in reports
- Debugging business logic
- Unit testing business logic
- Creating a report using the controller and the UI builder class

Introduction

In the previous chapters, report basics and graphical representations have been discussed extensively. In this chapter, we will discuss the report programming model using Dynamics AX 2012 R3 in greater detail. This chapter will give you a deeper understanding of how the reporting framework is modeled for report execution, and how to use report models to develop a complex report. The execution of a report not only involves designing the model but also involves receiving inputs and presenting these to the user. The recipes discussed in this chapter will assist you in making better choices on how to use the reporting framework to present and get inputs for the reports. The two important contracts—**Report Data Providers** (**RDP**) and **Report Definition Language** (**RDL**)—have been compared in detail for clarity. The later sections have recipes that detail how C#-based business logic can be designed, debugged, and tested in the report model.

Opening a report through a controller

A controller plays a key role in defining the entire report life cycle. It extends the `SrsReportRunController` base class. A controller class is used to control the execution of a report and preprocessing of data in a report. In Dynamics AX 2012 R3, the SSRS reporting framework uses this class to modify and call the report dialogs and pre/post processing the given parameters.

This recipe will be the first step in using the controller and will explain how a report can be invoked from a controller class. The *How it works...* section of this recipe will give you a detailed picture of the report programming model, which will help you understand the other recipes discussed in this chapter.

Getting Ready

To work with this recipe and the others explained here, it is required that you get familiar with the reports discussed in *Chapter 1, Understanding and Creating Simple SSRS Reports*, and *Chapter 2, Enhancing Your Report – Visualization and Interaction*.

How to do it...

To implement the recipe discussed here along with those that follow, create a report with the following steps:

1. Create a query called **PktRdlItemTransList** with limited selection fields as detailed in *Chapter 1, Understanding and Creating Simple SSRS Reports*.

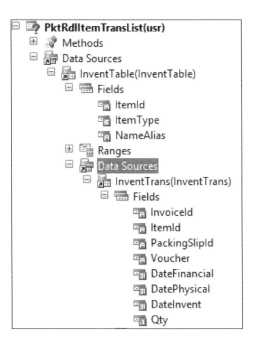

2. Create a new report by the name **PktRdlItemTransList** in Visual Studio using query.

3. Add an **Auto design** with grouping by **Item Id**.

4. Go to the **Parameters** node in the report and add the following unbound parameters:

Name	Type	Property "Nullable"
FromDate	DateTime	True
ToDate	DateTime	True
ShowApproved	Boolean	True

5. Build and deploy the report to AX.

6. Create a `PktRdlItemTransController` class that extends the `SRSReportRunController` class.

7. Add a new main method as shown in the following snippet:

```
public static void main(Args args)
{
    PktRdlItemTransController controller;
    controller = new PktRdlItemTransController ();
    controller.parmReportName(ssrsReportStr
        (PktRdlItemTransList, ItemTransList));
```

```
    //PktRdlItemTransList is report name while
      ItemTransList is report design name.
        controller.parmArgs(args);
        controller.startOperation();
    }
```

8. Save your changes and compile the class.

9. Now this controller class can be used to run the report. Press *F5* to run the **PktRdlItemTransList** report through this controller class.

How it works...

Though we have added only a few lines of code to identify our report, the whole process is flowing smoothly. This is made possible by the SSRSReportRunController class that is extended by the controller created in this recipe. The detailed description that follows should help you understand the report programming model clearly.

Report programming model

The report programming model in Dynamics AX 2012 R3 adopts the **Model View Controller** (**MVC**) pattern to decouple the user interface and business logic. An MVC pattern, in simple terms, improves abstraction and creates clarity on responsibilities. Consequently, it brings down the growing complexity caused by mashing up the logic that drives the user interface and the business logic. The RunBase framework in AX 2009 is an example of how business logic and UI are put together in the patterns and adopted by legacy systems.

The MVC pattern, when applied to a reporting framework, distributes the responsibilities as specified here:

- ▸ **Model**: Represents the data that is generated by processing the parameters
- ▸ **Controller**: Represents the parameters and UI builders that will be used to generate the report
- ▸ **View**: Represents the visualization of the report

Model

A model for an SSRS report can be an AOT query/RDP/business logic.

AOT queries are queries modeled using the MorphX IDE, while RDPs are classes that extend `SRSReportDataProvider`. An RDP model is used where complex business logic is involved in computing the data to be rendered. The data is modeled from different sources before it is sent to the report.

 For more details on the RDP class visit `http://technet.microsoft.com/en-us/library/gg724119.aspx`.

Controller

The controller is implemented in a report through a group of classes that are bounded under the report controller.

Report data contract

Implemented by `SRSReportDataContract`, this is the class that holds the different contracts used in a report. Each contract has its designated access method, such as `ParmQueryContract` and `ParmRDLContract` in the report data contract class. Here is a list of contracts present in a report data contract:

Contract	Purpose
RDLDataContract SRSReportRDLDataContract	Holds all the parameters related to the report including the system parameters, such as company, report context, user context
RDPDataContract	Holds the parameters related to an RDP class
Query Contract	Manages parameters for a query, including the dynamic filters and static ranges
PrintingContract SRSPrintDestinationSettings	Manages the print settings, such as destination, format, and so on

Report controller

This is the main controller that binds different contract classes and controls the execution of the report, starting from parsing the report `rdl`, binding the contracts, UI builder classes to the report, rendering the UI, invoking the report viewer, and post processing actions after the report is rendered. It is implemented by the `SRSReportRunController` base class and can be extended to apply report-specific controls.

We can use a controller class in the following scenarios:

  ▸ To open different reports/designs from the same menu item based on the input data

  ▸ To record base reports that are opened from a form

  ▸ To modify a report query based on the input data

  ▸ To modify report contract data based on the input data

The report controller uses different contract classes, each aimed at different purposes. All contracts involved in a report are referenced through the report data contract.

Report UI builder

This is another controller class that is responsible for building the UI based on related contracts. Implemented by `SRSReportDataContractUIBuilder`, this class extends the `SysOperationAutomaticUIBuilder` class and can be modified for report-specific implementation. Overridden to handle UI events such as validate, modified, and more.

View

The report model or the design is the representation of the view and it is designed through the Visual Studio extension for Dynamics AX. (Designing a report model was discussed in the previous chapters.)

The following diagram will help to understand the flow from the time a request to open a report is invoked till it is rendered, and after it is rendered as well.

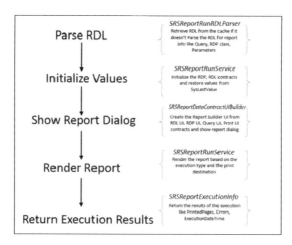

Modifying the report query in controller

Queries present the ability to add dynamic ranges to a report. Some situations demand ranges or sorting orders to be filled in, making it easier for the user. A good example would be an instance when a report is opened from the customer from which the range customer is prefilled. This recipe will handle this scenario of modifying queries through the controller class.

Getting Ready

This and the following recipes will use the **PktRdlItemTransList** report created in the first recipe.

How to do it...

1. In your controller class, override the `prepromptModifyContract` method and write the following code:

```
protected void prePromptModifyContract()
{
    Query                   query;
    QueryBuildDataSource    qbds;
    InventTable             inventTable;

    //if an argument is received then see if it is inventTable
    inventTable = args ? args.record() as inventTable : null;

    if (inventTable.RecId)
    {
        //get the query associated with the report
        query = this.getFirstQuery();
        qbds  = query.dataSourceTable(tableNum(InventTable));
        qbds.addRange(fieldNum(InventTable,
           ItemId)).value(inventTable.ItemId);
    }

}
```

2. Create a new menu item and add it to the **InventTable** form. Verify that the data source property on the button is set to **InventTable**.

3. Click the button to see that item name is pre-filled in the range in the report dialog.

In the `prepromptModifyContract` method, do not call the `super()` method.

For more details on the ternary operator (?), visit `http://msdn.microsoft.com/en-in/library/aa552755.aspx`.

How it works...

The `prePromptModifyContract` method available in the `SrReportRunController` class as we extend this class in our report controller class we are able to override this. The `prePromptModifyContract` method in the controller class is the designated location to place the code for modifying queries before they are displayed in the dialog. So any caller-based modification, or locking of ranges based on a caller, or the addition of other data sources can be done here.

The code discussed here could be applied to the `preRunModifyContract` method as well, but this method is invoked after the report dialog. Thus, the user never gets an option to modify or see the changes to the query.

Opening a report with a dialog

In Microsoft Dynamics AX R2 and R3, we can run an SSRS report with the help of a dialog. Dialogs help the user print the SSRS report on the basis of the parameters defined in the report dialog. Suppose a user wants to print the details of a selected customer, they will select the parameter, run the report, and print the desired result. The dialog of an SSRS report can be opened through a menu item.

How to do it...

1. In this recipe, the user will print the SSRS report which shows the customer's details on the basis of the customer account and customer group. So, the first step is to create an SSRS report using a query (as explained in *Chapter 1, Understanding and Creating Simple SSRS Reports*), giving the range as `AccountNum` and `CustGroup`.

2. The next step is to create a new menu item. Go to **AOT** | **Menu items** | **Output** and right-click on it. Click on **New Menu Item**, as shown in the following screenshot:

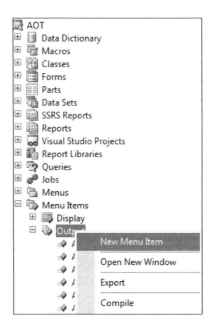

3. Now assign the SSRS report to the menu item.

4. The last step is to open the SSRS report through the menu item. The dialog looks like this:

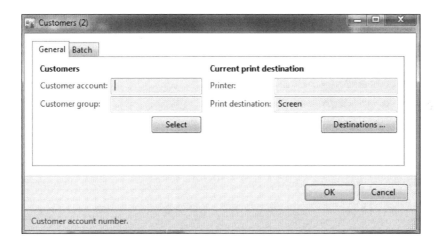

How it works...

To print an SSRS report in Microsoft Dynamics AX R3, the user requires a menu item so that they can run the report. We have three different types of menu items in Dynamics AX R3: **Display**, **Output**, and **Actions**. When creating a menu item for an SSRS report, you should choose the **Output** menu item, because output menu items have a purpose to print a result, mostly used for referencing classes.

Creating a report using the UI Builder class

SSRS reports can be created using UI Builder classes. UI builder classes are used to customize and add parameters to the dialog box at runtime, which opens before the report runs in Microsoft Dynamics AX R3. The UI Builder is used to define the layout of the parameter dialog box which pops up when an SSRS report is open. We can add the parameter in the dialog box and modify those parameters at runtime. With the help of the UI Builder, we can add the lookup in the dialog box, which will be created in the next recipe.

In this recipe, we will create a new SSRS report through the UI builder in Microsoft Dynamics AX R3 and customize the dialog box which opens the SSRS report. To create the UI builder class, it must extend the `SRSReportDataContractUIBuilder` class.

Getting Ready

To work with this recipe, we need to create a UI builder that extends the `SRSReportDataContractUIBuilder` class. In the UI builder class, we have a build method which is used to create a dialog through which the user can open the report.

How to do it...

1. The first step is to add a `UIBuilder` class that extends the `SRSReportDatacontractUIBuilder` class as follows:

```
class PktRdlWarehouseUIBuilder
extends SrsReportDataContractUIBuilder
{

}
```

2. The next step is to create a contract class named `PKTRdlWarehouseContract` and add the parameters using this contract class. Also, it is important to validate the contract parameters so that all the parameters have a value as shown in the following code snippet:

```
[
    DataContractAttribute,
    SysOperationContractProcessingAttribute
(classstr(PktRdlWarehouseUIBuilder))
]
public class PktRdlWarehouseContract implements
SysOperationValidatable
{
    TransDate                       fromDate;
    TransDate                       toDate;
    InventtransferUpdateType    status;
}


    [
        DataMemberAttribute('ToDate'),
        SysOperationLabelAttribute(literalStr("ToDate"))
    ]
public ToDate parmToDate(ToDate _toDate = toDate)
{
    toDate = _toDate;
    return toDate;
}


[
    DataMemberAttribute('FromDate'),
    SysOperationLabelAttribute(literalStr("FromDate"))
]
public FromDate parmFromDate(FromDate _fromDate = fromDate)
{
    fromDate = _fromDate;
    return fromDate;
}


    [
```

```
        DataMemberAttribute('Status'),
        SysOperationLabelAttribute(literalStr("Status"))
    ]
    public InventTransferUpdateTye
      parmStatus(InventTransferUpdateTye _status = status)
    {
        status = _status;
        return status;
    }


    public boolean validate()
    {
        boolean isValid = true;

        if (fromDate && toDate && fromDate > toDate)
        {
            isValid = checkFailed("From date cannot be
              greater than to date");
        }

        if (!fromDate)
        {
            isValid = checkFailed("From date must
              be filled in");
        }

        if (!toDate)
        {
            isValid = checkFailed("To date must
              be filled in ");
        }

        return isValid;
    }
```

3. Next, declare the variables in the class declaration of the UI builder class as follows:

```
    public class PKTRdlWarehouseUIBuilder extends
      SrsReportDataContractUIBuilder
    {
        DialogField        dialogStatus;
        DialogField        dialogFromDate;
        DialogField        dialogToDate;
    }
```

4. Now, we will override the `build` method—which is used to build the layout of the SSRS report—of the UI builder class as shown in the following snippet:

```
public void build()
{
    PktRdlWarehouseContract     pktRdlWarehouseContract;

    pktRdlWarehouseContract = this.dataContractObject() as
        PktRdlWarehouseContract;

    dialogStatus = this.addDialogField
        (methodStr(PktRdlWarehouseContract, parmStatus),
        pktRdlWarehouseContract);

    dialogFromDate  = this.addDialogField
        (methodStr(PktRdlWarehouseContract,parmFromDate),
        pktRdlWarehouseContract);

    dialogToDate  = this.addDialogField
        (methodStr(PktRdlWarehouseContract,parmToDate),
        pktRdlWarehouseContract);
}
```

5. The last step is to override the `postBuild` method—which initializes the dialog field after the fields have been built—of the UI builder class method as follows:

```
public void postBuild()
{
    PktRdlWarehouseContract     pktRdlWarehouseContract;
    super();

    pktRdlWarehouseContract = this.dataContractObject() as
        PktRdlWarehouseContract;

    dialogStatus = this.bindInfo().getDialogField
        (pktRdlWarehouseContract,
        methodStr(PktRdlWarehouseContract, ParmStatus));

    dialogFromDate = this.bindInfo().getDialogField
        (pktRdlWarehouseContract,
        methodStr(PktRdlWarehouseContract, parmFromdate));

    dialogToDate  = this.bindInfo().getDialogField
        (pktRdlWarehouseContract,
        methodStr(PktRdlWarehouseContract, parmTodate));
}
```

How it works...

The three report parameters namely, `FromDate`, `ToDate`, and `Status` are added to the report, on the basis of which the report is printed. The methods that have been added in the contract class are created with the attributes. The UI and the controller are bounded by the `SysOperationContractProcessingAttribute` class while the contract associated with a report is determined by the `SRSReportNameAttribute` class.

The UI builder works with different scenarios, such as grouping dialog fields, overriding dialog events, creating a customized lookup in the dialog field, changing the layout of the report dialog, and binding the UI builder class with the data contract class.

Adding a lookup on a report dialog using the UI Builder class

The UI builder class is used to customize the layout of the report dialog through which the report is run. In the report dialog, we can add a lookup using this class. In the previous recipe, we created a dialog using the UI builder class. In the same recipe, we will add another field to create a lookup in the dialog.

Getting Ready

The prerequisites for creating this recipe are Microsoft Dynamics AX R3, reporting extensions must be installed, and the contract class.

How to do it...

1. The first step is to create a new `parm` method for a new parameter in the contract class made in the previous recipe. Add the method, named `parmECCNumber`, to the contract class as follows:

```
[
    DataMemberAttribute('ECCNumber'),
    SysOperationLabelAttribute(literalStr("ECC Number"))
]
public TaxRegistrationNumber_IN
  parmEccNumber(TaxRegistrationNumber_IN _eccNumber =
  eccNumber)
{
    eccNumber = _eccNumber;
    return eccNumber;
}
```

The `SysOperationLabelAttribute` class is an attribute that is used to specify the label of the data member of the contract class. We are using the ECC number as the label of the data member of the contract class.

2. The next step is to create a lookup method in the UI builder class made in the previous recipe. We will create a lookup method using the `syslookup` class:

```
public static void eccNumberLookUp(FormControl
  _formControl)
{
    SysTableLookup sysTableLookup =
      SysTableLookup::newParameters(tablenum
      (TaxRegistrationNumbers_IN), _formControl);
    Query                   query           = new Query();
    QueryBuildDataSource    queryBuildDataSource;
    QueryBuildRange         queryBuildRange;

    queryBuildDataSource =
      query.addDataSource(tablenum
      (TaxRegistrationNumbers_IN));
    queryBuildRange =
      queryBuildDataSource.addRange(fieldnum
      (TaxRegistrationNumbers_IN, TaxType));
    queryBuildRange.value(queryValue(TaxType_IN::Excise));

    sysTableLookup.addLookupfield(fieldnum
      (TaxRegistrationNumbers_IN, RegistrationNumber));
    sysTableLookup.addLookupfield(fieldnum
      (TaxRegistrationNumbers_IN, Name));
    sysTableLookup.parmQuery(query);
    sysTableLookup.performFormLookup();
}
```

In this method, we have created a lookup method for the ECC number. In the lookup method, we have stated that the range for the tax type should be equal to excise. So, using this lookup method will return the lookup with the ECC number of the excise tax type.

3. In the UI builder class, add a variable in the class declaration method of the class:

```
DialogField   dialogECCNumber;
```

4. To add the customized layout of the dialog of the report, we will override the build method of the UI builder class as follows:

```
public void build()
{
    PKTRDLWarehouseContract    pKTRDLWarehouseContract;
```

```
pKTRDLWarehouseContract = this.dataContractObject()
    as PKTRDLWarehouseContract;

dialogECCNumber =
    this.addDialogField(methodStr
    PKTRDLWarehouseContract , parmECCnumber),
    pKTRDLWarehouseContract );
}
```

5. Now, we will override the `postBuild` method—which is called when the dialog is created—of the UI builder class, as shown in the following snippet:

```
public void postBuild()
{
    PKTRDLWarehouseContract      pKTRDLWarehouseContract;
    super();

    pKTRDLWarehouseContract = this.dataContractObject()
     as PKTRDLWarehouseContract;

    dialogECCNumber =
      this.bindInfo().getDialogField
      (pKTRDLWarehouseContract,
      methodStr(PKTRDLWarehouseContract, ParmEccNumber));
    dialogECCNumber.registerOverrideMethod(
      methodStr(FormStringControl, lookup),
      methodStr(PKTRDLWarehouseUIBuilder_IN,
      eccNumberLookup),this);
}
```

The `BindInfo` method returns the object of `SysOperationUIBindInfo`, which contains information about the dialog controls bounded to a report contract.

6. After running the report, the dialog will look like the following screenshot:

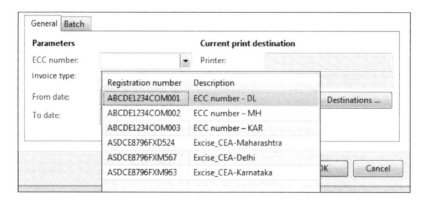

How it works...

We have just finished adding another parameter of ECC number into the dialog box. By giving the lookup on the ECC number, the user will be able to choose the value from the multiple options. Lookup can easily be added to the report dialog using the UI builder class. To make the lookup, we need to write the query to get the lookup and then bind the lookup method with the contract `parm` method. The `RegisterOverrideMethod` is used to create a lookup which registers the runtime overridden method and object for the given method.

Connecting the UI builder class with a contract class

A contract class is used to define one or more parameters that are used in an SSRS report. It consists of `parm` methods with `DataMemberAttribute`, which is defined at the beginning of the `parm` method. If users want to customize the parameters in the report dialog, then they will require the UI builder class and will need to connect the UI builder class with the contract class. The `SysOperationContractProcessingAttribute` class is used to link the UI builder class with the contract class in an SSRS report in Microsoft Dynamics AX R3.

Getting Ready

In this recipe, we will link the contract class with the UI builder class. This can be done by using the `BindInfo` method of the UI builder class, which binds the dialog controls bounded to a report contract.

How to do it...

Create a contract class to link with the UI builder class as follows:

```
[
    SysOperationContractProcessingAttribute
(classStr(PKTRDLCustInvoiceUIBuilder))
]
public class PKTRDLCustInvoiceContract
{
    FromDate        fromDate;
    ToDate          toDate;
}
```

The `SysOperationContractProcessAttribute` is used to bind the contract class with the UI builder class. It tells the contract class to build the parameter dialog.

In the earlier recipe, we used the `bindInfo` method in the UI builder class, which binds the report dialog controls with the report data contract parameters.

How it works...

Linking the UI builder class with the contract class of an SSRS report in Microsoft Dynamics AX R3 is necessary so that report parameters can be customized and shown in the report dialog. `SysOperationContractProcessingAttribute` is written above the class declaration of the data contract class in square brackets, which tells the data contract class that the UI builder class is linked to the contract class.

Adding ranges from unbound parameters to a query

SSRS reports support using parameters that are not part of a dataset. This recipe will attempt to use the unbound parameters `FromDate` and `ToDate` added to the report to set the ranges in the report query. These parameters are added to the report and are not connected to any dataset. The values in these controls will be received and set in the report query.

How to do it...

1. The first step is to create a contract and UI builder class and bind them together (assuming you have created the parameters as discussed in the first recipe *Opening a report through a controller*).

2. Add a `UIBuilder` class that extends `SRSReportDatacontractUIBuilder` as follows:

```
public class PktRdlItemTransListUIBuilder extends
   SrsReportDataContractUIBuilder
{

}
```

3. Add a contract class that extends `SRSReportRdlDataContract` as shown in the following snippet:

```
[
    SrsReportNameAttribute(ssrsReportStr
      (PktRdlItemTransList, ItemTransList)),
    SysOperationContractProcessingAttribute(classstr
      (PktItemTransUIBuilder),
      SysOperationDataContractProcessingMode::
      CreateSeparateUIBuilderForEachContract)
]
public class PktRdlItemTransListRdlContract extends
   SRSReportRdlDataContract
{
```

```
    TransDate    fromDate;
    TransDate    toDate;
    #define.FromDate('FromDate')
    #define.ToDate('ToDate')
}
```

4. The next step is to show these values in the UI. If the report is previewed in Visual Studio, the **FromDate** and **ToDate** parameters appear as shown in the following screenshot. This may not be a convenient way for the end user to specify date ranges.

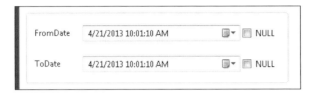

5. To add the date fields to the report dialog, add the following method and call it from the overridden method `PktItemTransListUIBuilder\build` as follows:

```
class PktRdlItemTransListUIBuilder extends
   SrsReportDataContractUIBuilder
{
    DialogField dialogFromDate;
    DialogField dialogToDate;

//identifier text for retrieving the value
//from the parameter map in RDL data contract
//The names must match the name provided in the report //model

    #define.FromDate('FromDate')
    #define.ToDate('ToDate')
}

private void addDateFields()
{
    dialog                         dialogLocal;
    PktRdlItemTransListRdlContract   transContract;

    dialogLocal = this.dialog();
    transContract = this.getRdlContractInfo()
      .dataContractObject()
      as PktRdlItemTransListRdlContract;

    dialogFromDate = dialogLocal.addFieldValue(
      extendedTypeStr(FromDate),
```

```
//set the value from the contract.
//is equivalent of unPack and initialize in ax 2009
        DatetimeUtil::date(transContract.getValue(
        #FromDate)), "@SYS5209");

    dialogToDate = dialogLocal.addFieldValue(
        extendedTypeStr(ToDate),
        DatetimeUtil::date(transContract.getValue(
        #ToDate)), "@SYS14656");
}
public void build()
{
    super();
    this.addDateFields();
}
```

6. Run the report to see the result, which will look like the following screenshot:

The report image shows four controls. This is the result of the framework adding two controls for the type `Datetime` and two controls being added by the extended class for type `Date`. To make only the controls added by the child class visible, comment `super` in the build method. This turns out to be a disadvantage, as every other control such as `showApproved` present in the report dialog field must be added explicitly in the same way as `FromDate` and `ToDate` are added.

The report image shows three controls. This is the result of the framework adding two controls for the type `UTCDatetime` and customer account controls being added by the extended class for type `CustAccount`.

7. After the controls have been added, these values must be saved in the contract to be set in the query. Override the `getFromDialog` method in the UI builder class and write the following code to save the value to the contract:

```
public void getFromDialog()
{
    PktRdlItemTransListRdlContract  transContract;

    transContract = this.getRdlContractInfo()
        .dataContractObject() as
        PktRdlItemTransListRdlContract;

    transContract.setValue(#FromDate, DateTimeUtil::
        newDateTime(dialogFromDate.value(), 0));
    transContract.setValue(#ToDate, DateTimeUtil::
        newDateTime(dialogToDate.value(), 0));
}
```

This completes adding the `Date` field to the UI, storing, and showing back the values from the data contract.

8. The values from the dialog should be set in the query to make it complete. This must be done after the user clicks **OK** on the report dialog. The `preRunModifyContract` method on the controller is invoked after the user clicks **OK**, so the `preRunModifyContract` method will be appropriate to use in this case. Override this method with the following code:

```
protected void preRunModifyContract()
{
    #define.parameterFromDate('FromDate')
    #define.parameterToDate('ToDate')

    SrsReportRdlDataContract    contract;
    contract = this.parmReportContract().parmRdlContract();

    Date fromDate =
      contract.getParameter(#parameterFromDate)
      .getValueTyped();
    Date toDate =
     contract.getParameter(#parameterToDate)
     .getValueTyped();
```

```
        Query query = this.getFirstQuery();

    //Modify the query contract based on fromDate & toDate.
        SrsReportHelper::addFromAndToDateRangeToQuery(
          query, fromDate, toDate,
          tableNum(InventTrans),
          fieldNum(InventTrans, DatePhysical));
    }
```

9. The last part is to ensure that the value of `FromDate` is less than `ToDate`. Any validations in the contract values can be placed in the contract class. Override the `PktRdlItemTransListRdlContract\Validate` method with the following code:

```
public boolean validate()
{
    boolean isValid = super();
    fromDate = this.getValue(#FromDate);
    toDate = this.getValue(#ToDate);

    if(fromDate && toDate)
    {
        if(fromDate > toDate)
        {
            isValid = checkFailed("@SYS120590");
        }
    }

    return isValid;
}
```

How it works...

The two report parameters `FromDate` and `ToDate` that are added to the report directly are accessed through the controller. Since the report model only supports `DateTime` and not `Date`, the report dialog when previewed shows a control of type `DateTime`. The `Datetime` field type in the UI may not be convenient to enter inputs and the date value alone is required in this case. This can be done through adding custom controls of type `Date` to the UI. By blocking the `super` call, the controls are prevented from being added to the report dialog. Alternative date controls are added through the code and are bounded to the report parameters. The values from these overridden controls are then added to the query. This way we understand how we can create an unbounded control and override the type of control that is rendered to the UI.

The classes created in this recipe are decorated with attributes. The attributes attached to the contract class create the necessary binding. The UI and the controller are bounded by the `SysOperationContractProcessingAttribute` while the contract associated with a report is determined by the `SRSReportNameAttribute`. As seen in the previous screenshot, a control of `DateTime` type is shown. To be able to do this, it is important to understand the parameters and contracts along with how they are stored.

RDP vs RDL data contract

This chapter will largely use the RDL contract to control report parameters. In this section, the major contract types have been discussed to create clarity in understanding. Contracts are used to share input values between the controller, UI builder, and the report at runtime. The RDL and RDP contracts are very important as these carry user inputs. RDP and RDL have been compared here to give a detailed understanding (RDP contracts have been discussed in detail in *Chapter 4, Report Programming Model – RDP*):

RDL data contract	RDP data contract
A report is bound to a query, data method, or OLAP data source and validation logic must be added to the parameters.	A report is bound to an RDP class and validation logic must be added to the parameters.
It holds system parameters and report model parameters.	It holds contract-specific parameters.
Parameters are accessed by their identifier name; for example, `Contract.get("FromDate")`, `Contract.set("FromDate")`.	Parameters are accessed by the corresponding parm method; for example, `Contract.ParmFromdates`.
Contracts are stored in Maps.	Contracts are stored in corresponding variables.
It is weakly typed.	It is strongly typed.
It is used in all reports.	It is only used for RDP-based reports.
The parameter map consists of all parameters, including the RDP parameters.	It holds reference only to its own parameters.
It is bounded to a report.	It can be shared across reports.
It stores system parameters, such as **Company name**, **Report context**, and others.	System parameters are not accessible through this contract.

 An RDP report can have both RDL and RDP data contracts. Each data contract can have its own UI builder, but care must be taken that events are carefully delegated and handled.

Modifying the UI by caller

This recipe will discuss how the controls in the report dialog can be added or removed based on the caller. For this purpose, the third parameter `ShowApproved` added in the first recipe will be used. `ItemTrans` has an **Approved** field and the idea is to link this unbound parameter to this field in the dataset so that users can easily choose it in the report dialog rather than adding it through the dynamic filters in the query.

How to do it...

1. The `build` method from the UI builder class will be the ideal choice to handle any changes to the UI. Create a method called `enableApprovedFlag()` and call this method from the build method in UI builder. This can alternatively be invoked from the `postBuild` method of the UI builder.

```
private void enableApprovedFlag()
{
    Dialog        dlg;
    TableId       tableId;
    PktRdlItemTransController transController;
    DialogField dialogApproved;

    dlg = this.dialog();
    //add the field since the super call is blocked
    in the build method
    //dialogApproved is a global variable
    dialogApproved  = dlg.addFieldValue(
      extendedTypeStr(NoYesId), this.dataContractObject()
      .getValue(#ShowApproved), "Include Approved");
    //if super is not blocked then get the dialog field
    using this syntax

    transController = this.controller() as
      PktRdlItemTransController;

    if (transController.parmArgs())
    {
        tableId =
          transController.parmArgs().record().TableId;
        if (tableNum(InventTable) == tableId)
        {
            dialogApproved.visible(false);
        }
    }
}
```

2. As we have learnt in the *Adding ranges from unbound parameters to a query* recipe, the methods `getDialogField` in the UI builder (`PktRdlItemTransUIBuilder`) and `preRunModifyContract` in the controller classes must be modified to retrieve the value and to set the value in the query correspondingly.

3. Save and compile the classes and now run the report. When the report is invoked from the **InventTable** form, the report dialog will now display the **Show approved** flag.

How it works...

The visibility of control can be easily switched, as shown here, thus helping in creating a dynamic and context-specific report dialog. If you wish a report parameter to be completely hidden, it is recommended that you use the visible property in Visual Studio.

Turning off a report dialog

When no user interaction is required, the report can be run directly without the report dialog. This short recipe will show how this can be done.

How to do it...

1. In the controller class of the report, add the following code:

```
public static void main(Args args)
{
    PktRdlItemTransController controller;

    controller = new PktRdlItemTransController();
    controller.parmReportName(ssrsReportStr
        (PktRdlItemTransList, ItemTransList));
    controller.parmArgs(args);
    //turn off dialog
    controller.parmShowDialog(false);
    controller.startOperation();
}
```

2. Run the report to see that the report opens up directly without any prompts.

Setting up security for reports

Security set up for a report is significant as it helps apply the right control. As a developer, it is important to understand the right security approach during development. Through this recipe, we will learn how to properly set up security for reports.

How to do it...

1. Go to the **Action** menu item and add a new menu item.

2. In the properties of the menu item, set the properties as follows:

Property	Value
Name	PktItemTransList
Object Type	Class
Object	PktItemTransController
LinkedPermissionType	SSRSReport
LinkedPermissionObject	PktItemTransList
LinkedPermissionObjectChild	ItemTransList
ViewUserLicense	Functional
MaintainUserLicense	Functional

How it works...

The `LinkedPermissionType` properties control the security of a report. They tell the security framework where the security for this menu item must be inferred from. The framework tries to retrieve the associated report from the object attached to the entry points, which is a menu item in this case. When there is no controller class, the steps discussed in this recipe can be applied to the display menu item that invokes the report.

Adding up the report menu item into privilege

The security privileges in Microsoft Dynamics AX R3 basically constitute a group of permissions. The entry points below each privilege identify the objects that the user can access. By using a privilege, we give permissions to forms, menu items, tables, and SSRS reports. A privilege provides multiple access levels to securable objects. These levels are `Read`, `Update`, `Delete`, `Create`, `Correct`, and `NoAccess`. In this recipe, we will learn how a menu item can be added into a privilege. We will create a new privilege and add a menu item into it.

How to do it...

1. The first step is to create a new menu item in the SSRS report. Go to **AOT | Menu Items | Output** and right-click on it. Click on **New Menu Item**. Name the new menu item as `PKTRDLMenuItem`.

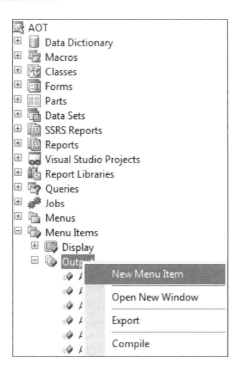

2. Assign the properties of the menu item as follows:

Properties	Values
Name	PktRdlMenutItem
LinkedPermissionType	SSRSReport
LinkedPermissionObject	PKTRdlCustInvoiceReport
LinkedPermissionObjectChild	Report

3. The next step is to create a new privilege. Go to **AOT** | **Security** | **Privileges** and right-click on it. Click on **New Privilege** and name it as `PktRdlPrivilege`.

4. Now drag and drop **PKTRdlMenuItem** into the entry point of **PKTRdlPrivilege**. Assign the access level of the menu item to **Read**. This is how we assign the level of the menu item in the privilege.

How it works...

Privileges are a group of related permissions that are required to perform a duty. We can apply access levels to securable objects. In the standard Microsoft Dynamics AX R3 application, there are several existing privileges that meet the business requirements. However, if these requirements are not met, then users can make their own privileges. We can assign the privilege directly to security roles if needed. In Microsoft Dynamics AX R3, there are duties that are predefined by the application, which is the group of privileges. Now, the administrator no longer has the need to identify the application objects and can grant access to objects.

Find more information on creating new duties, roles, and privileges at `http://technet.microsoft.com/en-us/library/hh556870.aspx`.

Calling multiple reports from a controller

A single controller can be used to invoke multiple reports. This recipe will discuss how to use the same controller for different reports and the security set up for multiple reports from a single controller.

How to do it...

1. Here we have modified our method to choose two different reports: one developed in *Chapter 2, Enhancing Your Report – Visualization and Interaction* and the other from the current chapter. In this we will invoke the multiple reports using the single controller:

    ```
    public static void main(Args args)
    {
        PktRdlItemTransController controller;

        controller = new PktRdlItemTransController();
        if (args && args.record())
        {
            switch (args.record().TableId)
            {
                case tableNum(InventTable)):
                    controller.parmReportName(ssrsReportStr
                    (PktRdlItemTransList, ItemTransList));
                        break;
                case tableNum(CustGroup)):
                    controller.parmReportName(ssrsReportStr
                    (PktItemTransList, TransList));
                        break;
            }
        }
        controller.parmArgs(args);
        controller.startOperation();
    }
    ```

2. When the controller is connected to more than one report, the permission setup for the menu item differs. It involves creating a security permission object and linking it to the report controller.

3. Go to **AOT | Security | Code Permissions** and right-click on it. Then select **New Code Permission**.

4. Create a new permission object called `PktItemTransReport`. Expand the **Associated Objects** node, select **Reports**, and add the reports that are used in the controller.

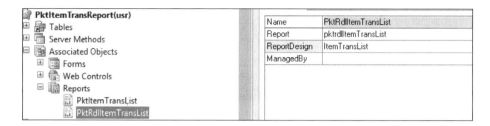

5. Create an action menu item and set the following properties:

Property	Value
Object Type	Class
Object	PktRDLItemTransController
LinkedPermissionType	CodePermission
LinkedPermissionObject	PktRDLItemTransList

How it works...

The permission object bundles all the reports and helps the menu item determine the security rights that must be assigned to a role that will use these report bundles. Use the main method in the controller class to select the appropriate report based on context.

Calling multiple reports simultaneously using a single controller

In the previous recipe, we explained how to call multiple reports using a single controller. But in this recipe, we will explain how we can call multiple reports simultaneously. This means we will print multiple reports from a single trigger point.

In this recipe, we will show how to print the two SSRS reports together using a single controller in Microsoft Dynamics AX R3.

How to do it...

1. Suppose on the clicked method of any control of a form, we need to print two SSRS reports simultaneously. For that, firstly we need to create two menu items to call two SSRS reports. To create the menu item, follow these steps:

2. Go to **AOT** | **Menu Item** | **Output** and right-click on it. Create a new menu item named `PKTRDLCustListMenu`. Similarly, create another menu item and name it `PKTRDLVendListMenu`.

3. Assign the SSRS report to both the menu items (as discussed in the previous recipe).

4. The controller class extends the `SRSReportRunController` class. In the controller, override the `dialogShow()` method as follows:

```
protected void dialogShow()
{
    SysOperationDialog   sysOperationDialog;
    FormRun              formRun;

    dialog.run();
    this.dialogPostRun();
    sysOperationDialog = dialog as SysOperationDialog;
    formRun = sysOperationDialog.formRun();
    formRun.detach();
}
```

This method will detach the form run and run another dialog of the report.

5. Now, override the `dialogClose()` method of the controller class and comment the `Super()` method of this method because in this method in the parent class, until the dialog is not closed, another report cannot be run. So we have to override this method and comment the `Super()` method as follows:

```
protected void dialogClose()
{
    //super();
}
```

6. Now we will modify the main method of the controller class as follows:

```
public static void main(Args _args)
{
    PKTRdlController formLetterController =
      new PKTRdlController();

    if(_args.menuItemName() ==
      menuitemOutputStr(PktRdlCustListMenu))
    {
        formlettercontroller.parmReportName
          (ssrsReportStr(PktRdlCustReport, Report));
    }
    if(_args.menuItemName() ==
      menuitemOutputStr(PktRdlVendListMenu))
    {
```

```
        formlettercontroller.parmReportName
          (ssrsReportStr(PKTRdlVendReport, Report));
    }

    formLetterController.parmShowDialog(false);
    formLetterController.startOperation();
}
```

7. Finally, we call the controller class using the menu item on the clicked method of form control:

```
void clicked()
{
    Args                args = new Args();
    Args                args1 = new Args();

new MenuFunction(menuitemOutputStr(PktRdlCustListMenu _IN),
    MenuItemType::Output).run(args);
new MenuFunction(menuitemOutputStr(PktRdlVendListMenu _IN),
    MenuItemType::Output).run(args1);
}
```

How it works...

To control the report execution and processing of the report data, the controller class is being used. The controller class extends the SRSReportRunController class. To call the reports through the menu item, the controller class is used. Using the two menu items for two reports corresponding with the single controller, both reports can be printed simultaneously. By overriding the dialogClose() and dialogShow() methods, multiple SSRS reports can be printed simultaneously.

Debugging a report model

One challenge that comes along with the new reporting model is debugging. Different approaches for debugging issues must be taken based on the context. This is a short recipe that will tell you the configurations to debug the report model and the possible methods where the debugging points would be appropriate to start.

How to do it...

To debug framework-related classes the AX debugger can be used:

1. Under developer options, make sure the **Execute business operations in CIL** flag is unchecked to enable you to debug the code in X++ debugger.

2. The following methods are ideal to place your debugger to examine the execution:

    ❑ **Controller**: `PrePromptModifyReport, PreRunModifyReport`

    ❑ **UI Builder**: `build`

 You must first open your debugger manually to use it. Then run your code.

Changes to model and adding new classes

This subsection is about refreshing the code when you make changes to the model or framework classes.

When changes are made to the query by adding ranges or fields, ensure that you open Visual Studio. On the dataset, select refresh and then redeploy the project.

The report model is cached inside AX to ensure faster operation. In the event of changing the report model or introducing a new UI builder or contract class, it is important to refresh the cached elements under **Tools | Caches | Refresh elements**.

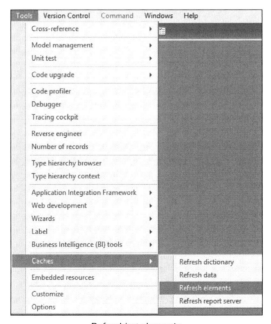

Refreshing elements

If this still doesn't reload the changes, resolve the problem by attempting to log in to AX again. This will definitely refresh the cache.

How it works...

Unlike AX 2009, every part of a report cannot be debugged by a unified approach like using the AX debugger. This specific recipe suggests how the report modeling framework inside AX, which comprises the controller and UI builder, can be done.

Adding data methods in business logic

While display methods in AX can be accessed through the table methods exposed in the **Query** window, there can be small computational needs in every report. If these small computations cannot be implemented by expressions, then they can be handled by data methods. These are based on C# and can be used to leverage the C# framework capabilities for small computations. This recipe will showcase adding a data method to the report where a text in a selected field is made upper case.

How to do it...

1. Right-click on the **Data Methods** node of your report data model to add a new data method.

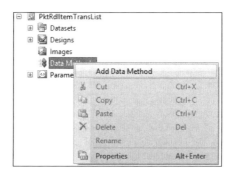

Adding a data method

2. Rename the data method to `changeCase`.

3. Double-click on the new data method and a new C# project with the name of the report will be added to the solution.

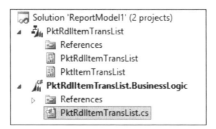

4. The cursor will point to a plain implementation method that appears similar to this:

```
[DataMethod (), PermissionSet (SecurityAction.Assert,
  Name = "FullTrust")]
    public static string DataMethod1()
    {
    throw new NotImplementedException("The method or
      operation is not implemented.");
    }
```

5. The `[DataMethod]` attribute indicates that this is a data method. The default return value is string, but this method can return any .Net supported types.

6. Rewrite the logic to convert the voucher number to upper case:

```
[DataMethod(), PermissionSet(SecurityAction.Assert,
  Name = "FullTrust")]
    public static string changeCase(string value)
    {
        return value.ToUpper();
    }
```

7. Compile the code and it is ready to be used. Verify to see the report model showing the new parameters as sub nodes, as seen in the following screenshot:

8. To use the business logic that was created previously, expand the **Data** node under **AutoDesign** and add a new field.

9. Go to the property expression, open the expression dialog and key in the following code:

```
=changeCase(Fields!Voucher.Value)
```

This way the expression is tied to the data method that has been added.

10. Run the report and notice the new field showing the voucher number in upper case.

How it works...

Data methods in the report model provide the ability to manipulate and modify the report data. They can be used for:

- Implementing expressions
- Returning a `DataTable` that can be used as a dataset
- Building URLs for the drill-through action connecting to a SubReport or a URL

It is wise to remember that these data methods are not alternatives to the AX business logic. Avoid using data methods to implement business logic or query the AX database. Simple data methods can be achieved using expressions as well, but the choice has to be made based on the requirement.

Data method vs Expressions

Chapter 1, Understanding and Creating Simple SSRS Reports and *Chapter 2, Enhancing Your Report – Visualization and Interaction*, detailed how the expressions window can be used to write simple logic, but they are limited to the number of lines that can be used. These logics are not reusable, and do not have the option of including any external references from the .NET framework to compute. A data method overcomes these disadvantages.

Data methods can be invoked from expressions and they offer the flexibility to include external references and write bigger computations, and the compiler indicates any break in the code with greater detail. A data method can be accessed and called via the expression.

Adding a URL drill through action in reports

A URL drill through action is similar to the **View Details** option in a form. AX supports a URL mechanism that can be processed to open a form with the appropriate record highlighted.

How to do it...

1. The first step is to identify the URL builder that will be used to construct the URL. The **SRSDrillThroughCommon** project consists of a list of helper classes for different modules.

2. In Visual Studio, go to **AOT | Visual Studio Project | C Sharp Project | SRSDrillThroughCommon**.

3. Right-click and select **Edit**. This will add the project to the current report solution.

4. Search through the **drillThroughCommon** C# class for prebuilt methods for the field.

5. In this case, the field is **Voucher** and the finance helper classes have a prebuilt function that can handle drill through for vouchers.

6. Navigate back to the **PktRdlItemTransList.BusinessLogic**, right-click, and add the **SRSDrillThroughCommon** project as a reference.

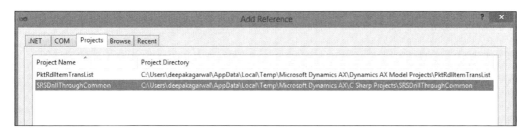

7. Add the following namespace to the **PktRdlItemTransList** C# class:

```
using Microsoft.Dynamics.AX.Application.Reports;
```

8. Add this code to generate the URL to open the **Voucher Transactions** from the **Voucher** column in the report and build the solution:

```
[DataMethod(), PermissionSet(SecurityAction.Assert,
    Name = "FullTrust")]
public static string DrillVoucher(string      reportContext,
    string     VoucherNum, DateTime  ADate,
    String     CompanyValue)
    {
        return DrillThroughCommonHelper
          .ToLedgerTransVoucherForm(reportContext,
          VoucherNum, ADate, CompanyValue);
    }
```

9. Move to the report model and right-click on the **Voucher** field. Select **Add | URL drill through action** and name it URLDrillAction.

10. In the new node properties node, select the expression and enter the following statement:

```
=drillVoucher(!Parameters.AX_ReportContext.Value,
              !Fields.ItemTrans.VoucherNum.value,
              !Fields.ItemTrans.TrandDate.value,
              !Parameters.AX_CompanyName.Value);
```

11. Rebuild the solution and deploy the report to see **Drill Through** in action.

How it works...

A typical URL to open a currency form appears as `menuitemdisplay://currency/+47+%5B1:USD%5D`. These URLs are processed by the `SysHelp::processStandardLink()` method to open the appropriate forms and highlight the selection.

AX automatically adds drill through action to fields with foreign key relations, such as customer, vendor, and so on. In the case of specific fields such as **Voucher Number**, where finding the record involves more than one field or is different, a drill through action needs to be added. AX has built-in classes that have helper classes that can handle a majority of the drill through actions.

Debugging business logic

Business logic can be debugged using the Visual Studio debugger. Follow this recipe to activate debugger and debug the report.

How to do it...

1. Ensure that you are on the same server where the reporting services is installed.
2. Set the project configuration to point to debug mode, and rebuild and deploy the solution including the report model and the included business logic.
3. This will deploy the necessary symbols for debugging.
4. Open **Tools | Attach to Process**, and make sure **Show Process** from **All users** and **Show Process** from **All sessions** is checked.
5. Under the displayed process select **ReportServicesService.exe** and click **Attach**.
6. Open the report through the report services in the web browser or in AX.
7. After specifying the parameter values in the dialog, the reporting services will activate the debugger.

How it works...

The business logic for a report is stored along with the report as a DLL. These DLLs are deployed along with the RDL. To debug the data method, the debug files are loaded. If the files are not loaded, debugging is impossible. It is preferable to use the unit testing approach which is defined in the following recipe.

Unit testing business logic

Debugging can be a time-consuming task as it is required to re-deploy the reports for every change that is made. An alternate way to reduce this cycle and make it easier to test is by creating unit test cases. Visual Studio has handy tools that can create a unit testing project. This recipe will implement unit testing for the drill-through action implemented in the *Adding a URL drill through action in reports* recipe.

How to do it...

1. Select the **DrillVoucher** method in the business logic class. Right-click and select **Create Unit Tests**.

2. A **Create Unit Tests** dialog will appear with the **DrillVoucher** method selected by default. If additional methods are present, check them and click on **OK**.

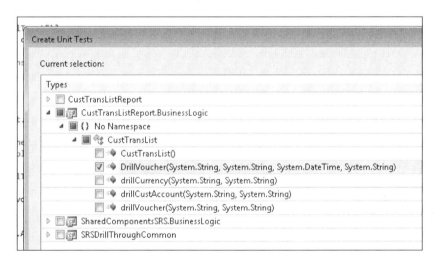

This will create a unit test project and a specific implementation to invoke the DrillVoucher method like this:

```
[TestMethod()]
        public void DrillVoucherTest()
        {
            string reportContext =
              "?RunOnClient=1&PrintMediumType=Screen"
            string VoucherNum = "ARPM000004";
            DateTime ADate = new DateTime(200, 02, 28);
            string CompanyValue = "USSI";
            //initialize if you want use assert
            //string expected;
```

```
                    string actual;
                    actual =
                       ItemTransList.DrillVoucher(reportContext,
                       VoucherNum, ADate, CompanyValue);
                    //initial approach would be test using
                    //Ax Class SysHelp::ProcessStandardLink
                    //Once the link is verified it can be added to
                    the expected.
                    //Assert.AreEqual(expected, actual);
             }
```

3. Place the debugger anywhere in the method. In the tool bar, select **Test** | **Debug** | **All Tests** in **Solution**. This will activate the debugger.

4. The business logic tested in the previous recipe is a drill through URL. Copy the returned URL from the unit test and run the following job in AX to see if it opens the right form and highlights the selection.

```
static void JobTestURL(Args _args)
{
    //Add the URL fetched through the unit test results
    SysHelp::processStandardLink('menuitemdisplay:
       //ledgertransvoucher/+3123+%5B63:ARPM000004%5D%5B2:
       02/28/2011%2000:00:00%5D%5B64:USSI%5D', null);
}
```

How it works...

The unit testing framework comes as part of Visual Studio and helps test code units. Most of the process is automated here and requires minimal effort to get it working such as passing the input parameters and validating the output parameters. This also helps in achieving better coverage of the logic since some logic never gets tested during functional testing. This unit test can be maintained or discarded after this testing, but opt to discard it as it can always be regenerated, unless you have huge prerequisites that are difficult to recreate, such as inserting records.

Creating a report using a controller and the UI Builder class

The controller class is primarily used to manage the report execution. This class is used in the SRS reporting framework to modify the dialog of a report, process the parameters of a report, as well as call SQL Reporting Services.

In this recipe, we will generate an SSRS report in Microsoft Dynamics using the controller class and UI builder class. The controller class extends SRSReportRunController.

How to do it...

1. The first step is to create a contract class which implements
   `SysOperationValidatable` to validate all the report parameters (explained in
   the previous recipe).

2. The next step is to create a controller class which extends the
   `SRSReportRunController` class. The `Main()` method is used in the controller
   class of the report execution.

   ```
   public client static void main(Args _args)
   {
       PktRdlCustomerVendorController controller = new
   PktRdlCustomerVendorController ();

       controller.parmReportName(ssrsReportStr(PktRdlCustomerVendorRe
   port, Report));

       controller.parmArgs(_args);
       controller.startOperation();
   }
   ```

   The `ParmReportName` method is used to define the name of the report and the
   design of the corresponding SSRS report.

3. The next step is to create a UI builder class which extends
   `SRSReportDataContractUIBuilder` class. In the UI builder, we will change
   the range of the query being used in the SSRS report depending upon the
   parameter selected.

   ```
   public boolean TypeModified(FormComboBoxControl _control)
   {
       boolean                 ret = true;
       QueryBuildDataSource    qbds;

   Map queryContracts =
     PktRdlCustomerVendorController.parmReportContract()
    .parmQueryContracts();
       MapEnumerator mapEnum;

       if(queryContracts)
       {
           mapEnum = queryContracts.getEnumerator();
           if(mapEnum.moveNext())
           {
               query = mapEnum.currentValue();
           }
   ```

```
    }

    ret = _control.selectionChange();

    if (ret)
    {
        qbds =
          query.dataSourceTable(tableNum(TaxTrans_IN));
        qbds.clearRanges();
        if (dialogField.value() == Type::Customer)
        {
            qbds.addRange(fieldNum(TaxTrans_IN, Customer));
        }
        else
        {
            qbds.addRange(fieldNum(TaxTrans_IN, Vendor));
        }
        this.rebuildQueryControl(this.getQueryBuilder());
    }
    return ret;
}
```

This method is used to modify the range of the query based on the parameter selected. If the user selects customer, then the range of the query will be customer, and if the user selects vendor, then the range of the query will be vendor.

4. Now create a new method named getQueryBuilder to get the query as follows:

```
private SysDataContractQueryUIBuilder getQueryBuilder()
{
    Map contractObjects;
    MapEnumerator contractEnumerator;
    SysOperationDataContractInfo contractInfo;
    SysOperationUIBuilder builder;

    contractObjects =
      PktRdlCustomerVendorController
      .getDataContractInfoObjects();
    if (contractObjects)
    {
        contractEnumerator =
          contractObjects.getEnumerator();

        while (contractEnumerator.moveNext())
        {
```

```
            contractInfo =
              contractEnumerator.currentValue();

            builder =
              PktRdlCustomerVendorController
              .getUIBuilderForContractObject(contractInfo
              .dataContractObject());
            if (builder is SysDataContractQueryUIBuilder)
            {
                return builder;
            }
        }
    }

    return null;
}
```

5. Next, create a method named `rebuildQueryControl` to rebuild the query on the basis of the parameters, as follows:

```
public void rebuildQueryControl(SysDataContractQueryUIBuilder _
queryUIBuilder)
{
    FormBuildControl          queryBuildControl;
    FormGroupControl          queryControl;
    Form                      form = this.dialog().form();
    FormRun                   formRun = this.dialog().formRun();

    SRSReportRunBuilder       queryHelper;

    #SrsFramework

    if (formRun)
    {
        formRun.lock();

queryControl = form.design().control(#GroupPrefix + _
queryUIBuilder.dataContractInfo().key());

        queryControl = formRun.control(queryControl.id());

        queryHelper = PktRdlCustomerVendorController.queryHelper
(_queryUIBuilder.dataContractInfo().key());
        queryHelper.updateQueryGroupControl(
            queryControl,
```

```
            new QueryRun(query));

        formRun.unLock();
    }

}
```

6. Finally, override the post build method of the UI builder class:

```
public void postBuild()
{
    PktRdlCustomerVendorController = this.controller();
    dialogField  = this.bindInfo().getDialogField(
      this.dataContractObject(), methodStr(
      PktRdlCustomerVendorContract, parmType));

    super();

    dialogField.registerOverrideMethod(
        methodStr(FormComboBoxControl, Modified),
        methodStr(PktRdlCustomerVendorUIBuilder,
          TypeModified),
        this);
}
```

Open the report dialog; it will look like the following screenshot:

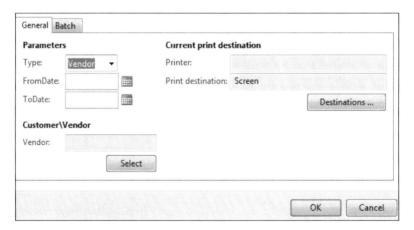

How it works...

In the main method of the controller, the `startOperation()` method is called, which starts the execution of the SSRS report. The controller class can be used before the report dialog is shown to the user, and this can be done by overriding `prePromptModifyContract`. It can be used before the report is run using the `preRunModifyContract` method. Controller classes are mostly used when reports are opened from the form to show the selected details. In this recipe, using the controller class and UI builder, the range of the query changes as the user modifies the parameters of the dialog.

4
Report Programming Model – RDP

This chapter will discuss the following recipes:

- Creating a simple RDP report
- Testing the RDP report
- Creating a simple precision design
- Creating an advanced RDP report
- Creating a report with multiple data sources in a single table
- Creating a group view report
- Adding headers and displaying company images
- Using an existing temp table in RDP
- Pre-processing reports

Introduction

In the earlier chapters, we have discussed how to create SSRS reports using queries in Microsoft Dynamics AX R3. In this chapter, we will discuss creating an SSRS report using the **Report Data Provider** (**RDP**) class. RDP-based SSRS reports are used when complex business logic cannot be achieved using an AOT query. When designing reports, not all the data can be retrieved through queries. Many reports involve analysis and consolidation of data that comes through business logic. RDP enables the use of existing business logic in reports but in an abstract manner.

We will discuss the working pattern of the RDP class and determine how to make the choice of using it in reports. The samples discussed in the chapter detail the different approaches and patterns to use RDP. This chapter will introduce you to precision design in SSRS, which offers a lot of flexibility and control in rendering a report. It will also discuss the widely used tabular design in greater detail.

Creating a simple RDP report

In this recipe, we will help you to understand the concept of the RDP class. We will create a simple SSRS report using the RDP class and write a simple business logic in the RDP class to calculate the compounded interest and print it in the report.

Getting ready

To be able to do this recipe and the others involving RDP in this chapter, you need a basic understanding of X++, data contracts, and data attributes.

How to do it...

1. An RDP uses a temporary table to store data. So the first step in RDP development is to identify the fields involved in the report and create them as part of a temporary table.

2. For the present scenario, we will create a temporary table called **PKTInterestCalcTmp** with the fields **Amount**, **Interest**, **Total**, and **Year**.

3. In the table, set the property **TableType** as **InMemory** to make it temporary.

> There are three types of **TableType** properties: **Regular**, **InMemory**, and **TempDB**. **Regular** tables are standard physical tables, while **InMemory** and **TempDB** are the temporary tables. **InMemory** tables are held in memory and written to the local disk file once they grow beyond a certain point. **TempDB** tables are held in the SQL server database. For more information, visit `https://msdn.microsoft.com/en-us/library/gg863308.aspx`.

4. After creating the table, the next step is to define the contract. The contract must contain all the parameters that are exposed to the user as well as those that are hidden. Here, based on the user inputs, the parameters would be the initial amount, interest rate, and total number of years. Create the contract class using the code here:

```
[
    DataContractAttribute
]
```

```
classPktInterestCalcContract
{
    Amount arcmount, interest;
    Yr      yr;
}


[
    DataMemberAttribute('Amount')
]
public Amount parmAmount(Amount _amount = amount)
{
    amount = _amount;

return amount;
}


[

    DataMemberAttribute('Interest'),
    SysOperationLabelAttribute(literalStr("Interest")),
    SysOperationHelpTextAttribute(literalStr("Rate of
       Interest")),
    SysOperationDisplayOrderAttribute('1')
]

public Amount parmInterest(Amount _interest = interest)
{
    interest = _interest;
    return interest;
}


[

    DataMemberAttribute('Year'),
    SysOperationLabelAttribute(literalStr("Period")),
    SysOperationHelpTextAttribute(literalStr("Number of
       years")),
    SysOperationDisplayOrderAttribute('0')
]
public Yr parmYear(Yr _year = Yr)
{
    yr = _year;

return yr;
}
```

5. The attribute `DataContractAttribute` at class declaration indicates that this is a contract. If the contract requires a UI builder, that must also be defined in the class declaration.

6. Each `parm` method has the attribute `DataMemberAttribute` indicating it as a contract member. This helps having methods internal to the contract class, which don't have a decorator, and are not accessible by other components, say the controller.

7. The remaining attributes in the contract methods, as seen in the previous code, are used to set UI-specific values.

Attribute Name	Description
SysOperationLabelAttribute	Specifies the label for the data members in the data contract
SysOperationHelptextAttribute	Specifies the help text for the data members in the data contract
SysOperationDisplayOrderAttribute	Shows the data members of the data contract in a particular order
SysOperationGroupAttribute	Groups the data members of the data contract

8. The contract class is used by the UI builder to construct the report dialog automatically, unlike in AX 2009, where the dialog field must be added for each field that is exposed to the user.

9. The next step involves the creation of the RDP class. Create the RDP class using the following code, where the `SRSReportParameterAttribute` decorator in the class declaration binds the contract and the RDP class:

```
[
    SRSReportParameterAttribute(classStr
       (PktInterestCalcContract))
]
class PktInterestCalcDp extends SRSReportDataProviderBase
{
    PktInterestCalcTmp interestCalcTmp;
}
```

10. The `ProcessReport` method is decorated with the `SysEntryPoint` attribute to be invoked from the services framework. The temporary table must be filled in the `ProcessReport` method.

```
[SysEntryPointAttribute(false)]
publicvoid processReport()
{
    PktInterestCalcContract  contract;

    Amount  amount, total, oldTotal;
    Amount  interestRate, interest;
    percent interestPct;
    yr      yr, yrCount = 1;

    contract = this.parmDataContract() as
      PktInterestCalcContract;

    amount      = contract.parmAmount();
    interestPct = contract.parmInterest();
    yr          = contract.parmYear();

    interestRate = interestPct / 100;
    oldTotal     = amount;

while (yrCount <= yr)
    {
        interest = (oldTotal*interestRate);
        total    = oldTotal +  interest;

        this.insertInTmp(yrCount, oldTotal,
          interest, Total);
        oldTotal = total;
        yrCount++;
    }
}

privatevoid insertInTmp(
        Yr             _yr,
        Amount         _amount,
        Amount         _interest,
        Total          _total)
{
```

```
        interestCalcTmp.clear();
        interestCalcTmp.Year = _yr;
        interestCalcTmp.Interest = _interest;
        interestCalcTmp.Amount    = _amount;
        interestCalcTmp.Total     = _total;
        interestCalcTmp.insert();
    }
```

11. Any method that is decorated with `SRSReportDataSetAttribute` will be used to identify the temporary tables returned by RDP. There can be more than one method with this attribute, but in this case there is only one table.

```
[
    SRSReportDataSetAttribute(tableStr(PktInterestCalcTmp))
]
public PktInterestCalcTmp getInterestCalcTmp()
{
select interestCalcTmp;
return interestCalcTmp;
}
```

This completes the design of RDP. The next recipe will use this RDP class to create a simple precision design-based report.

How it works...

In this section, we will discuss all the classes which we used in making SSRS reports in Microsoft Dynamics AX R3 using the RDP class.

RDP

To be able to set RDP as your data source type on your report with parameters, there are two required classes:

1. **Data Contract Class**: It defines the parameters in the report.
2. **RDP Class**: It processes the business logic based on a query and parameters defined in the data contract class, and then returns the data in temporary tables as a dataset for the report.

The concept of RDP is very simple. We need a temporary table of either `InMemory` or `TempDB` type that has all the necessary fields that store all the required values which need to be shown on the report. While using the RDP concept, the temporary table is used as a data source in the SSRS report. All the required values are filled through the business logic in the temporary table. This temporary table is used as a data source and the report is rendered. An RDP comprises the following components:

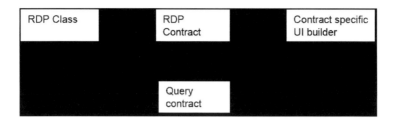

RDP class

The RDP class is a major component in an RDP. Any class that extends `SRSReportDataProviderbase/SRSReportDataProviderPreprocess` can act as an RDP. As per the best practice, if our temporary table is of the `TempDB` type, then the RDP class must extend `SRSReportDataProviderPreProcessTempDB`. If our temporary table is of `InMemory` type, then the RDP class must extend `SRSReportDataProviderPreProcess`. The RDP class resides inside the AX, executes the business logic, processes the data, and stores the data in the temporary table which is rendered in the report. An RDP receives its inputs optionally through a contract or a query and implements the logic involved in filling the temporary table. The reporting services invoke the data provider through the query services framework to fetch the data.

The RDP class uses two important attributes:

- ▸ **SRSReportQueryAttribute**: This attribute specifies which AOT query is used in the report. If the RDP class uses the AOT query, then this attribute must be specified at the beginning of the class.

- ▸ **SRSReportParameterAttribute**: This attribute is used to link the data contract class with the RDP class. This defines that the data contract class will be used by the report to prompt for parameter values. To link the RDP class and contract class, this attribute must be defined at the beginning of the RDP class.

RDP data contract

The RDP data contract class is used to define one or more parameters in the SSRS report. The data contract class contains the `parm` method with `DataMemberAttribute`, which specifies the data member of the contract class written at the beginning of the `parm` method. The data contract is also used by the report UI builder to render the form controls for user inputs. A contract can use its own UI builder, which is bound through `SysOperationContractProcessingAttribute`. A data contract can include or extend other contracts; for example, `SalesFormLetterconfirmcontract` and `InventDimviewcontract`.

UI builder

Similar to an RDL contract, an RDP contract can also bind itself to a UI builder. The UI builder class is used to customize the report dialog through which a user opens the SSRS report. The UI builder class extends the `SRSReportDataContractUI` builder class. If a report has both RDL and RDP contracts with each bounded to a UI builder, then the system invokes both in a sequence. A report dialog is built by several UI builder classes, such as query, print destination, and the contract UI builders. This class is responsible for grouping dialog fields, adding a customized lookup to a dialog field, grouping and handling form control events, adding custom controls to the dialog, and binding the dialog fields with the data contract member in the data contract class. The following figure will give you a clear view of how the report programming flow works with RDP:

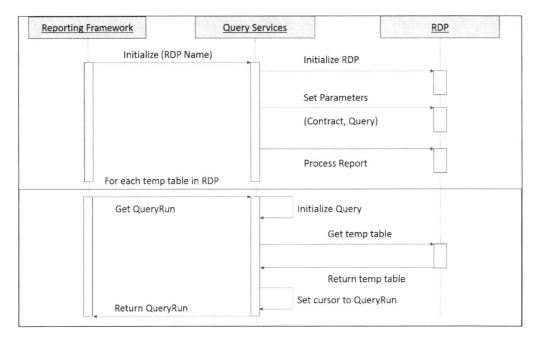

Choosing RDP for a report

A report can be designed to use an RDP data source type in the following cases:

▶ Data to be rendered cannot be constructed as a query

▶ Business logic to be processed depends on the parameters

▶ Data can be rendered using existing business logic

▶ More filters are to be added at runtime

 Did you know that the majority of the reports in AX 2012 are RDP-based reports?

See Also

▸ The *Adding ranges from unbound parameters to a query* recipe in *Chapter 3, Report Programming Model.*

Testing the RDP report

In this recipe, we will explain about testing the RDP class using the code. The RDP class can be tested even without hooking it to a report. This has the advantage of testing it faster and ensuring that it works reliably before connecting it to a report. This topic is explained in details in a later chapter.

How to do it...

1. Create a new job as shown in the code here:

```
static void TestInterestCalcRDP(Args _args)
{
    //initialize contract
    PktInterestCalcContract cont = new
      PktInterestCalcContract();
      PktInterestCalcDp dp;
    //fill the contract
    cont.parmAmount(2000);
    cont.parmInterest(10);
    cont.parmYear(5); //instantiate
    dp = new PktInterestCalcDp();
    //pass the contract
    dp.parmDataContract(cont);
    //fill the table
    dp.processReport();
}
```

2. Change the temporary table used for this RDP to a persistent table by setting the table type property as `Regular`.

3. Run the job and verify that the data is filled in the table. If the RDP works well, then data must be filled in the table created. After verifying, change the property of the table back to `InMemory`.

How it works...

This is an effective way of testing your RDP even before the report is made. This can also be applied in a different instance where you don't want the RDP logic to be executed every time. When testing reports that have longer execution time, make the table permanent and execute the report once. Once the table is filled, the entire RDP logic can be commented. This allows only the reporting logic to be executed, making it easier and faster to test.

Creating a simple precision design

Precision designs are the most flexible and creative design in SSRS reporting in which you can design your report in a flexible manner. Precision design is a report design created by the SQL Report Designer in Visual Studio. It is like a pre-defined format, in which you know the format of the report and are designing it according to that format. Precision designs are flexible and offer abundant options to customize your report by allowing you to decide the location, font, and much more.

Getting ready

This recipe will use the RDP created in the *Creating a simple RDP report* recipe to create a precision design report.

How to do it...

1. Open Visual Studio and create a reporting project. Add a report and name it `PktInterestCalcReport`.

2. Add a dataset and change the property **Data Source Type** to **Report Data Provider**. Click on the **Query** property button to view the list of the RDP classes.

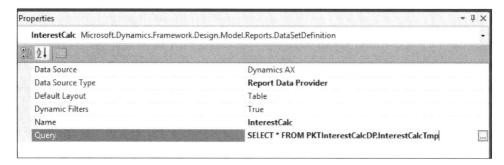

3. Select the RDP class created and click on **Next** to add the fields. Expand the dataset to see the fields from the temporary table and the parameters listed from the data contract.

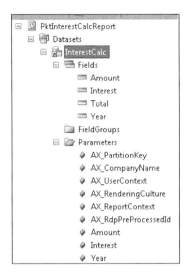

4. To start with precision design, right-click on the **Design** node and select **Precision Design**.

5. Select the precision design node and set the following properties:

Property	Value
Name	InterestReport
Style Template	TableStyleTemplate

6. Right click on **Precision Design** and select **Edit Using Designer**. This opens the designer. The left side of the designer holds the report data, which lists all the fields available for use in the report design. Right-click on the design area and select **Insert | Table**.

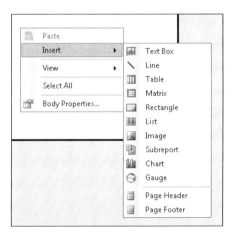

7. Drag the fields from the RDP table and drop them into the table.

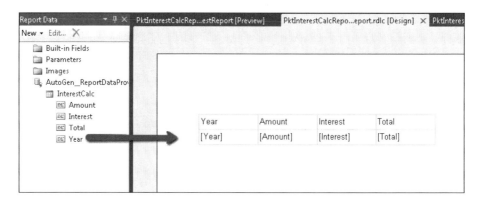

8. Save the report design, and in the report model, click on **Preview** to see the report as shown here:

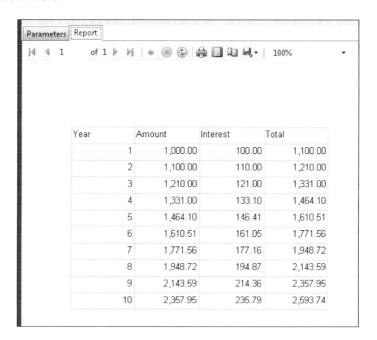

9. Now deploy the report and create a menu item to use the report in AX.

How it works...

This report shows how RDP can be used as a data source. The RDP doesn't necessarily require a query or contract; the key part is the content in the temporary table.

Did you know that an actual SSRS has no concept called auto design?

Creating an advanced RDP report

In the earlier recipe, we created a very simple SSRS report using the RDP concept. In this recipe, we will create an advanced SSRS report using RDP. This recipe is more practical in nature. The goal is to build a report for the customer desk where the user can key in the manufacturing date and find the batches manufactured on that date. On selection of a batch or batches, the user can print a report with the batch and its transactions to track its history. This report will be implemented through the next two recipes. The first recipe will involve creating the RDP for the business functionality while the next recipe discusses the report design part.

How to do it...

1. As seen in the last RDP recipe, the first step is to identify the fields involved in the report and create a table for it. Create a table named **PktInventBatchTransTmp** with the fields indicated here:

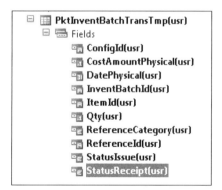

2. The contract class is to be created next. The parameters required are the manufacturing date and batch number. Create a data contract as shown here:

```
[
    DataContractAttribute,
]
class PktInventBatchTransContract
{
    InventDimViewContract        inventDimViewContract;
    InventBatchProdDate          prodDate;
```

```
        InventBatchId                    batchId;
}


[DataMemberAttribute('Batch')]
public InventBatchId parmBatchId(InventBatchId _batchId =
  batchId)
{
    batchId = _batchId;


return batchId;
}


[DataMemberAttribute('ProdDate')]
public InventBatchProdDate parmProdDate(InventBatchProdDate
  _prodDate = prodDate)
{
    prodDate = _prodDate;


return prodDate;
}
```

3. The next step is to fill the data in the temporary table. A select statement (DML) can be used to fetch the data, but using a query would mean that the report ranges (parameters) can be extended later. So design a query named **PktInventBatch** as seen in the following screenshot:

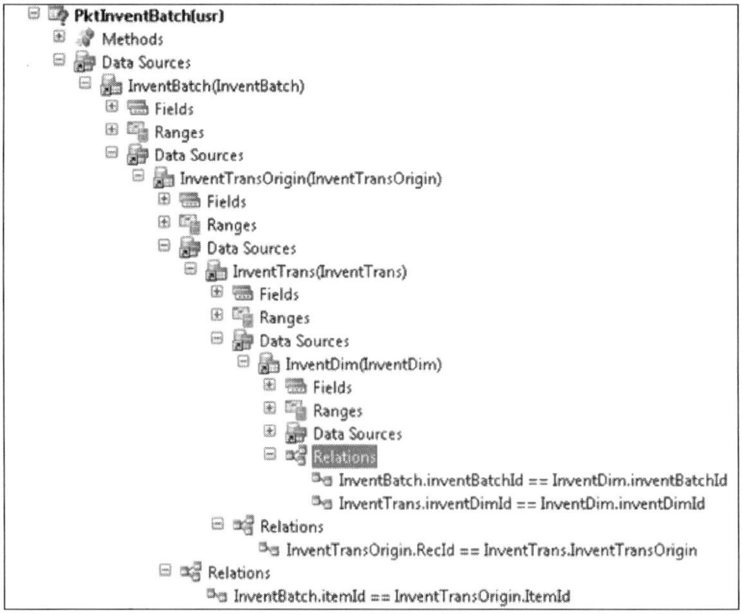

4. An RDP must be created with a binding to the contract. The query created can also be bound to be exposed in the report dialog. We bind query and contract class in the `ClassDeclarion` method of RDP as shown in the following code:

```
[
//bind query - shows in the report dialog
    SRSReportQueryAttribute(queryStr(PktInventBatch)),
//bind the contract
    SRSReportParameterAttribute(classStr(
      PktInventBatchTransContract))
]
class PktInventBatchTransDP extends
  SRSReportDataProviderBase
{
    PktInventBatchTransTmp tmpBatchTrans;
}
```

5. The `processReport` method must be designed to receive the parameters from the contract and set them on the query. This query must be executed further to insert the data in the tables.

6. The `processReport` method as seen here will get the RDP query and set the range from the contract for the batch ID and the production date. This is followed by the execution of the query to insert the records in the temporary table.

```
[
SysEntryPointAttribute(false)
]
publicvoid processReport()
{
    Query                    query;
    QueryRun                 queryRun;
    QueryBuildRange          batchRange, dateRange;
    QueryBuildDataSource     qbds;

    InventBatch              inventBatch;
    InventTrans              inventTrans;
    InventTransOrigin        transOrigin;

    InventDimViewContract    viewContract;

    batchContract = this.parmDataContract() as
      PktInventBatchTransContract;

    query = this.parmQuery();
    qbds = query.dataSourceTable(tableNum(InventBatch));

//set the range
```

```
batchRange = SysQuery::findOrCreateRange(qbds,
  fieldNum(InventBatch, InventBatchId));

batchRange.value(batchContract.parmBatchId());

if (batchContract.parmProdDate())
    {
dateRange = SysQuery::findOrCreateRange(qbds,
  fieldNum(InventBatch, ProdDate));
    dateRange.value(SysQuery::value(
      batchContract.parmProdDate()));
    }

    queryRun = new queryRun(query);

while (queryRun.next())
    {
        if (queryRun.changed(tablenum(InventBatch)))
        {
            inventBatch =
              queryRun.get(tableNum(InventBatch));
        }

        if (queryRun.changed(tablenum(InventTransOrigin)))
        {
            transOrigin =
              queryRun.get(tableNum(InventTransOrigin));
        }

        inventTrans = queryRun.get(tableNum(InventTrans));

        this.insertTmpTable(inventBatch,
          transOrigin, inventTrans);
    }

}
```

7. The `insertTmpTable` method is invoked from the process report to simply insert the records into the temporary table:

```
privatevoid insertTmpTable(
    InventBatch          _inventBatch,
    InventTransOrigin    _transOrigin,
```

```
    InventTrans            _inventTrans,
    InventDim              _inventDim
    )
{
    tmpBatchTrans.clear();
    tmpBatchTrans.ItemId = _inventTrans.ItemId;
    tmpBatchTrans.InventBatchId =
      _inventBatch.inventBatchId;

    tmpBatchTrans.ReferenceId = _transOrigin.ReferenceId;
    tmpBatchTrans.ReferenceCategory =
      _transOrigin.ReferenceCategory;

    tmpBatchTrans.StatusIssue = _inventTrans.StatusIssue;
    tmpBatchTrans.StatusReceipt =
      _inventTrans.StatusReceipt;
    tmpBatchTrans.DatePhysical = _inventTrans.DatePhysical;
    tmpBatchTrans.Qty = _inventTrans.Qty;
    tmpBatchTrans.CostAmountPhysical =
      _inventTrans.CostAmountPhysical;

    tmpBatchTrans.insert();
}
```

8. The following method is used by the reporting extension to retrieve the data from temptable:

```
[
    SRSReportDataSetAttribute(tableStr(
      PktInventBatchTransTmp))
]
public PktInventBatchTransTmp getinventOnhandTmp()
{
select  tmpBatchTrans;
return  tmpBatchTrans;
}
```

9. All the artifacts to enable a proper RDP are complete.

10. There is one UI related change that needs to be incorporated, that is, when a manufacturing date is chosen, the batch displayed must be from the same date. This change deems a UI builder that must be bound to the contract. The approach is to override the postRun method in the UI builder and build a local lookup method for the batch ID field.

11. The UI builder `PktInventBatchTransUIBuilder` must be designed as shown here:

```
class PktInventBatchTransUIBuilder extends
  SysOperationAutomaticUIBuilder
{
    DialogField batchDialog, dateDialog;
}

publicvoid build()
{

super();

    batchDialog = this.bindInfo().getDialogField(
      this.dataContractObject(),
      methodStr(PktInventBatchTransContract, parmBatchId));

    dateDialog = this.bindInfo().getDialogField(
      this.dataContractObject(),
      methodStr(PktInventBatchTransContract,
      parmProdDate));
}

publicvoid postRun()
{
super();

    //setup the event routing
    batchDialog.registerOverrideMethod(
      methodStr(FormStringControl, lookup),
      methodStr(PktInventBatchTransUIBuilder, batchLookup),
      this);
}

publicvoid batchLookup(FormStringControl _control)
{
    Query              query;
    SysTableLookup     sysTableLookup;
    QueryBuildDataSource qbds;

    sysTableLookup =
      SysTableLookup::newParameters(tableNum(InventBatch),
      _control);
```

```
    sysTableLookup.addLookupfield(fieldNum(InventBatch,
        InventBatchId));

    query = new Query();
    qbds = query.addDataSource(tableNum(InventBatch));
//if no date is specified show all batch
if (datedialog.value())
    {
        qbds.addRange(fieldNum(InventBatch,
            prodDate)).value(queryValue(datedialog.value())));
    }

    sysTableLookup.parmQuery(query);
    sysTableLookup.performFormLookup();
}
```

12. Decorate the class declaration of the contractor class to bind the UI builder:

```
[
    DataContractAttribute,
    SysOperationContractProcessingAttribute(
        classStr(PktInventBatchTransUIBuilder),
    SysOperationDataContractProcessingMode::
        CreateUIBuilderForRootContractOnly)
]
class PktInventBatchTransContract
{
    InventDimViewContract        inventDimViewContract;
    InventBatchProdDate          prodDate;
    InventBatchId                batchId;
}
```

This completes the design of the RDP.

Testing the RDP

As performed in the previous recipe, write a test job and validate the RDP. This completes all coding-related modifications for the report. The next recipe will model a report using this RDP.

How it works...

The RDP designed here uses a query to iterate through the data and insert into a temporary table. The query is bounded to the report through the query attribute in the class declaration of the RDP. However, if the business logic doesn't demand a lot of dynamic behavior, opt to use a DML (select statements) to fetch the information. This can speed up the report process.

When designing a temporary table for an RDP, remember to add replacement keys for any surrogate key, and add relations to the table to enable drill through.

 RDP classes can be used for multiple purposes and need not be restricted to only reporting. The `TrialbalanceDP` class is used by the trial balance report and form.

Creating a report with multiple data sources in a single table

In this recipe, we will create an SSRS report using the RDP concept with multiple data sources. The process method of the RDP class is used to write the business logic in the report and to insert the data into the temporary table. In the previous recipe, we took only one temporary table, but in this recipe, we will take one more temporary table and use both the temporary tables in a single table in the SSRS report.

How to do it...

1. The first step is to create a new temporary table called **PktItemTableTmp** with the fields indicated here:

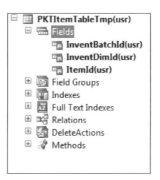

2. Now we will insert the data into this temporary table in the RDP class. Add another line of code in the `ProcessReport` method.

   ```
   this.insertItemTmpTable(inventBatch,  inventTrans);
   ```

3. Add a method in the RDP class named `insertItemTmpTable`, which is used to insert the data into **PKTItemTableTmp** invoked from the `ProcessReport` method:

   ```
   privatevoid insertItemTmpTable(
       InventBatch          _inventBatch,
   ```

```
    InventTrans            _inventTrans
    )
{
pktItemTableTmp.clear();
pktItemTableTmp.ItemId = _inventTrans.ItemId;
pktItemTableTmp.InventBatchId = _inventBatch.inventBatchId;
pktItemTableTmp.InventDimId = _inventBatch.InventDimId;

pktItemTableTmp.insert();
}
```

4. Now get the temporary table from the RDP class:

```
[
SRSReportDataSetAttribute(tableStr(PKTItemTableTmp))
]
public PKTItemTableTmp getPKTItemTableTmp()
{
select pKTItemTableTmp;
return pKTItemTableTmp;
}
```

5. Next, add a new dataset in the visual design in the SSRS report:

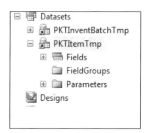

6. Now edit the precision design in the SSRS report. Add a table in the report and assign its `PKTInventBatchTransTmp` as a dataset of that table. In the report, we will get the `itemid` and `inventBatchId` from `PKTItemTableTmp` table and other data from `.PKTInventBatchTransTmp`. We have just created the table and assigned the fields of the `PKTInventBatchTransTmp` table:

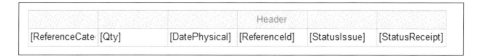

Header						
[ReferenceCate	[Qty]		[DatePhysical]	[ReferenceId]	[StatusIssue]	[StatusReceipt]

7. Now, we will get the details of `ItemId` and `InventBatchId` from `PKTItemTableTmp` in the same table used in step 6 in the header row. In the first column of the header row, right-click and go to **Expression** and write the code as seen in the following screenshot:

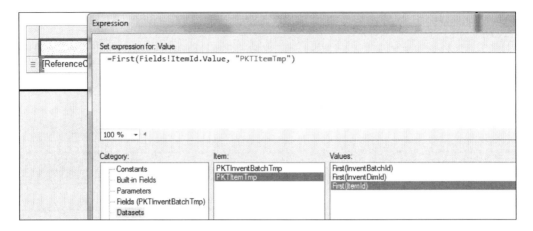

8. Similarly, write the code for `InventBatchId`:

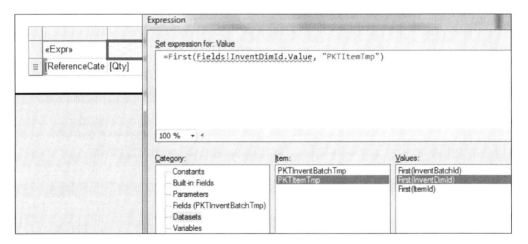

How it works...

Precision design allows you to modify the report in your own report format. Using multiple data sources in a single table helps a lot in showing complex data in a single table. This will help the developers to break the code into smaller pieces and insert the data into multiple data sources.

Creating a group view report

We have started using precision design. The most prominently used reporting technique in precision design is tabular grouping. Grouping helps render the data hierarchy, and precision design leverages the capability manifold when compared to auto design in this respect. The RDP created in the previous recipe will be used here as the source of data.

How to do it...

1. Create a new precision design and set the property name as `BatchTransReport` and style as **TableStyleAlternatingRow**. Double-click on **Design** to open the designer.

2. In the designer area, right-click on the report page and select **Insert New Table**.

3. A header and detail row will appear. Drop the header by selecting the header row and right-click delete rows.

4. Place the cursor in the column to see this icon ▣ . Click on this to get the list of fields and select the required field.

5. To add a new column, right-click and insert a column to the right.

Insert a new Column

6. This shows all the detail lines. To add a grouping on batch, go to the **Grouping** tab at the bottom (if grouping is not visible select **Report | Grouping** from **Menu**). Click on the downward arrow in the right corner of the row that says **Details**, as shown in the following screenshot:

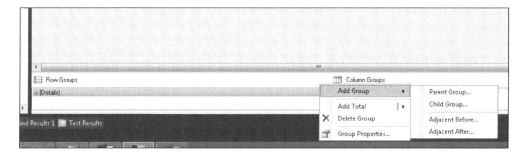

7. Select **Add Group | Parent Group...** and in the prompted dialog, select **[InventBatchId]**. This sets the grouping based on the selected field.

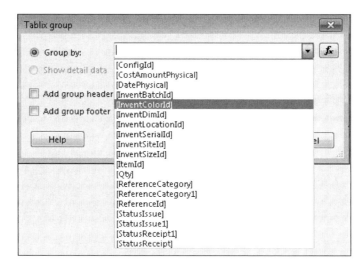

8. A new column **InventBatchId** is added to the design. Preview the report. It will appear as seen in the following screenshot:

000001	M2002	Purchase order	000002	None	Purchased	117,000.00	64,350.00
000002	M2002	Production line	B-000015	Sold	None	-60,469.41	-33,258.18
	M2002	Purchase order	000002	None	Purchased	61,962.48	34,079.36
000003	P5000	Production line	B-000005	Sold	None	-646,190.90	-545,746.66
	P5000	Production line	B-000006	Sold	None	-342,461.88	-289,229.43
	P5000	Production line	B-000003	Sold	None	-123,550.24	-104,345.53
	P5000	Production line	B-000004	Sold	None	-969,404.84	-818,720.07
	P5000	Production	B-000001	None	Purchased	2,081,607.86	1,758,041.69
000004	P5000	Production	B-000002	None	Purchased	1,958,057.62	1,653,696.16
	P5000	Production line	B-000003	Sold	None	-1,958,057.62	-1,653,696.16
000005	P5006	Production	B-000003	None	Purchased	1,400.00	516,097.12
	P5006	Sales order	000332	Sold	None	-1,400.00	-516,097.12
000006	M5001	Purchase order	000001	None	Purchased	143,000.00	127,270.00

9. This view takes up one column for the batch, reducing the space for details. A better idea would be displaying the batch at the top. Also missing are the labels for the detail lines. In the steps to follow, let's work this out.

10. Select the header of the **InventBatchId** column, right-click on it, and select **Delete Columns**. In the delete dialog, choose the **Delete columns only** option. This option will retain the grouping but delete only the fields.

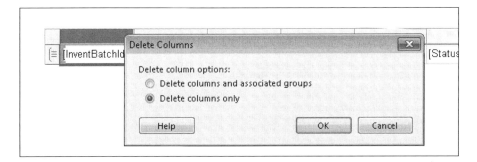

11. In the table row, select the row and right-click and select the **Insert Row | Outside Group - above** option. This will add a new row. Add two rows: one for the labels and the other for the group header displaying the batch.

12. To create labels in the row immediately above the data fields, double-click the cell, right-click and select **Create Placeholder**. A property window for the cell will open. Click on the ![fx] button next to the value field and enter the following expression:

    ```
    =Labels!@sys13647
    ```

    Repeat this for each column header. (Identify the label ID from the label editor in the rich client before entering it.)

13. Of the two rows inserted, the top row will be used to display the group header. Select the first cell and enter the label for **InventBatchId** in the same manner as explained earlier. In the top-most row, the first cell is used for the expression label for the batch. Select all the remaining cells and right-click and select **Merge Cells**. In the merged cell, click the ![icon] icon and select the field **Invent Batch**.

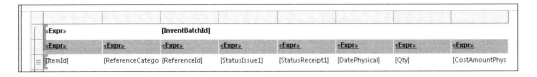

14. This will display a batch at the top followed by the transaction with labels. You can collectively change the font, color, and size of each cell by selecting all of them. The sample here uses **Segoe UI font**, **8pt** for values and **Grey** color background for the header cells. Precision design gives the comfort of setting up the properties collectively by multi-selection.

15. Set the property **Can Shrink** in the cells to **True**. This will allow automatic report sizing.

16. To add totals to each group in the **Grouping** node, at the bottom select **Group1** and click on the small arrow at the end. Select **Add Totals | After**. This will insert a new row at the bottom and add two sum fields for **Quantity** and **CostAmountPhysical**. Delete **Quantity** since we don't need it, and instead, modify the expression to set the label as **Total**. This will print the label after each group.

Adding a total

17. To add a grand total, insert a row at the bottom outside the group. Right-click on the cell below the group total and select **Expression**. In the expression window, set the label expression as **Grand Total** and enter the following expression:

```
=Sum(Fields!CostAmountPhysical.Value)
```

18. The following screenshot shows how the final report will appear:

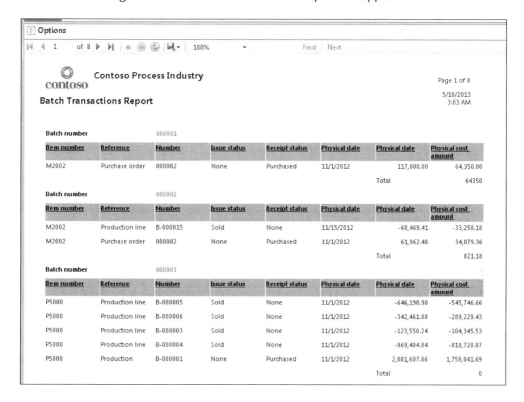

How it works...

Precision design allows in-detail modeling of a report, thus offering more flexibility and control. However, when the design is simple, opt to use auto design. In many reports, we need to add a company logo in a report header. This can only be added using precision design. The next topic will discuss adding a company logo to the header in a report. So you may have to make this choice even in this case.

When using expressions in precision design, be specific to ensure that they are right. Since the compiler doesn't indicate where these errors occur, it might result in opening every expression window. However, you will get an error message in Visual Studio while building/rebuilding or deploying the solution. Though precision design might look exhaustive at first sight, it is more convenient and easier to control than auto design.

 Use the document outline view to see the controls in precision design to identify the name of the controls in the design. The document outline view can be opened by using *Ctrl + W, U*.

Adding headers and displaying company images

Images and headers give a report a professional appearance. This interesting recipe will guide you to build a report with company images and headers. It is good to add a header and company logos for all reports which will be used outside the company; for example, purchase orders, vendor/customer account statements, and statutory reports.

How to do it...

1. To insert a header, right-click **Insert | Header**. In the header, add a textbox each for company name, page, date, and report name as shown in the following screenshot:

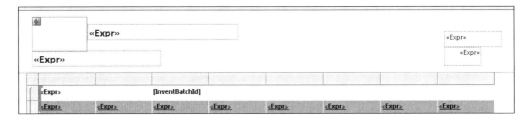

2. In the expression field of these controls, add the following code:

Controls	Code

Company name	`=Microsoft.Dynamics.Framework.Reports.`
	`DataMethodUtility.GetFullCompanyNameForUser(`
	`Parameters!AX_CompanyName.Value,`
	`    Parameters!AX_UserContext.Value)`

Report name	`="Batch Transactions Report"`

Page	`=System.String.Format(Labels!@SYS182566, "" &`
	`    Globals!PageNumber & "", "" &`
	`    Globals!TotalPages & "")`

Date	`=Microsoft.Dynamics.Framework.Reports.`
	`DataMethodUtility`
	`ConvertUtcToAxUserTimeZoneForUser(Parameters!AX_`
	`CompanyName.Value,Parameters!AX_UserContext.Value,`
	`System.DateTime.UtcNow, "d", Parameters!AX_`
	`RenderingCulture.Value) & vbCrLf & Microsoft.Dynamics.`
	`Framework.Reports.DataMethodUtility.`
	`ConvertUtcToAxUserTimeZoneForUser(Parameters!AX_`
	`CompanyName.Value, Parameters!AX_UserContext.Value,`
	`System.DateTime.UtcNow, "t", Parameters!AX_`
	`RenderingCulture.Value)`

3. Adding a company image starts with defining a query. Create a query called **PktCompanyImage** and add a table called **CompanyImage**. Come back to your Visual Studio report and add the query as a data source. Set the **Dynamic Filter** property to **False**, save the report, and open the designer.

4. In the designer, the new data source will appear in the report data view. In the page header, create a new field of type image. In the prompting window, select the image source as **database** and point the value field to **image** field from the **companyImage** datasource. Set the MIME type based on the image you have added. Resize the image and place it before the company name. Save and preview it to see the image.

5. Deploy the report and create a menu item to see the report working.

How it works...

The company logo query that was created for this report can be reused for other reports that require the same. If there are images that are specific to this report then the field can be directly added to the temporary table field used by the RDP. You can also use embedded images in precision design, as seen in *Chapter 2, Enhancing Your Report – Visualization and Interaction*.

Precision design enables copying controls from one report/report design to another report/report design, so you can copy the header field if the same alignment is required in other reports.

Debugging RDP

The most preferable mode to debug an RDP report would be to use the test job discussed in the *Testing the RDP report* recipe. However, if you prefer to debug it in the `processReport` method of your RDP class, type the keyword `breakpoint`. Open the debugger even before opening or previewing the report by running the `axdebug.exe` file in the client installation. Once the execution reaches the debugging point, the debugger will be activated.

See Also

▶ The *Adding an image in auto design* recipe in *Chapter 2, Enhancing Your Report – Visualization and Interaction*

Using an existing temp table in RDP

Temporary tables in AX are used in existing business logic and also as a data source in some forms. The reporting framework provides the ability to use these temporary tables filled outside in a form or a business logic, to be copied to the RDP without re-implementing the business logic. The reporting framework offers the ability to do this through a set of helper classes: `SRSTmpTableMarshaller` and `SRSTmpTblMarshallercontract`.

This recipe will simplify and make it easy to understand the temporary table pattern. This pattern helps in designing RDP reports faster when the temporary table and logic to fill it already exists.

How to do it...

1. To better understand the `Marshaller` class and its usage, we will use the interest calculation example. In this example, the interest calculation is done in a form using a temporary table. The simulation in the form must be printed in a report. We will use the `Marshaller` class to pass the prefilled table to the RDP.

   We have used the interest calculation example where the calculation is already done using the temporary table and shown in the following screenshot:

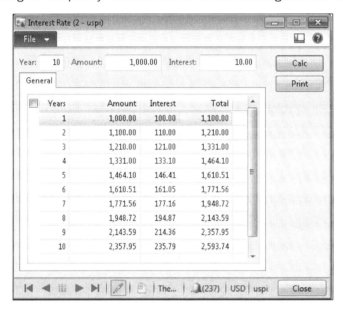

2. The user enters the value in the **Amount**, **Interest**, and **Years** input boxes and clicks on the **Calc** button. The simulation is shown in the form. When the user clicks on the **Print** button, the temporary table must be passed to the RDP and rendered in the report.

3. The first step begins with creating a contract since the temporary table already exists. This step can be surpassed. There are no further inputs from the user to be received. So our contract class needs no parm methods except the one for holding `RecId` from the data source. So the `SRSTmpTableMarshallerContract` contract can be directly used as the contract for RDP. (In situations where you have your own contract class, `SRSTmpTableMarshallerContract` must be used as a nested data contract. See the *Inventory dimensions in reports* recipe in *Chapter 7, Upgrading and Analyzing Reports*.)

4. The RDP for a pre-populated temp table is much simpler. The only logic to be performed is to retrieve the data from the database. The `processReport` method of RDP appears as seen here:

```
[SysEntryPointAttribute]
publicvoid processReport()
{
    SrsReportRunPermission   permission;

    SrsTmpTblMarshallerContract contract =
        this.parmDataContract() as
        SrsTmpTblMarshallerContract;
breakpoint;

    tmpTableDataRecId   = contract.parmTmpTableDataRecId();
    permission          = new SrsReportRunPermission();
    permission.assert();

//Temp Table Object that was returned from
  SRSTmpTblMarshaller
    tmpCalc =
        SRSTmpTblMarshaller::GetTmpTbl(tmpTableDataRecId);
    //drop the temp table from data store since it is
    //copied to the local buffer
    SRSTmpTblMarshaller::deleteTmpTblData(tmpTableDataRecId);
    CodeAccessPermission::revertAssert();
}
```

Bind the contract class `SRSTmpTableMarshallerContract` in the class declaration and create a data return method as in the previous RDP classes.

5. The controller class owns the responsibility of storing the temp table. Create a controller class and override `preRunModifyContract` with the following code:

```
publicvoid preRunModifyContract()
{
    RecId recid;
    PktInterestCalcTmp tmp;

    SrsTmpTblMarshallerContract contract;

new SRSReportRunPermission().assert();

    tmp.setTmpData(this.parmArgs().record());

//store the data in data store and retrieve the recid
```

```
        recid =
          SRSTmpTblMarshaller::sendTmpTblToDataProvider(tmp);
        CodeAccessPermission::revertAssert();

    //set the recid in contract to be used in RDP
        contract = this.parmReportContract().parmRdpContract()
          as SrsTmpTblMarshallerContract;
        contract.parmTmpTableDataRecId(recid);
    }
```

6. In the main method, switch off the dialog since no user input is needed:

```
publicstaticvoid main(Args args)
{
    PktMarshallCalcController control;


    control = new PktMarshallCalcController();
    control.parmArgs(args);
    control.parmReportName(
      'PktMarshallCalc.InterestReport');
    control.parmShowDialog(false);
    control.startOperation();
}
```

7. Once all the code artifacts are ready, design the report to look similar to the one in the first recipe in this chapter. The final part is to hook the controller to the clicked event in the button. Override the **Print** button and call the controller:

```
void clicked()
{
    PktMarshallCalcController cont;
    Args args;

super();

    args = new args();
//pass the temptable buffer from the form
//to the contract class
    args.record(PktInterestCalcTmp);
    PktMarshallCalcController::main(args);
}
```

8. Click the **Print** button to run the report.

How it works...

The contents of the temporary table are transferred to a container and stored in a table in the SQL called the data store. The data is identified by the **Recid** of the record in the data store. This **Recid** is stored in the contract and passed to the RDP. The RDP again retrieves the data from the data store by using the **Recid** when required. Once the data is retrieved, it must be explicitly deleted from the data store. The deletion is performed in the `processReport` method in the RDP class.

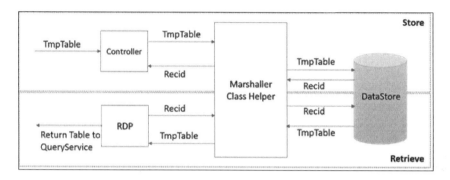

Pre-processing reports

SSRS uses the **Windows Communication Foundation** (**WCF**) to connect to the AOS for data access. This connection has a threshold limit and might fail if a report takes a longer time to execute. The report server execution waits for the RDP to process the data and return. In the event where the RDP takes a longer time to execute the reporting service might fail. Pre-processing is a strategy to beat this issue. This recipe will help you understand how to enable pre-processing for any RDP report.

How to do it...

When a report processes a huge amount of data or is found to take considerable time during execution, you can decide to incorporate pre-processing. Follow these steps to enable pre-processing:

1. Extend the RDP class from the `SrsReportDataProviderPreProcess` class.

2. Set the following properties in the temp table used by RDP:

Properties	Value
Table Type	Regular
CreatedBy	Yes
CreatedTransactionId	Yes

3. The crucial portion of RDP is inserting records in the table with the scope. In order for the tables to automatically generate the `TransactionId` in the beginning of the process report, set the `userconnection` as shown here:

```
Public void processReport()
{
InventBatchTransTmp.setConnection(
  this.parmUserConnection());
}
```

This sets a scope and generates a `TransactionId` which is valid only for that scope; for example, `AgreementConfirmationDP`.

4. Open the report in Visual Studio and refresh the data source to include the new `CreatedTransactionId` field. To do this, in the Model Editor, right-click on the dataset and then click refresh.

5. In Solution Explorer, right-click on **Solution** and click **Deploy Solution** to deploy the new report.

How it works...

The AX reporting framework delays the invocation of the reporting framework until the data is processed. After the data is processed and inserted, the reporting framework is invoked, thus preventing timeouts. The hindrance here is that RDP uses a temporary table. Converting this to persistent introduces a different sort of problem with two different instances of the report inserting conflicting data.

The AX reporting framework solves this problem by making the table persistent and introducing a scope field called `TransactionId`. The `TransactionId` field allows the reporting framework to identify the records created for the session. In the case of pre-processed reports, the data is inserted in the table and the details of the pre-processing are stored in the **SRSReportPreProcessDetail** table. The `recid` of the record is passed as `preprocessid` to the report framework, and the data is fetched using this scope from the table.

Clean up

The data in these tables is cleaned up after the report is run automatically.

For more details on the use of WCF in SSRS reports, you may visit `http://www.codeproject.com/Articles/37270/Consuming-a-WCF-Service-from-an-SSRS-RDL-Server-Re.`

5
Integrating External Datasources

This chapter will cover the following recipes:

- Adding a datasource through business logic
- Using an XML feed as a datasource
- Building a parameter lookup using business logic
- Building a report through an external datasource
- Adding a parameter for an external datasource query
- Creating a customer summary OLAP report
- Adding a parameter lookup for OLAP
- Designing an OLAP table report with SQL Report Builder
- Designing a map sub-report with SQL Report Builder
- Creating a sub-report in auto design
- Creating a sub-report in precision design

Introduction

One of the main lookout features from the transformation to SSRS reports is the ability to support multiple sources to render data. An ERP is one of many single corporate systems, with the data involved in making decisions spread across multiple systems. It is important that the reports are able to pull through data from different sources. For example, when a company switches to a new ERP, the legacy system is still kept alive for transactional data references. This chapter will focus on offering recipes that involve different sources of data, such as XML feeds, SQL databases, and OLAP that can be used as a datasource for the report.

Adding a datasource through business logic

This recipe will show how a simple datasource can be created and used as a source of data through the business logic option in reports.

Getting ready

This recipe requires that you have access to Visual Studio with the Dynamics AX reporting extension.

How to do it...

1. Create a new reporting project called **PktExchRateReports** in Visual Studio.

2. Add a report and name it **PKTExchRateDataTable**.

3. Right-click on the **Data Method** node and create a new method as shown in the following screenshot:

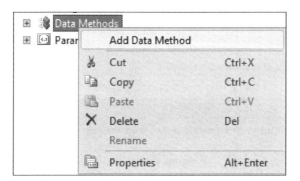

4. Double click the **TestMethod** node. This adds a new C# project to the solution and a C# class with the same name as the report.

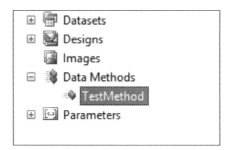

5. Replace the empty data method with the business logic shown here:

```
[DataMethod(), PermissionSet(SecurityAction.Assert,
  Name = "FullTrust")]
Public static DataTable ExchangeRateDataset(string _stest)
    {
DataTable dt;
// Adding rows and columns in DataTable
dt = new DataTable();
dt.Columns.Add("Category", typeof(string));
dt.Columns.Add("Base Currency", typeof(string));
dt.Columns.Add("Currency", typeof(string));
dt.Columns.Add("Base Rate", typeof(double));
dt.Columns.Add("Rate", typeof(double));

dt.Rows.Add("Australia", "USD", "AUD", 1, 1.03);
dt.Rows.Add("Asia", "USD", "SGD", 1, 1.26);
dt.Rows.Add("Europe", "USD", "EUR", 1,0.77);
dt.Rows.Add("Middle East", "USD", "AED", 1, 3.67);

return dt;
    }
```

6. Save and build the solution. This will refresh the data method in the report model.

7. Open the report model, select the **Datasets** node, and create a new dataset. In the new dataset **Properties**, set the **Data Source Type** to **Business Logic**.

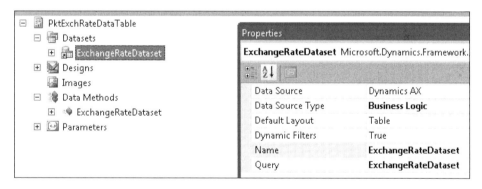

8. Now click the ellipsis (...) button on the **Query** property and select the business logic that was just created. Click the exclamation on the right corner to validate the data retrieval. This action will add the fields from the data table and the parameters of the method (if any will be added as parameters).

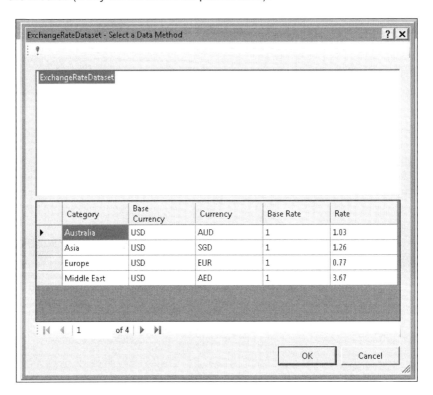

9. Drag the dataset to the report design. Apply templates, align the controls, and specify the labels for rendering. Save and preview the report. It should look like the following screenshot:

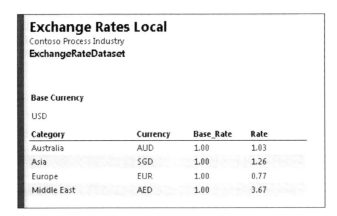

How it works...

Any data method that returns a data type of `System.data` can be added as a dataset to the report. The datatable filled in the data method is used by SSRS to identify fields of the table. If there are parameters for the data method, then they are added as parameters for the dataset. The program logic creates a datatable instance and adds columns with the data type, and then inserts rows in the table. The row details are hardcoded in the table in this recipe.

See Also

- ▶ The *Expressions in reports* recipe in *Chapter 2, Enhancing Your Report – Visualization and Interaction*

- ▶ The *Adding data methods in business logic* recipe in *Chapter 3, Report Programming Model*

Using an XML feed as a datasource

In the previous recipe, the entire data for the report was hardcoded. In this recipe, we will continue to use the data table as a datasource, but the data for this report will come through an XML feed. The XML is retrieved at runtime, and parsed and filled in a data table, which is then rendered in the report.

Getting ready

This recipe requires the machine on which you work to be connected to the Internet. The XML feed (`http://themoneyconverter.com/rss-feed/USD/rss.xml`) used in this report is downloaded at runtime.

How to do it...

1. In the existing project, **PKTExchRateReports**, add a new report called **PKTExchRateFromWeb**.

2. Add a new data method and double-click on it to create the business logic.

3. Replace the empty method with the logic given here:

```
[DataMethod(), PermissionSet(SecurityAction.Assert,
  Name = "FullTrust")]
Public static DataTableExchangeRateData()
    {
DataTable dt;

dt = new DataTable();
```

```
dt.Columns.Add("Category", typeof(string));
dt.Columns.Add("Base Currency", typeof(string));
dt.Columns.Add("Currency", typeof(string));
dt.Columns.Add("Base Rate", typeof(string));

Xdocument xdoc =
  XDocument.Load("http://themoneyconverter.com/rss-
  feed/USD/rss.xml");


var q = from c in xdoc.Descendants("item")

select new {
title     = c.Element("title").Value,
pubDate  =c.Element("pubDate").Value,
desc      = c.Element("description").Value,
cat       = c.Element("category").Value
         };

foreach (var obj in q){

dt.Rows.Add(obj.cat,
obj.title.Substring(0, 2),
obj.title.Substring(4, 3),
obj.desc);
         }

return dt;
      }
```

4. Before adding this as a datasource, it is important to ensure that this method works well, since any runtime issues might prevent it from adding this data method as a datasource.

5. Create a unit test method (refer to the *Unit testing business logic* recipe in *Chapter 3, Report Programming Model*) and run the test to ensure execution at runtime.

6. Add the data method as a datasource and then add it to the report design.

7. Remember to set the templates and adjust fonts and labels before you run the report. The report preview should be as seen in the following screenshot:

Exchange Rates from Xml Feed

Contoso Process Industry

Category	Currency	Rate
Africa	EG	1 United States Dollar = 6.98753 Egyptian Pound
Africa	GH	1 United States Dollar = 1.99331 Ghana Cedi
Africa	GM	1 United States Dollar = 35.98998 Gambian Dalasi
Africa	KE	1 United States Dollar = 85.16999 Kenyan Shilling
Africa	MA	1 United States Dollar = 8.51679 Moroccan Dirham
Africa	MG	1 United States Dollar = 2,189.87071 Malagasy Ariary
Africa	MU	1 United States Dollar = 31.22997 Mauritian Rupee
Africa	NA	1 United States Dollar = 9.90858 Namibian Dollar
Africa	NG	1 United States Dollar = 158.64999 Nigerian Naira
Africa	SC	1 United States Dollar = 11.80002 Seychellois Rupee
Africa	TN	1 United States Dollar = 1.63346 Tunisian Dinar
Africa	UG	1 United States Dollar = 2,581.79994 Ugandan Shilling
Africa	XA	1 United States Dollar = 501.84148 Central African Franc

How it works...

The data table is initialized with columns followed by the logic to access the XML feed. The XML feed is downloaded at runtime and parsed. Parsing is done using **Language Integrated Query** (**LINQ**) to XML in C# and is inserted into the data table. LINQ offers a robust retrieval mechanism by abstracting the source of data.

It is good to keep in mind that the method must return a type of `system.datatable`, otherwise it will fail to show up as a datasource. The unit test can be used to debug the logic during design without much hooking involved in services, such as the reporting service for debugging.

Spin-off recipes

This business logic idea can be further extended to create and insert data in tables at runtime using other sources, such as web services, JSON API, and even AX queries.

 Do not modify the design in the report model when the precision design editor is open. Close the precision design editor before modifying the report model, otherwise the changes will not be stored.

Building a parameter lookup using business logic

In the last two recipes, there was no user interaction, but real-time scenarios will demand that a user input be taken. Adding a parameter doesn't make it usable, as the user might be left clueless about what the possible values are. This is because there is no lookup available for the external data. This recipe will show you how a dataset can be used just for the purpose of creating parameter lookups. The parameter here will be the category field that indicates the geographical location of the country. Apart from adding a parameter, this recipe will also discuss how to show the report parameter lookup from business logic. The report built through this recipe will provide a parameter category and the lookup for the parameter through which the user can view the exchange rate data only for the selected category.

Getting ready

This recipe requires the machine on which you work to be connected to the Internet. The XML feed (`http://themoneyconverter.com/rss-feed/USD/rss.xml`) used in this report is downloaded at runtime.

How to do it...

1. Create a report called **PKTExchRateDataLookup** in the project **PktExchRateReports**.

2. Create a data method, which receives a string parameter category and applies it to the category field in the XML, using the code here:

```
[DataMethod(), PermissionSet(SecurityAction.Assert,
  Name = "FullTrust")]
Public static DataTable ExchangeRateDataFilter(string
  category)
    {
DataTable dt;

dt = new DataTable();
dt.Columns.Add("Category", typeof(string));
dt.Columns.Add("Base Currency", typeof(string));
dt.Columns.Add("Currency", typeof(string));
dt.Columns.Add("Base Rate", typeof(string));

Xdocument xdoc =
  XDocument.Load("http://themoneyconverter.com/rss-
  feed/USD/rss.xml");

var q = from c in xdoc.Descendants("item")
where (c.Element("category").Value == category ||
string.IsNullOrEmpty(category))

select new
              {
title = c.Element("title").Value,
pubDate = c.Element("pubDate").Value,
desc = c.Element("description").Value,
```

```
              cat = c.Element("category").Value
                       };

          foreach (var obj in q)
                 {

          dt.Rows.Add(obj.cat,
          obj.title.Substring(0, 2),
          obj.title.Substring(4, 3),
          obj.desc);
                 }

          Return dt;
             }
```

3. Rebuild the solution.

4. The next step is to build a lookup for this parameter. Create a new data method and place the business logic shown here:

```
          Public static DataTable CategoryData()
             {
          DataTable dt;

          dt = new DataTable();
          dt.Columns.Add("Category", typeof(string));

          Xdocument xdoc =
            XDocument.Load("http://themoneyconverter.com/rss-
            feed/USD/rss.xml");
          XNamespace space = xdoc.Root.GetDefaultNamespace();

          IEnumerable<string> q =
            xdoc.Descendants("item").Descendants("category").Select(
            pn =>pn.Value).Distinct().ToList();

          foreach (string category in q)
                 {
          dt.Rows.Add(category);
                 }

          return dt;
             }
```

5. Rebuild the solution. Add the business logic as datasets. The parameter that was added in the `ExchangeRateDataFilter` data method should now be seen in the **Parameters** node of the dataset and the report parameter.

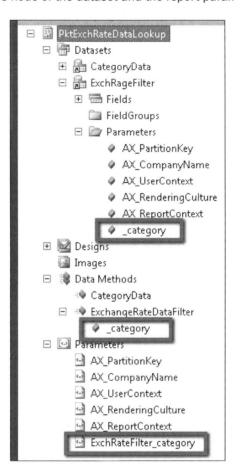

6. Under the **Parameters** node, select the parameter **ExchRateFilter_category** and on the **Values** property click the button. A dialog box opens up; fill the dialog box with the values shown in the following screenshot. This hooks up the category dataset to the lookup.

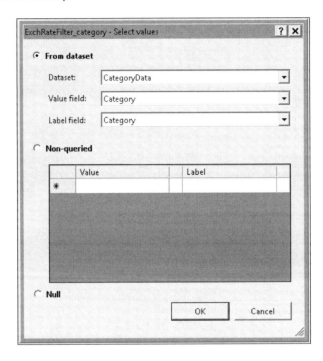

7. Preview the report after setting the template, font, label, and alignment. In the preview, you should notice that the category shows the geographical classification, as seen in the following screenshot:

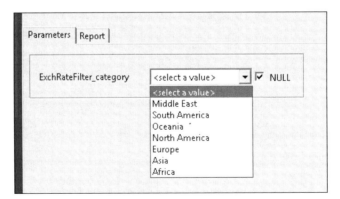

How it works...

When executed, the value for the lookups appears through the dataset category. Once the user selects a value, this is passed as a parameter to the business logic that returns the data for the report.

Business logic

The business logic for the exchange rate filter uses LINQ to read data. The difference here from the business logic used in the previous recipe is the additional `where` condition that determines if the node has a category that is equal to the parameter received. The `OR` condition in the logic is to deactivate this conditional check when the parameter is null and will retrieve all the data from the XML lookup.

The business logic for category lookup uses LINQ to identify all the distinct values from the XML. Since there can be more than one node in the XML with the same category, the category dataset that is created using the business logic is used as a lookup source. This should give you an idea of how a lookup can be built using business logic.

Building a report through an external datasource

In this recipe, we will create a report that connects to an **Online Transaction Processing** (**OLTP**) datasource and retrieves data through an SQL query. You will learn how to add a generic report datasource that can be used across all reports. The report here will retrieve the employee information from the Adventure Works sample database.

Getting Ready

In order to execute this recipe, you will need the Adventure Works database installed in the SQL server. This is available for free to download from Microsoft at `http://technet.microsoft.com/en-us/library/ee873271.aspx`.

How to do it...

1. Open Visual Studio and create a project with the name **AdventureWorkDatasoure**. This project is created to hold the new report datasource in AX.

2. In the project, add a new element of type **ReportDatasource**.

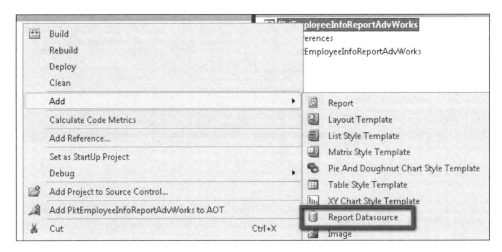

3. Open **ReportDatasource** and set the following properties:

Property	Value
Name	AdventureWorks
Connection String*	Server=AX2012R2A;Database=AdventureWorks2008R2;Integrated Security=SSPI
Provider	SQL

 '*' – The database name and server name must be modified according to your setup.

4. The reason to add it as a separate project is so that you can later easily identify the project that holds the report data source to change its properties; for example, connection string. This report datasource is now ready to be used across all reporting projects.

5. Create a new project with the name **PktEmployeeInfoReportAdvWorks**.

6. Add a new dataset, and in the **Data Source** property, select **AdventureWorks**. The new data source that was added must be visible along with other data sources.

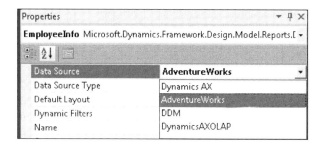

7. Select this as a datasource and click on the ellipsis (...) button on the **Query** property. This opens a new editor window.

8. It is advisable to design your query in SQL Server Management Studio before you apply it here. In the editor window, key in the following SELECT statement:

```
SELECT NationalIDNumber, LoginID, JobTitle,
    BirthDate, MaritalStatus, Gender, HireDate,
    VacationHours, SickLeaveHours

FROM HumanResources.Employee
```

9. Click the exclamation button to validate the query.

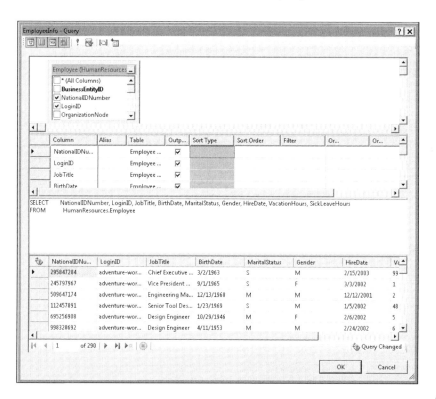

10. Click **OK** to see the fields added to the new dataset.

11. Now drag it to the auto design node. Set the template and appropriate labels to present the rcport.

12. Run the report preview.

EmployeeInfo
Contoso Process Industry
EmployeeInfo

National ID Number	LoginID	Job Title	Birth Date	MaritalS tatus	Gender	HireDate
10708100	adventure-works\frank1	Production Technician - WC50	8/24/1965 12:00:00 AM	S	M	3/27/2003 12:00:00 AM
109272464	adventure-works\bonnie0	Production Technician - WC10	10/11/1980 12:00:00 AM	M	F	2/2/2004 12:00:00 AM
112432117	adventure-works\brian3	Vice President of Sales	7/8/1971 12:00:00 AM	S	M	3/18/2005 12:00:00 AM
112457891	adventure-works\rob0	Senior Tool Designer	1/23/1969 12:00:00 AM	S	M	1/5/2002 12:00:00 AM
113393530	adventure-works\hung-fu0	Production Technician - WC20	11/23/1965 12:00:00 AM	S	M	2/7/2004 12:00:00 AM
113695504	adventure-works\alice0	Production Technician - WC50	2/27/1972 12:00:00 AM	M	F	1/8/2003 12:00:00 AM
121491555	adventure-works\wendy0	Finance Manager	11/12/1978 12:00:00 AM	S	F	1/26/2003 12:00:00 AM
1300049	adventure-works\nicole0	Production Technician - WC40	5/10/1980 12:00:00 AM	M	F	3/26/2003 12:00:00 AM
131471224	adventure-works\andreas0	Quality Assurance Technician	4/29/1983 12:00:00 AM	M	M	3/6/2003 12:00:00 AM
132674823	adventure-works\jeffrey0	Production Technician - WC10	8/12/1950 12:00:00 AM	S	M	3/23/2002 12:00:00 AM
134219713	adventure-works\ranjit0	Sales Representative	10/31/1969 12:00:00 AM	S	M	7/1/2006 12:00:00 AM
134969118	adventure-works\dylan0	Research and Development Manager	3/27/1981 12:00:00 AM	M	M	3/12/2003 12:00:00 AM
138280935	adventure-works\carole0	Production Technician - WC30	11/19/1977 12:00:00 AM	M	F	1/20/2003 12:00:00 AM
139397894	adventure-works\shu0	Sales Representative	4/10/1962 12:00:00 AM	M	M	7/1/2005 12:00:00 AM
141165819	adventure-works\gary1	Facilities Manager	3/21/1965 12:00:00 AM	M	M	1/3/2004 12:00:00 AM
14417807	adventure-works\guy1	Production Technician - WC60	5/15/1976 12:00:00 AM	M	M	7/31/2000 12:00:00 AM
152085091	adventure-works\sameer0	Production Technician - WC50	7/27/1972 12:00:00 AM	M	M	3/15/2003 12:00:00 AM
153288994	adventure-works\houman0	Production Technician - WC50	9/30/1965 12:00:00 AM	M	M	2/26/2003 12:00:00 AM
153479919	adventure-works\io1	Janitor	5/25/1948 12:00:00 AM	M	F	4/7/2004 12:00:00 AM

How it works...

The report uses the `Reportdatasource` connection string to establish a connection with the report datasource. Ensure the necessary permission for the database is set up and is accessible. The query that is specified in the editor is an SQL query and not one from AX. It is a good practice to design the query in the Management Studio and verify it before specifying it here. The editor in the database can be used to select fields, join tables, specify conditions, and validate them.

 Global values such as company name and report name can be used only in headers and footers in precision design.

Adding a parameter for an external datasource query

This recipe will extend the previous recipe to add a parameter that will influence the data retrieved through the SQL query.

Getting Ready

This recipe requires that you have the Adventure Works database installed and you have ready access to the SQL server. This is a continuation of the report developed in the *Building a report through an external datasource* recipe in this chapter.

How to do it...

1. Open the project and the report associated with the project.

2. Select the dataset and open the query editor window to modify the query as shown here:

```
SELECT NationalIDNumber, LoginID, JobTitle,
   BirthDate, MaritalStatus, Gender, HireDate,
   VacationHours, SickLeaveHours
FROM HumanResources.Employee
WHERE (NationalIDNumber LIKE @Id)
// @ID will be treated as a variable
```

3. Click OK to see the parameter reflected in the **Parameters** node in the dataset and report parameters in the report model. A new popup will show up asking for the parameter; you can key in a valid ID or %.

4. Optionally, you can attach a lookup to the parameter by creating an additional dataset that filters **NationalIdNumber** from the table as was done in the *Building a parameter lookup using business logic* recipe.

5. Save and preview the report.

How it works...

The SQL statement uses a `like` condition to make it work more like a search rather than look for a match. The parameter to retrieve all the employees is not * as in AX and should be %.

Creating a customer summary OLAP report

Online Analytical Processing (**OLAP**) helps create interesting data mash-ups that can show trends, distribution, and various other dimensions summarized for top-level management. Dynamics AX offers many different ways to represent OLAP reports, such as SQL Report Builder, Power View, and Excel. But when it comes to exposing the reports over the Web or deploying them to a role center, then SSRS reports are an ideal choice. In this recipe, we will get into the details of creating a simple OLAP report that will summarize the total transaction value across customer groups quarterly in a year.

Getting Ready

To be able to implement this recipe, you need OLAP configured for Dynamics AX. You must have a basic understanding of OLAP and the ability to write **Multidimensional Expressions** (**MDX**) queries.

How to do it...

The goal of the recipe is to display the total value of transactions for a customer group represented quarterly in the year 2012:

1. The first step is to create an MDX query, and the best place to do this is in the management studio. Open the Analysis Service MDX Query Editor.

> For more details on the MDX Query Editor, follow these links:
>
> https://msdn.microsoft.com/en-us/library/hh231197.aspx
>
> https://msdn.microsoft.com/en-us/library/ms187058.aspx

2. In the Microsoft Dynamics AX Query Editor, run the following query and ensure that it works fine:

```
SELECT {[Measures].[Accounts receivable amount -
   transaction currency]} oncolumns,
nonempty(
[Transaction date].[Quarter].[Quarter].Members*
[Customer].[Customer group].[Customer group].Members*
[Customer].[Customer group name].[Customer group
   name].Members,
```

```
{([Measures].[Accounts receivable amount - transaction
currency])})
onrows
FROM [Accounts Receivable Cube]
WHERE( [Transaction date - fiscal
  calendar].[Year].&[USPI]&[2012],
  [Company].[Company].&[USPI])
```

3. The query editor lists all the available cubes and their dimensions and measures. As you execute the query, the results can be viewed at the bottom, as seen in the following screenshot:

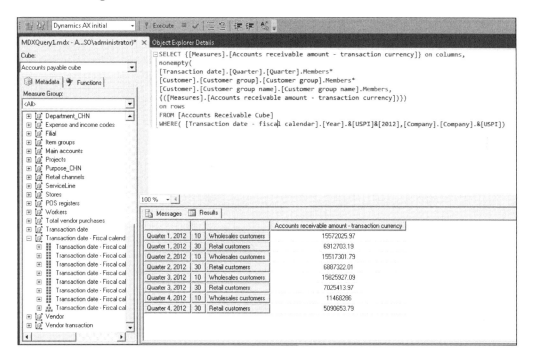

4. Create a new reporting project in Visual Studio and add a report called **PKTCustgroupSalesSummary**.

5. Add a dataset and set the **Data SourceTypeas** property to **DynamicsAxOLAP**.

6. Now copy the MDX query from the Management Studio and paste it in the report query editor that is opened by clicking the ellipsis (...) button in the **Query** property.

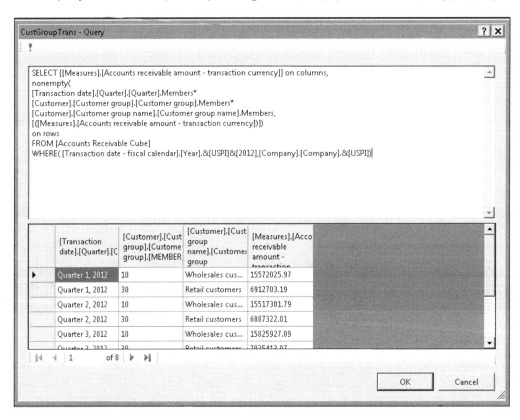

7. Click the exclamation button to validate the query. This should display the data in the data editor window at the bottom. Click **OK** to add the dataset.

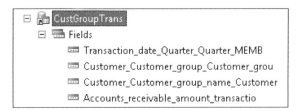

8. Add a precision design node **CustGroupSummary** and double-click to open the designer.

9. Insert a new table and add the following fields as seen here:

Customer Group	Name	Amount
[Customer_Customer_grc	[Customer_Customer_group_n:	[Accounts_receivable_amount_transacti:

10. Add a **Parent Group...** field in **Row Groups** as shown in the following screenshot:

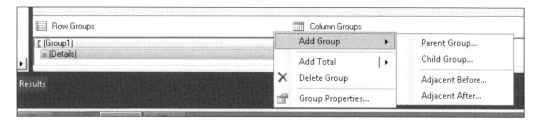

11. Select **Transaction_date_Quarter_Quarter_MEMB** in the group by option dialog.

12. Preview the report after adding labels and setting fonts.

How it works...

The MDX query used in this report uses the account receivable cube that comes along with standard AX. It tries to represent the total amount in transaction currency for each quarter against each customer. The nonempty function ensures that the query doesn't return any blank values.

 Did you know you can copy and paste controls from precision design in one report to another precision design?

See also

▶ The *Creating a group view report* recipe in *Chapter 4, Report Programming Model – RDP*

Adding a parameter lookup for OLAP

The previous recipe was a simple implementation of a static MDX query. This recipe will further extend it to influence it through parameters. We will parameterize both transaction year and company under the WHERE condition. Users will be able to do a lookup for these parameters that are again attached to MDX queries.

Getting Ready

To be able to implement this recipe, you need OLAP configured for Dynamics AX. You must have a basic understanding of OLAP and the ability to write MDX queries. This recipe extends the report built in the *Creating a customer summary OLAP report* recipe in this chapter.

How to do it...

1. The MDX query used in the existing report has two conditions hardcoded: one for the company and the other for the year. Modify the query as shown in the following code snippet to parameterize the hardcoded values:

```
SELECT { [Measures].[Accounts receivable amount -
   transaction currency] } oncolumns,
nonempty(
```

```
[Transaction date].[Quarter].[Quarter].Members*
[Customer].[Customer group].[Customer group].Members*
[Customer].[Customer group name].[Customer group
  name].Members,
{([Measures].[Accounts receivable amount -
  transaction currency])})
onrows
FROM [Accounts Receivable Cube]
WHERE( STRTOMEMBER(@EndDate),
  strtomember(" [Company].[Company].&[" + @Company + "]"))
```

2. Clicking **OK** in the query editor will prompt for the values. Fill in a valid value to proceed. For example, [Transaction date - fiscal calendar].[Year].&[USPI]&[2012] , USPI.

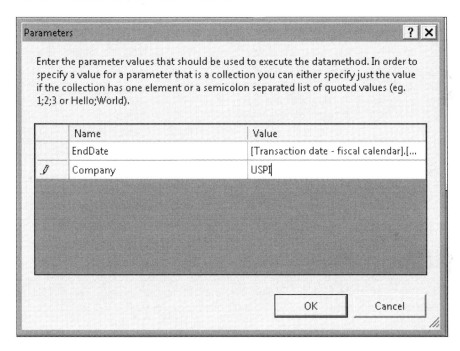

3. This adds the parameter to the dataset and report. Any error in the MDX query will fail to add it as a datasource, so double check it with the MDX Query Editor and make sure the right parameter values are entered. Entering wrong parameter values also stops adding the query to the dataset.

4. The two parameters `@Enddate` and `@Company` are now added to the **Parameters** node as shown in the following screenshot:

5. The next step involves creating the lookup for these parameters. Use the following MDX queries to create a report dataset to look up the company:

```
WITH
MEMBER [Measures].[ParameterCaption] AS
  '[Company].[Company].CURRENTMEMBER.MEMBER_CAPTION'
MEMBER [Measures].[ParameterValue] AS
  '[Company].[Company].CURRENTMEMBER.UNIQUENAME'
MEMBER [Measures].[ParameterLevel] AS
  '[Company].[Company].CURRENTMEMBER.LEVEL.ORDINAL'
MEMBER [Measures].[Key] AS
  '[Company].[Company].CURRENTMEMBER.PROPERTIES("Key")'
SELECT { [Measures].[ParameterCaption],
  [Measures].[ParameterValue],
  [Measures].[ParameterLevel],[Measures].[Key]}
```

```
ON COLUMNS ,
Except(
    [Company].[Company].ALLMEMBERS,{[Company]
    .[Company].[Unknown],[Company].[Company].[All]})
ON ROWS
FROM   [Accounts Receivable Cube]
```

6. In the **Report parameters** node, for the **CustGroupTrans_Company** parameter, set the following values for the parameter dialog that opens by clicking the **Values property** button. This links the dataset company to this parameter for lookup purposes.

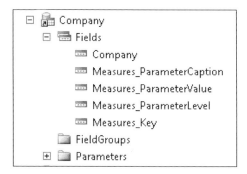

7. To set a default value for the **Company** parameter, modify the **Default value** property to the expression =Parameters!AX_CompanyName.Value.

8. For the **Enddate** parameter, create a dataset by using the following query:

```
WITH
MEMBER [Measures].[ParameterCaption] AS '[Transaction date
    - fiscal calendar].[Year].CURRENTMEMBER.MEMBER_CAPTION'
MEMBER [Measures].[ParameterValue] AS '[Transaction date -
    fiscal calendar].[Year].CURRENTMEMBER.UNIQUENAME'
MEMBER [Measures].[ParameterLevel] AS '[Transaction date -
    fiscal calendar].[Year].CURRENTMEMBER.LEVEL.ORDINAL'
MEMBER [Measures].[Key] AS
    '[Company].[Company].CURRENTMEMBER.Properties("Key")'
SELECT
{
[Measures].[ParameterCaption], [Measures].[ParameterValue],
    [Measures].[ParameterLevel]
}
ON COLUMNS,
{
[Transaction date - fiscal calendar].[Year].[All],
FILTER
(
    [Transaction date - fiscal calendar].[Year].MEMBERS,
```

```
     INSTR( [Transaction date - fiscal
       calendar].[Year].CURRENTMEMBER.UNIQUENAME,"&[" +
       [Measures].[Key] + "]"  ) > 0
     AND
     INSTR( [Transaction date - fiscal calendar].[Year].
  CURRENTMEMBER.UNIQUENAME,"&[1900]") = 0
  )
   } ON ROWS
  FROM [Accounts receivable cube]
  WHERE STRTOMEMBER("[Company].[Company].&[" +
    @Company + "]")
```

9. This dataset, used to look up `Year` for the `EndDate` parameter, has another parameter called `Company`, as seen in the MDX query. In the dataset for this MDX query, expand the **Parameters** node and select the **Company** parameter. Set the **Report parameters** property to **CustGroupTrans_Company**. This way, the company parameter is attached to the value set for the company parameter in `CustGroupTrans`, resulting in showing the years applicable for the selected company.

10. Bind the dataset to the **Enddate** parameter by modifying the **Values** property as shown here, to show up as lookup:

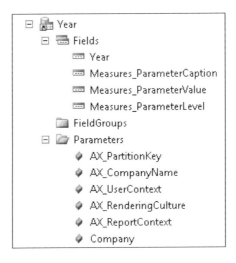

11. Select **From dataset** radio button from the **CustGroupTrans_EndDate - Select values** window and click on **OK**.

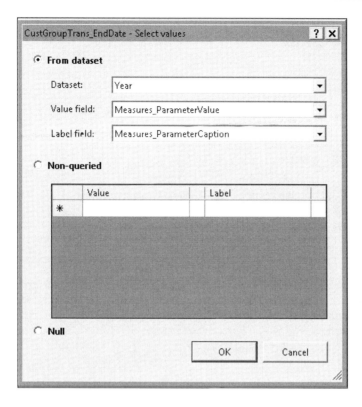

12. Preview the report and verify that the lookups show properly. Notice that the year value changes based on the company selected. This is because of the binding created between the parameters in the `CustGroupTrans` and `Year` datasets.

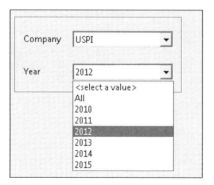

How it works...

Company parameter

The **Company** parameter uses the default value that comes from the system parameter `AX_company`. The user can alternatively choose the value from the lookup and that comes from the Company dataset.

EndDate parameter

The lookup dataset uses a query that also has a **Company** parameter. This is because the lookup should only show values that are applicable for a company selected by the user. So, a binding is created between this parameter and the company parameter. This dependency causes the **EndDate** parameter to be activated only after the company parameter value is set.

Main query

The main query has two conditions: company and end date (actually holds year value and not date). Both have different formats. This has mainly to do with how they are represented in the cube. Each dimension in a cube has different attributes, such as `Member_Name`, `UniqueName`, and `Ordinal`. To construct the company parameter, the `Member_Name` is sufficient; so, the parameter lookup values **Value field** and **Label field** are both set to **Measures_Parameter Caption**. For end date, the complete value must be constructed; so, the parameter lookup values **Value Field** is set to **Measures_ParameterValue** and the **Label Field** is set to **Measures_ParameterCaption**.

Designing an OLAP table report with SQL Report Builder

Ad-hoc reports using SQL Report Builder—the reports that we have designed so far—use Visual Studio based report development tools. This section will show how SQL Report Builder can be used to build ad-hoc reports to be viewed and published back to the reporting services. SQL Report Builder is not an AX-based solution but a generic reporting tool which can be used to generate reports. Designing reports using SQL Report Builder is so convenient and user-friendly that sometimes end users themselves can design reports. In the upcoming recipes, we will see how, with no coding or model changes, reports are developed with the help of inbuilt wizards.

This recipe will specifically show how the customer group cube report that was made using SSRS in the *Creating customer summary OLAP report* recipe can be designed and published using SQL Report Builder.

Getting Ready

This recipe requires that you have installed and have access to the Reporting Services Manager and the Report Builder.

How to do it...

1. Open the Reporting Services in the browser and click on the **Report Builder** icon at the top.

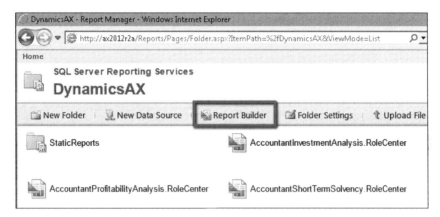

2. This opens up the **Report Builder** editor. In the wizard that shows up, select **Table or Matrix Wizard** and click on **Next**.

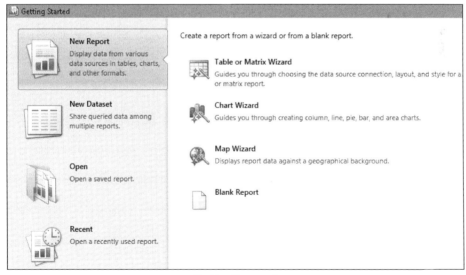

The New Report tab

3. The next tab is where the dataset must be defined. Select **Create a dataset** and click **Next**. The following tab is to choose the source of the report data. Click on **New**.

Selecting DynamicsAXOLAP

4. In create new connection for the **Data Source** property, give the connection a name, such as **AxOLAP**. Set the **Select connection type** to **Microsoft SQL Server Analysis Service** and click on **Build**.

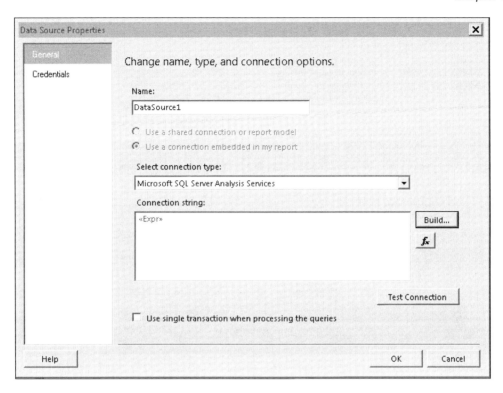

5. In the **Connection Properties**, type the name of the server and choose the database. Click on **OK** to return and press the **Next** button in the wizard.

6. The wizard displays the query designer. Since we will use the **Accounts receivable cube**, use the datasource selector to select the cube.

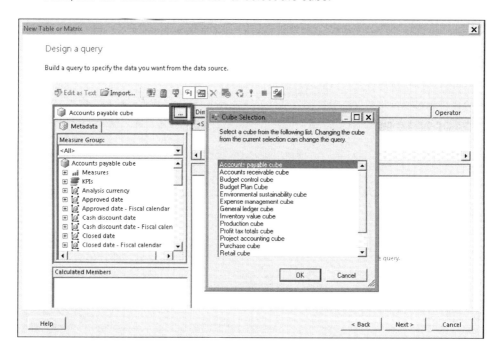

7. In the top dimension row, set the values, as seen in the following screenshot, by using the lookups in the columns:

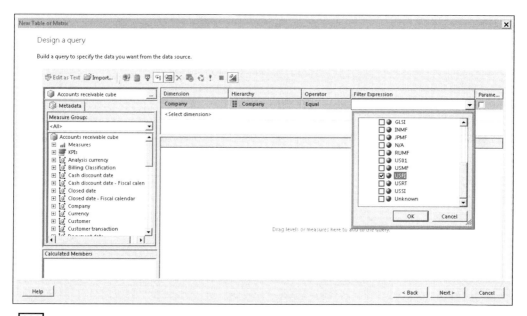

8. After completing this, in the empty space below, drag **Customer group name**, **Customer name**, and **State** from **Customer Dimension** from the left pane. Similarly, traverse to the **Dimension Transaction Date** node and drag **Transaction date** and **Year-Quarter-Month-Date** to the empty space.

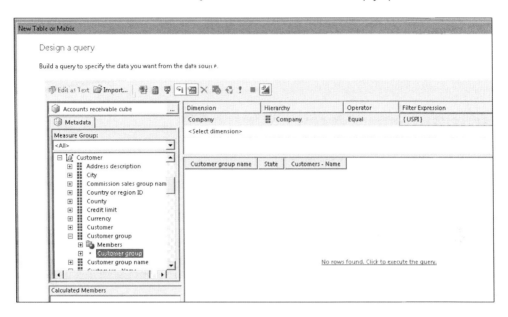

9. The next step is to go to **Measures** at the top in the left pane, expand **Customer transactions**, and drag **Accounts receivable amount currency** to the columns. The query automatically executes and shows the data returned in the screen:

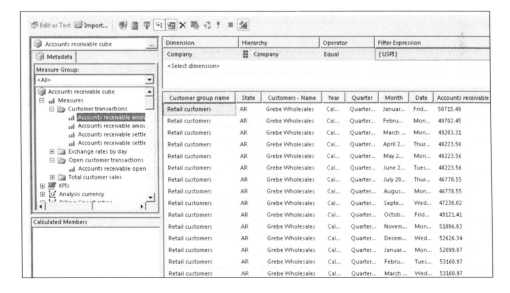

10. Click **Next** and from the available fields, drag and drop the fields as shown here:

11. Click on **Next**. The layout designer provides options to select Total and Subtotal.

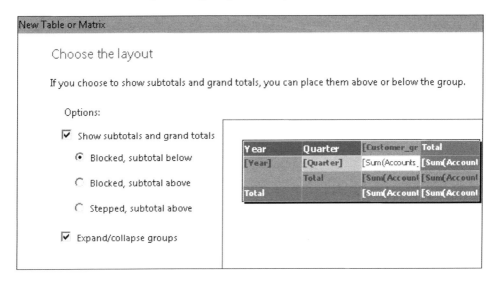

12. In the subsequent screen, select the theme and click on **Finish** to see the fully designed report in the editor.

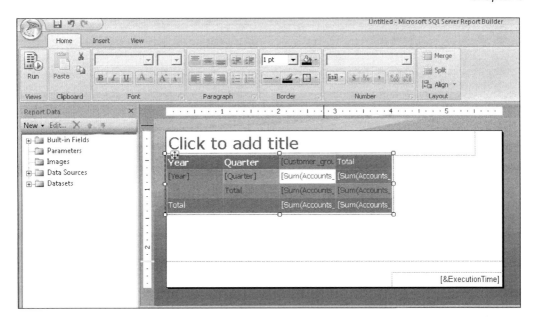

13. Click on **Run** to see the report preview.

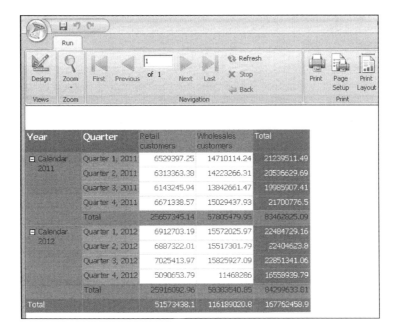

14. To save the report, publish this to the report server. From the menu, select the **File** | **Save As** option and choose the location in the report server, preferably the DynamicsAX folder. Once saved, the report can be accessed through the Reporting Services.

How it works...

SQL Report Builder also doubles as an easier way to verify a cube query before creating it using SSRS. The Report Builder can also be used against the OLTP database, but the label transformations and security might not be put to action, so care must be taken in using it.

Designing a map sub-report with SQL Report Builder

Though the AX SSRS extension has improved the capability of AX reports, it is still to catch up with the actual SSRS. Features such as map and a few other graphical additions to reports are yet to make way into it. However, there is a way to bring nice map reports to AX through SQL Report Builder. This recipe will extend our previous recipe to add a map data, which will then be added as a sub-report.

Getting Ready

This recipe requires that you have installed and have access the Report Server Manager and Report Builder. This recipe is a continuation of the recipe, *Designing an OLAP table report with SQL Report Builder*, in this chapter.

How to do it

1. Continue with your last report by stretching the borders of the report to make some space to insert a new control. On the **Insert** ribbon bar, select **Map | Map Wizard**.

2. In the wizard, choose **USA by State Exploded** and click on **Next**.

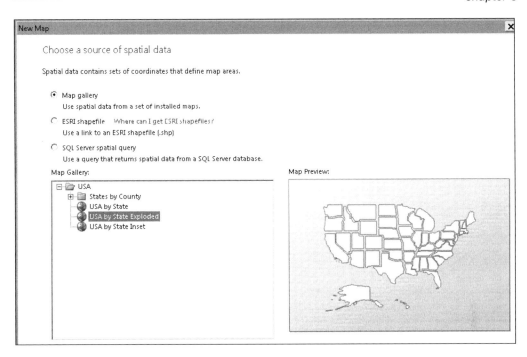

3. Let's use the same dataset that was added, so set the option to choose the already added datasource and click on **Next**.

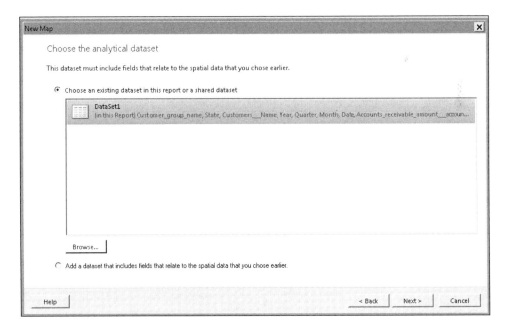

4. The next step is to relate the spatial data and the analytical data. In the below tab, choose the spatial data which identifies a geographical location. Select **STUSPS** in **Match Fields** and select the **State** field from the **Analytical Dataset Fields**.

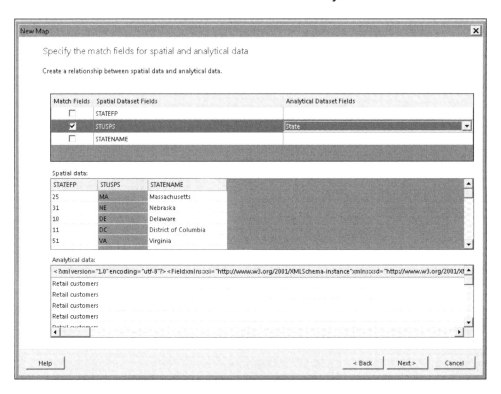

5. In the next tab choose a theme, preferably **Generic**, and choose the amount field sum for visualization. Set the **Color rule** to your preferred choice. Click on **Finish** to complete the wizard.

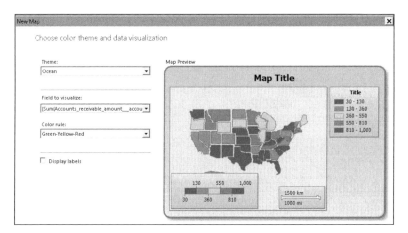

6. The map is inserted in the report. Before we make it a sub-report, it is necessary to drop all the extra add-ons in the map, such as **Title**, **Scale**, and so on. So, select each of them and uncheck the **Show Distance Scale** and **Show Color Scale** options.

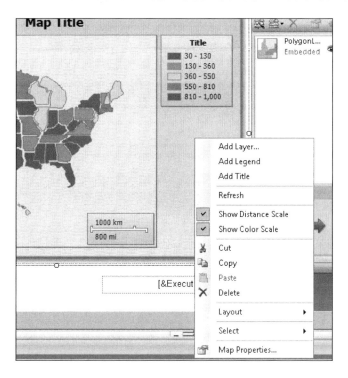

7. In the map area, right-click and select **Viewport Properties...**. In the properties, set the **Fill** and **Border color** to **None** and **Border size** to **0 pt**. The map should appear plain as seen in the following screenshot. Resize it to a smaller size so that it can be inserted as a sub-report.

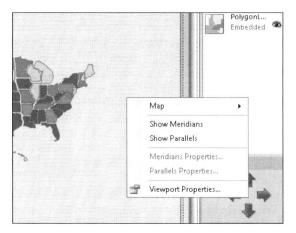

8. We have now added our map to the report.

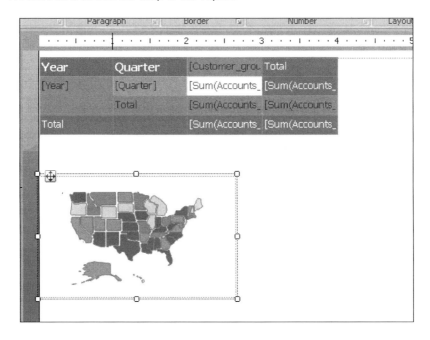

9. Now, in the tabular design, right-click on the **Sum** field as seen in the following screenshot. Insert a row by selecting **Inside Group - Below** in **Insert Row**.

10. Readjust the table design by stretching the columns and rows to build some space for the map. Cut the map and paste it in the new column. This automatically makes the map a sub-report.

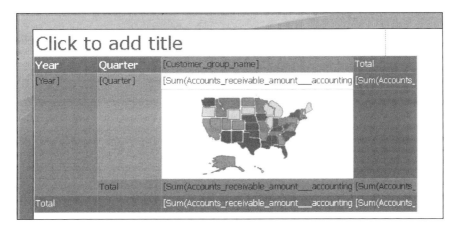

11. Run the report.

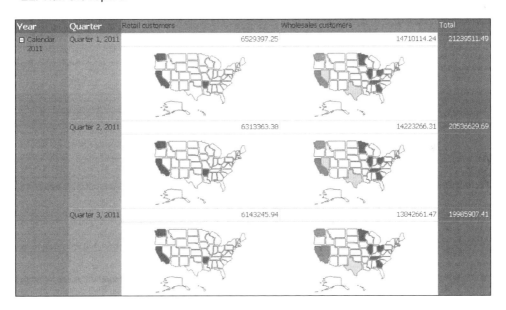

12. To save the report, publish this to the report server. From the menu, select the **File | Save As** option and choose the location in the report server, preferably the DynamicsAX folder. Once saved, the report can be accessed through Reporting Services.

How it works...

A sub-report reflects the data inside the slice in which it is placed. The sub-report option is automatically applied to the map when it is dragged and dropped into the existing table. The main report passes the relevant parameters to the sub-report to render the right data; all these settings are taken care of automatically by the Report Builder in this case.

These reports, once published, can be reused and made accessible to all users. To open the reports inside the rich client, modify the report viewer (`SRSReportViewer`) to pass the URL and the report name through the `SRSReportRunAdapter` class.

Creating a sub-report in auto design

Sub-reports can be compared to the **View Details** option in the Dynamics AX rich client forms. It is another way of adding drill down information to reports. In this recipe, we will see how to add sub-reports to auto design. The approach here is to create a report that shows the list of customer groups, and when the user clicks on a customer group, then a sub-report with all the customers belonging to the group.

Getting Ready

This recipe requires that you have access to Visual Studio, and the Dynamics reporting extension installed before you start.

How to do it...

1. Create a reporting project in Visual Studio and add a report **PktCustGroup**.
2. To this report, add a dataset through AX query to list all the customer groups.
3. Drag the dataset to the auto design and create a design. Preview the report.
4. Add another report to the project **PktCustReport**.
5. To the report, add **CustTable Ax query** to list all the customers.
6. Drag the dataset to the auto design and create a design.
7. In the **Parameters** node, create a new parameter called **CustGroup** of type **String**.

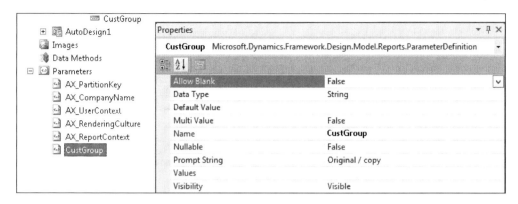

8. In the **Designs** node, expand the **Filters** node, create a new filter, and set the following properties:

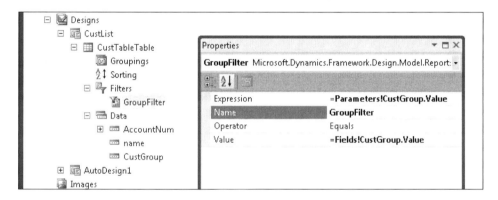

9. The columns are displayed as follows:

Property	Value
Name	GroupFilter
Expression	=Parameters!CustGroup.Value
Operator	Equals
Value	=Fields!CustGroup.Value

10. Open the report **PktCustGroup**. In the **Design** node, expand the data node and right-click on the **CustGroup** field. Select **Add | Report Drill Through Action**.

11. This will add a new **ReportDrillThroughAction** node. Open the properties of the node and click the button on the **ReportDesign** property. This will list all the reports in the same project. Expand **PktCustReport** and select the **Design** node. Then click on **OK**.

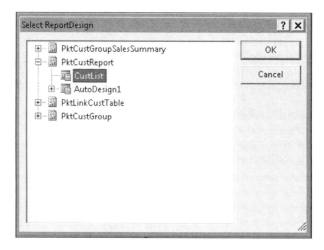

12. All the parameters—including **CustGroup**—that were created in **PktCustReport** will be added as sub-nodes. Navigate to each sub-report and set it to the system parameter of the current report in the **Value** field, except for the **CustGroup** parameter.

13. For the **CustGroup** parameter, set the value field to the expression `=Fields!CustGroup.Value`. Save and preview the report.

14. In the report preview, as you navigate to **CustGroup**, the cursor will change to indicate a link. Clicking on the link will open the customer list filtered by the customer group.

How it works...

The reports that are linked must be in the same project to make it work. The filter that is added to the **CustList** report will restrict the design to show only records whose customer group value is equal to the parameter, as the filter is mapped to the parameter. This parameter value is filled with the **CustGroup** field value in the **CustGroup** report. When the user clicks on the link, the corresponding field value is automatically passed as a parameter to the sub-report.

The link field (**CustGroup**) doesn't need to match with the parameter field. This means the drill through could be implemented for the **Name** field as well, since the link is governed by the expression that is set up for parameters under `ReportDrillThroughAction`.

Creating a sub-report in precision design

This recipe is to design a sub-report for precision design. To implement this recipe, let's use the cube report that was designed in the recipe *Creating a customer summary OLAP report* in this chapter.

Getting ready

This recipe extends the OLAP report developed in *Creating Customer Summary OLAP report* in this chapter and uses the report added in the recipe *Creating a sub-report in auto design* in this chapter.

How to do it...

1. Add **PktCustgroupSalesSummary** (OLAP report) to the **PktCustReport** project used in the previous recipe. We need to do this because the sub-reports and main report must exist in the same project.

2. Open precision design and navigate to the field for **Customer group**. Select the field, right-click, and choose **Textbox Properties...**.

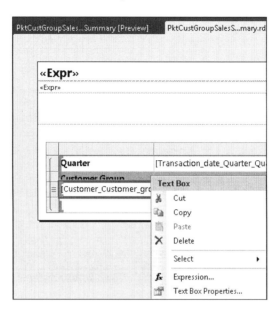

3. In the properties dialog, select the **Action** tab and choose **Go to Report** under **Enable as a hyperlink**.

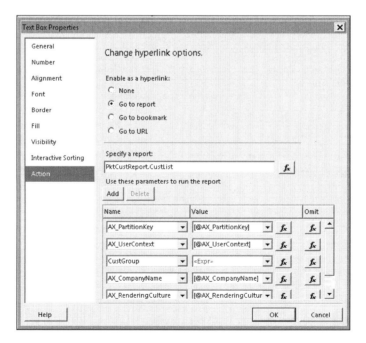

4. In the **Specify a report** field, manually fill the values with **PktCustReport.CustList** since no lookup is available as in auto design.

5. Click on the **Add** button to add parameters. In the **Name** field, type the parameter name used in **PktCustReport**, and in the **Value** field, use the expression button and select the appropriate values from the **PktCustgroupSalesSummary** report.

6. Rebuild and deploy the report.

How it works...

Sometimes in the preview option, the links may not work, resulting in an error. Go ahead and deploy the project to the report server and verify it in the report server to ensure that it works.

> Precision design can be created from auto design. This can be helpful as it is easier to add fields to auto design. Also, creating report drill through actions is manual in precision design but automatic in auto design. So, when auto design is converted to precision design, the drill through is automatically translated.

See also

▸ The *Adding Drill Up/Drill Down actions in reports* recipe in *Chapter 2, Enhancing Your Report – Visualization and Interaction*.

6
Beyond Tabular Reports

In this chapter, we will cover the following recipes:

- ▶ Creating a matrix report
- ▶ Creating a multicolumn matrix report
- ▶ Creating a column chart report
- ▶ Creating a line chart
- ▶ Gauges in the reports
- ▶ List and rectangle controls in the reports
- ▶ Adding reports to the role center

Introduction

The legacy reporting system in Dynamics AX, which used to develop through the MorphX IDE or X++, had very limited capabilities for rendering data. Something as simple as adding an image and placing it correctly was a massive task, while adding things like graphs and charts was not even imaginable. SSRS takes away this pain and makes it easy to represent data in different formats that offer convenient representation options, making it easier for the end-user to absorb the data. This chapter will discuss the recipes that cover the kinds of controls other than the table layout control discussed so far, and this can be used to represent data, such as matrix, charts, gauges, and more. The reader will be familiarized with the different controls and how these can be put to use in reports through this chapter.

Creating a matrix report

A matrix is an interesting representation format with a two-dimensional view of data, allowing capabilities to consolidate by row and column. This recipe will discuss how to add and use a matrix data region in reports. Totaling capabilities in the matrix reports will also be discussed.

How to do it...

The recipe is broken down into two sections. In the basic report design section, we will build a simple RDP that will be used in this recipe as well as in the other recipes found in this chapter; however, the actual recipe is given in the second section.

Basic report design

Before we start discussing this recipe, we will build an RDP class that can be used as a source for all the recipes in this chapter. This RDP will be used as the source of the dataset for all the reports in this chapter:

1. Create a query as seen here, the **InventItemGroupItem** table, which uses the existing join and is added for the purpose of limiting the sales lines data to certain item groups.

2. The goal of the RDP is to run across **SalesLine** in the system and retrieve the item, item group, and then confirm the shipping date. The shipping date that was confirmed is split into multiple parts like years, months, and days.

This RDP can be time consuming if you have a huge database of sales orders, so limit your data to certain item groups or a certain period, as required by the RDP `processReport` method.

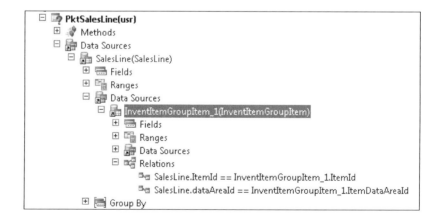

3. This RDP will fill a temporary table, as shown in the following illustration:

Temporary table creation

4. The RDP shown here will fill the temporary table by running through all the sales lines in the system.

 The general approach for an analysis like this is to use OLAP so that it is faster and provides multiple dimensions of consolidations, but uses an OLAP to demonstrate these report controls, which might stop several from practicing. This is because a majority of the AX developers are not BI experts. Keeping this in mind, this RDP has been used to demonstrate the following examples:

```
[
//bind query - shows in the report dialog
SRSReportQueryAttribute(queryStr(PktSalesLine))
]
Class PktItemSalesHistoryDP extends SRSReportDataProviderBase
{
PktItemSalesHistoryTmp salesHistoryTmp;
}


[
SRSReportDataSetAttribute(tableStr(PktItemSalesHistoryTmp))
]
public PktItemSalesHistoryTmp getItemSalesHistoryTmp()
{
Select salesHistoryTmp;
Return salesHistoryTmp;
}

private void insertTmpTable(SalesLine _salesLine)
  {
```

```
Qty qty;
Date shipDate;
InventItemGroupItem groupItem;

qty              = _salesLine.QtyOrdered;
shipDate         = _salesLine.ShippingDateConfirmed;
groupItem        = InventItemGroupItem::findByItemIdLegalEntity(
                                        _salesLine.ItemId,
                                        _salesLine.
DataAreaId);

salesHistoryTmp.clear();
salesHistoryTmp.ItemId          = _salesLine.ItemId;
salesHistoryTmp.ItemGroupId     = groupItem.ItemGroupId;
salesHistoryTmp.Price           = _salesLine.salesPrice;
salesHistoryTmp.Amount          = _salesLine.SalesPrice * Qty;
salesHistoryTmp.Qty             = qty;
salesHistoryTmp.Year            = year(shipDate);
salesHistoryTmp.MonthOfYearId   = mthOfYr(shipDate);
salesHistoryTmp.Days            = dayOfMth(shipDate);
salesHistoryTmp.insert();
}

[
SysEntryPointAttribute(false)
]
Public void processReport()
{
    Query          query;
QueryRun          queryRun;
SalesLine         salesLine;
InventItemGroup ItemitemGroup;

query = this.parmQuery();

queryRun = new queryRun(query);

while (queryRun.next())
    {
salesLine = queryRun.get(tableNum(salesLine));
this.insertTmpTable(salesLine);
    }
}
```

Creating a matrix report

1. Create a report in Visual Studio **PktMatrixReport** and add the RDP provider as the dataset.

2. Set the **Dynamic filter** property to **False**.

3. Create a new precision design and name it **MatrixDesign,** and then double click to open the editor.

4. Right-click and **Insert** a new **Matrix** data region, as shown in the following screenshot:

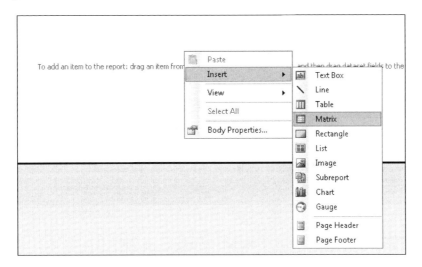

5. Use the field selector to set the fields; choose the **Qty** in the data section and it will automatically add the Sum function to it:

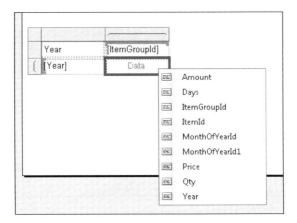

6. To add the total quantity for each row, navigate to **Row Groups** at the bottom, click on the small arrow, and then select **Add Totals | After**.

7. To add the total quantity for each column, on **Column Groups** at the bottom, click on the small arrow, and then select **Add Totals | After**.

8. There are a total of three boxes in the design, each represents the row total, the column total, and the grand total. The grand total tallies the sum of the rows and the sum of the columns.

9. As you can see in the following screenshot, the title rows and the grand total row are colored, and the font is set to bold. This will give a better appearance for the matrix.

10. The header for the row is present, but there isn't a similar header for the column group. So, right-click on the first column and select **Insert Row | Outside Group – Above**. This will give a header to the column; enter the expression string **ItemGroupId** using the label id or the static text. The design that appears will be as shown here:

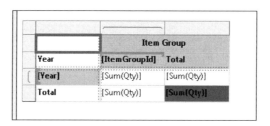

11. Save the report and preview it.

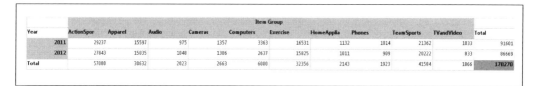

Year		ActionSpor	Apparel	Audio	Cameras	Computers	Exercise	HomeApplia	Phones	TeamSports	TVandVideo	Total
	2011	29237	15597	975	1357	3363	16531	1132	1014	21362	1033	91601
	2012	27843	15035	1048	1306	2637	15025	1011	909	20222	833	86669
Total		57080	30632	2023	2663	6000	32356	2143	1923	41584	1866	170270

How it works...

A matrix data region is a **tablix** control behind the hood. The tablix control combines the behavior of the table, the list, and the matrix reports. Though UI has the table and the matrix list, they are the same controls under the hood but they open with a different configuration. The matrix data region has both the row and column groups, whereas a table control only has a column group. Matrix helps in creating summary type reports.

Creating a multicolumn matrix report

This recipe will show you how a multicolumn matrix can be implemented. Here, we will expand our report to see how we can dissect it in detail, and see how the rows can be split by months, followed by years, and how the columns can show the average price and the quantity.

Getting ready

This recipe requires that you complete the *Creating a matrix report* recipe in this chapter.

How to do it...

Create a new design as done in the previous recipe, or extend the design created in the previous recipe with the help of the following steps:

1. From the **Report Data** toolbar, drag the **MonthOfYearId1** control to the **Row Group** control, which is next to the **Year**. When you drop, a blue bar appears, and it must face the year column as shown here:

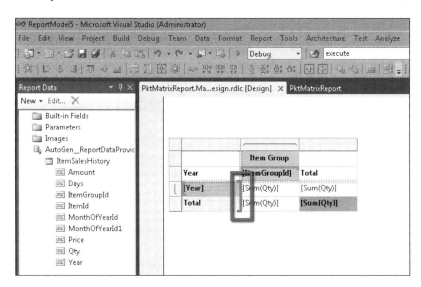

2. From the **Report Data** toolbar, drag the control **Price** to the **Column Group** that is next to the quantity field. A vertical blue bar appears, and it must face the quantity column, as illustrated in the following screenshot:

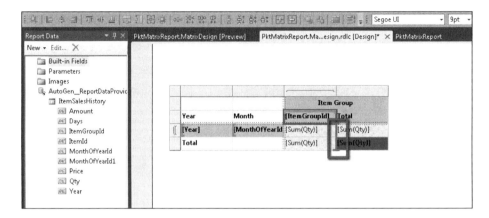

3. By default, the price field gets placed as a **Sum** operation; change it to **Average** by right-clicking on the cell and choosing **Expression**. In the expression field, modify the **Sum** and set it to **Average**.

4. Since the price can have decimal values, it is important to set the decimal ranges, otherwise it will have an improper formatting. Right-click on the **price control** and choose **Textbox properties**.

5. On the **Textbox properties**, set the **Formatting** to the **Decimal** and ensure that the decimal place is set to 2.

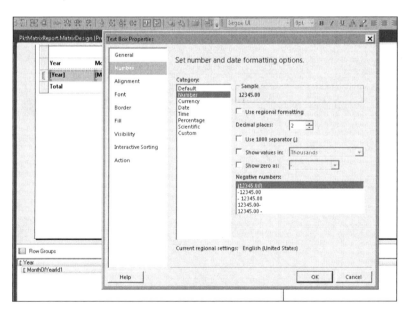

6. If you want to extend the previous recipe, drop the column totals before doing this, otherwise directly move to the column group at the bottom and click on the arrow button and then select **Add Totals | After**. This will add the total for the quantity and price fields.

7. The report design appears as shown here; save the report and preview it.

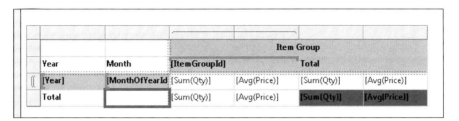

			Item Group		
Year	Month	[ItemGroupId]		Total	
[Year]	[MonthOfYearId]	[Sum(Qty)]	[Avg(Price)]	[Sum(Qty)]	[Avg(Price)]
Total		[Sum(Qty)]	[Avg(Price)]	[Sum(Qty)]	[Avg(Price)]

8. The first image shows the preview with a limited data (this is because the **load dataset** fully option is not activated).

Year	Month		Item Group		
		ActionSpor	Total		
2011	April	26	57.13	26	57.13
	August	39	61.74	39	61.74
	December	63	59.34	63	59.34
	February	29	60.35	29	60.35
	January	78	56.79	78	56.79
	July	39	59.22	39	59.22
	June	47	60.81	47	60.81
	March	45	59.28	45	59.28
	May	33	58.94	33	58.94
	November	39	57.43	39	57.43
	October	34	59.99	34	59.99
	September	42	61.05	42	61.05
2012	April	35	59.70	35	59.70
	August	28	63.43	28	63.43
	December	45	61.05	45	61.05
	February	36	62.28	36	62.28
	January	47	57.99	47	57.99
	July	28	58.85	28	58.85
	June	48	59.79	48	59.79
	March	51	58.74	51	58.74
	May	44	59.08	44	59.08
	November	30	64.54	30	64.54
	October	26	63.74	26	63.74
	September	34	62.28	34	62.28
Total		966	59.88	966	59.88

9. The second image shows the preview with the full dataset loaded:

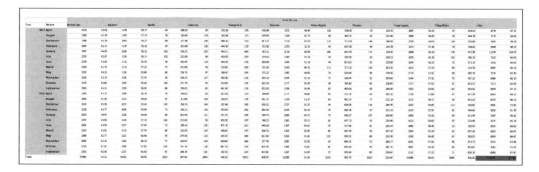

How it works...

In this report, the summary has been broken down by years and months, while the columns summarize the multiple values rather than just one value. This way the matrix can be used to build the detailed drilled summary reports.

The **report preview** option in Visual Studio always loads only a limited amount of sampled data and doesn't load the entire data on the system. This is not the case with small datasets. When using big datasets as we have been doing in this chapter, you will notice that the data changes every time. In that case, to confirm if everything has loaded, activate the **Load data set fully** option, which is available at the right corner of your preview window.

Creating a column chart report

This recipe will guide you in creating chart-based reports in Dynamics AX. Charts are an interesting pictorial representation of the data, and the SSRS reports support a multitude of chart types. It is easier to switch among the chart types in SSRS. In this recipe, we will create a column chart that represents the total sale of a quantity over a couple of years.

Getting ready

Complete the RDP defined in the getting ready section of the *Creating a matrix report* recipe in this chapter.

How to do it...

1. Since the RDP class can return a large number of item groups, it is ideal to limit it to two item groups, so as to test this recipe. This will make it faster and easier to work through the recipe.

2. Modify the `processreport` in the RDP to add the ranges for the item group in the query.

3. In Visual Studio, create a new report, **PktColumnChartReport,** and link the RDP class to it. Remember to set the **Dynamic filter** property in the dataset to **False**.

4. Create a new precision design and name it **ChartDesign**.

5. Open the editor, right-click and choose **Insert | Chart**. In the prompting dialog window that shows the different chart types available, choose the column chart, as shown in the following screenshot:

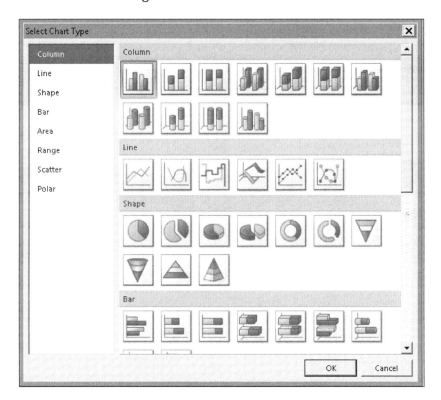

6. Resize the chart to the required size and double click on the chart area. This will display additional square boxes around the chart image, and there will be one each for category, series, and data. Drag the following fields to the specified region accordingly,

Field	Drop area
Year	Category
ItemGroupId	Series
Qty	Data

7. As the fields are dropped in the chart area, you can see the report changing at the design time. Though this may not reflect the exact data, it will give you a feeling of how it looks during run time.

8. Modify the chart and axis title. **Save** the report design.

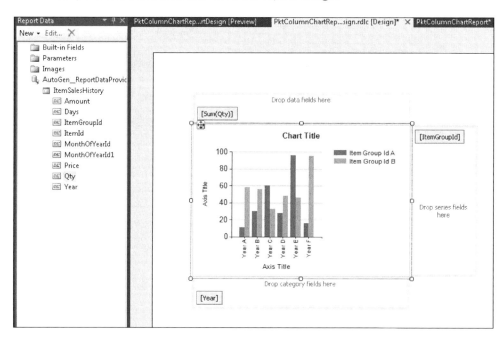

9. The report preview will appear as shown in the following screenshot:

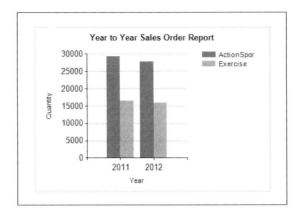

How it works...

The aforementioned report is a multi-series chart. This means that the category has been applied across the series. In a static series, we represent a single series item, for example, item group. In this case, if the item group is not restricted, then each year might be displayed for all the item groups in the system. Care has to be taken while considering what is added to the series, as it should make sense to the user when a comparison is made.

See also

▶   The *Creating a Chart Data region* recipe in *Chapter 2, Enhancing Your Report – Visualization and Interaction*.

Creating a line chart

This recipe will discuss another chart based report. Here, we will try to show the monthly quantity trend for the item groups over the years. The line chart is the best option for revealing the trends. This recipe will also focus on the aesthetic properties of the charts, such as color, axis design, and so on.

Getting ready

This recipe requires the *Creating a column chart report* recipe to be completed first.

How to do it...

1.   Create a new precision design for the report. Call it line design.

2.   Open the editor and insert a new chart.

3. Double click on the chart area to open the field editor. In the field editor, add the following fields as specified.

Field	Drop area
Year, MonthOfYearId	Category
ItemGroupId	Series
Qty	Data

4. In the steps discussed next, we will deal with how the aesthetics of a chart can be made better. In the **General Properties** window, set the **Palette** to **SeaGreen**, which will apply a different set of colors for each of the series.

5. To set up the markers for the series on the value points in the chart area, right-click and select **Series Properties**, and in the **Markers** tab, set the type of marker as **Square**:

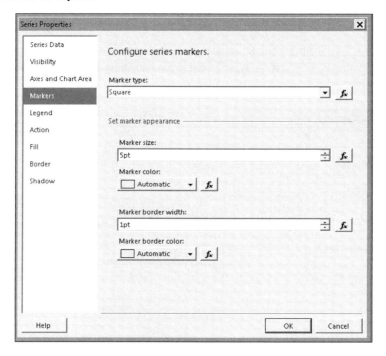

6. The axis may not show all the labels for the category axis. To make sure that it shows all the months as labels, right-click on the **Axis** and open the **Axis properties** form. In the property form, in the **Axis options** tab, under **Set axis scale and style,** set the Interval to **1**. This will ensure that all the labels are visible.

7. Right-click on the **Legend** and choose **Legend Properties**. In the **General** tab, under **Legend position**, choose the position of the legend from the circular radio buttons:

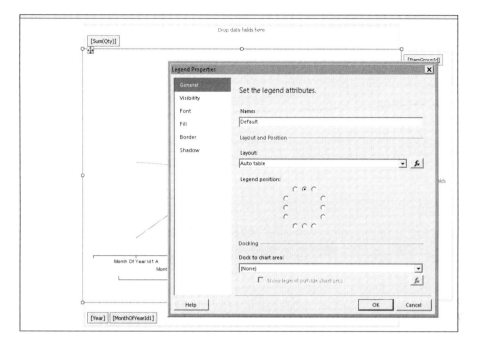

8. To disable the quantity axis, right-click on any axis and uncheck **Show Value Axis**, and then the design will be similar to the screenshot as shown here:

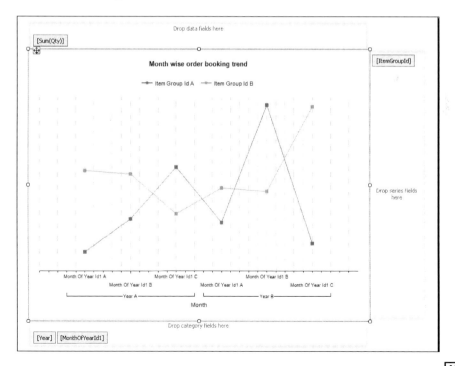

9. Save the report and preview it.

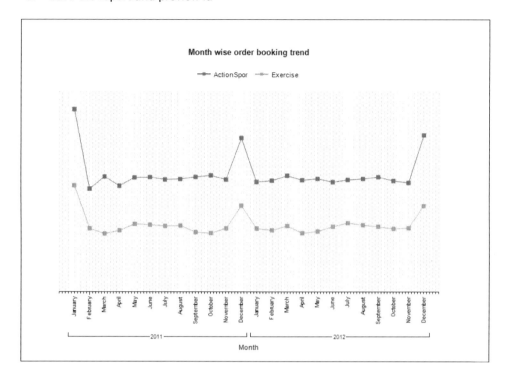

How it works...

The recipe provides details on the appearance of a report and how it could be controlled through the various properties associated with it. The recipe discusses only a limited set of options, while there are tons of other options, that you can explore.

There's more...

Though the chart design shown here is from the precision design, the auto design also supports charts.

Chart reports in auto design

In the auto design, the category, the series, and the data appear as a group node as shown in the upcoming screenshot. The chart type can be changed through the properties node of the chart control. The fields can be dragged into it from the datasets. The precision design is very flexible and convenient, as compared to the auto design, for the following reasons:

- ▸ Modifies and previews the chart in the design time
- ▸ Provides clarity for understanding the field and its corresponding axis

- ▶ Good extent of customization and visibility of the available charts
- ▶ More control of where and how the data is rendered, for example, the marker, the legend, and so on

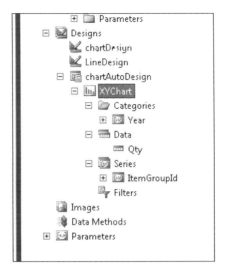

 It is preferable to use the precision design over the auto design when it comes to charts.

Gauges in reports

Gauges are one-dimensional data regions, which can display a single value in your dataset. A gauge can be used as a KPI, in the table or the matrix cells to indicate single values. This recipe will show you how a gauge can be added to a matrix cell for indicating the average price.

Getting ready

Complete a report design as specified in the *Create a multicolumn matrix report* recipe. The report design must appear as the following screenshot shows:

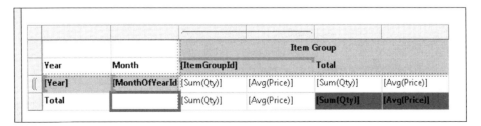

How to do it...

1. Open the precision design created in the matrix report recipe.

2. Select the **ItemGroupId** field, right-click and select **Insert Column | Inside group - Left**

3. In the newly created column, drag the gauge control from the report items in the toolbox. Select radial and choose the design highlighted in the screenshot:

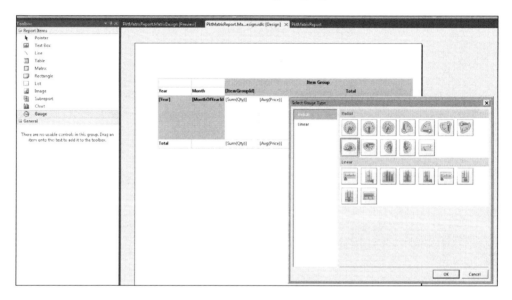

4. Stretch the box so that it allows you to resize the gauge control. Notice that the gauge control increases as the box expands. Stretch it to a visible limit.

5. Double click on the gauge control and on the **Drop data fields here** box that appears over the gauge, drop the field **Price** by dragging it from the report data. By default this value might appear as **Sum(Qty)**, in which case convert it to **Avg(price)**:

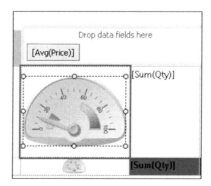

6. Right-click on the gauge and select **Pointer properties**. In the properties form in the **Pointer options** tab, click on the **Expression** button in the **value** field and then convert the **Sum** to **Avg** in the expression editor.

7. The gauge by default shows the max value in red but in case of the average price, the higher the value, the greener it is. To modify, select the range in red, followed by a right-click, and then open **Range properties**. In the range properties, set the **Secondary color** to **Green** in the default color option.

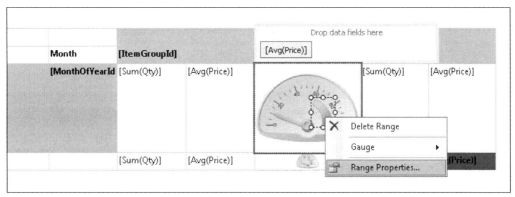

Selecting the range properties

8. To add a new range, right-click on the gauge and select **Add Range**. A new range will be added to the lower corner.

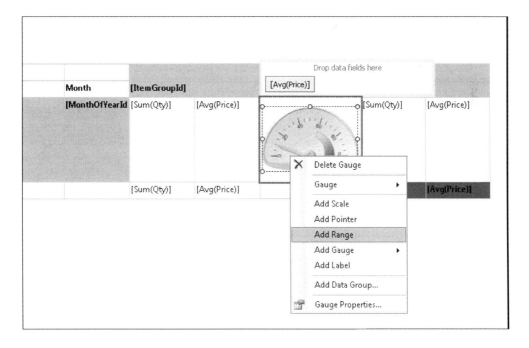

9. Select the range and open **Range properties** by right-clicking on the new range. In the **Range properties** form, set the **Start range at scale value** and **End range at scale value** to **1** and **20**, respectively, and change the **fill color** to **Red**. Any number of ranges with different scale values can be similarly added.

10. The final design appears as shown in the following screenshot:

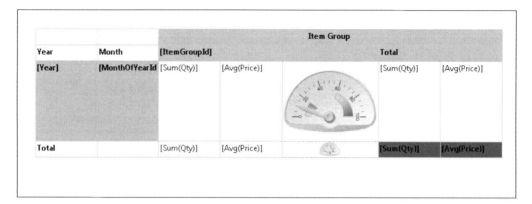

11. Save and preview the report.

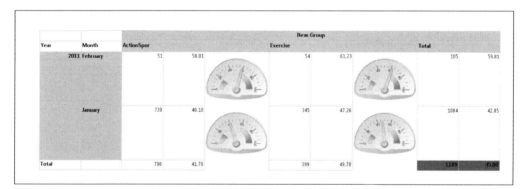

List and rectangle controls in reports

List and rectangle are types of container controls in SSRS. Rectangle control is used for the flow control, while the List data region is a kind of array control. The List region can help in creating very interesting representations of the report. In this recipe, we will discuss the idea of the list and rectangle controls in the process of building a summary sheet for each item group.

How to do it...

1. Create a new report with the RDP **PktItemSalesHistoryDP,** and add a new precision design.

2. In the editor window, insert a list region. Right-click on the control and select the **Tablix** properties. In the properties window, set the **dataset** to the RDP dataset **ItemSalesHistory**.

3. The **Row Groups** window, which is at the bottom, must indicate a details row. Click on the arrow at the corner and open **Group Properties**:

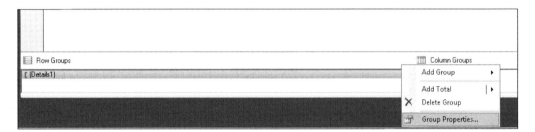

4. In **Group Properties**, add a new grouping by **ItemGroupId**:

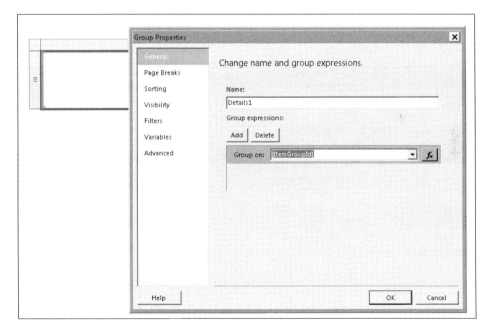

5. Stretch the list data region to fit the entire report. From the toolbox, drag the text box control and set the field to **ItemGroupId**. Also, enter the text title as **Summary Sheet** before **ItemGroupId** as illustrated in the following screenshot:

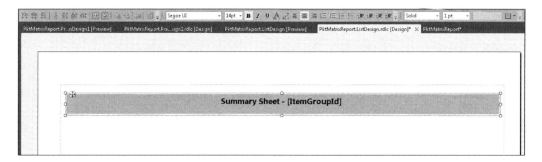

6. Increase the font size, set the alignment to center, and the back color using the text tool bar.

7. From the tool box, again drag the rectangle control to the list box. Add the quantity and price sum to the rectangle control. Also, add labels, header text, back color. The rectangle should reflect the total **Quantity** and **Amount** for the item group.

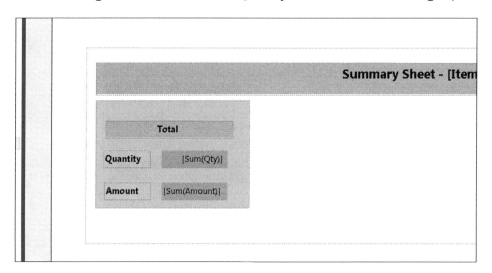

8. Stretch the list box to increase the height, and insert a radial gauge below the total. In the pointer properties, set the field to **Avg(Price)**. Add a text box for the title of the gauge, which is **Average Price**.

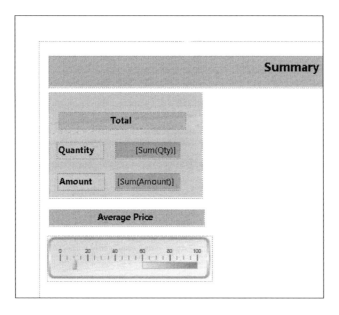

9. In the rest of the available area of the list, we will create two charts. One is a bar chart that indicates the quantity sold across items, and the other will be a line chart that indicates the price graph across items.

10. Insert a chart, choose the **Barchart option**, drop **ItemId** in the categories and **Quantity** in the **Data fields**. Delete the axis titles and legends to make space for the graph.

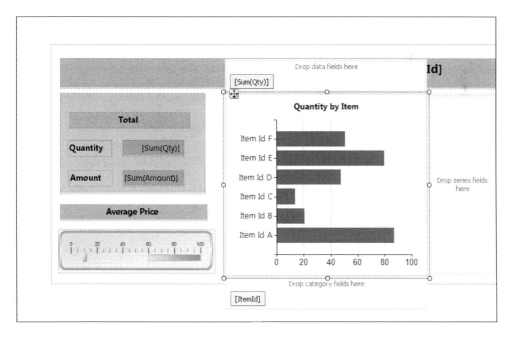

11. Similarly, insert a line chart and add **ItemId** to the categories and **Price** to the **Data fields**. Give it a title, after removing the axis titles and legend.

12. The final design of the report should look as follows:

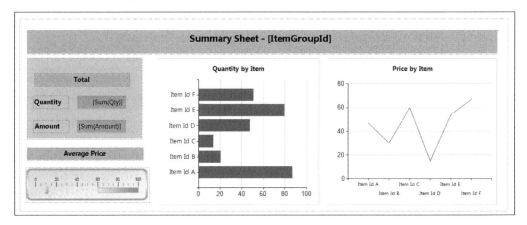

13. Since this is a summary, it is preferable to print each summary in a single sheet. To activate this, navigate to the **Group properties | Page breaks** tab and enable the **Between each instance of a group** flag. This will enable the printing of the summary in one sheet. Preview the report to see the summary print per page.

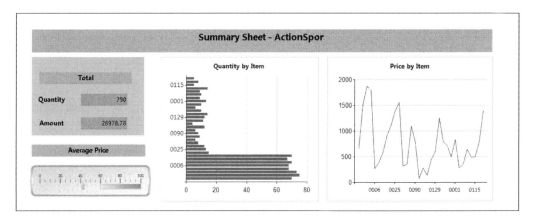

How it works...

Surprisingly, the list data region internally is also a Tablix control with altered configuration. The list data region helps in setting up a format that can be repeated for every record in the dataset. To experiment with how the list data region works, do the following: drag a list data region and connect it to a dataset; then add a field from the dataset. When previewed, you will see that the list is repeated for each record in the dataset. In the example discussed here, since a grouping is added to the **ItemGroupId,** it is only repeated for the number of item groups in the system.

Adding reports to the role center

The analysis or the consolidation reports are usually used by those higher up in the organization, and it will be easier for them if these analysis reports are visible in their integrated role center dashboard. This recipe will discuss how any report can be added to the role center page.

How to do it...

1. Deploy a report and create a menu item for the report. In this case, we will use the **PktColumnChartReport** from **Create ColumnChartReport**. Give the menu item a label, **Year To Year Sales Order Report**.

2. Open the role center page that you wish to edit and click on the **Personalize this page** option at the right corner. This opens a view that can be edited.

3. Click on **Add a web Part**.

4. A screen listing all the categories and web parts will appear. Select **Microsoft Dynamics AX** from the category and **Report from the Web Part**. Click **Add**:

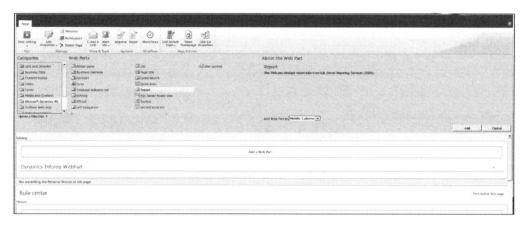

5. This adds the web part; the web part must be configured. Select the drop down box at the upper right corner, and then select **Edit My Web Part:**

6. A report bar will appear on one end of the web page. From this bar, select the report; in this case, it is the column chart. The list highlights the reports based on the report menu item label. Select the report and set the properties, such as parameter, layout, and so on. Click on **OK**:

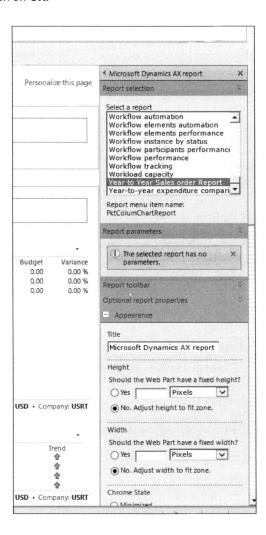

7. The report will show up in the role center. Click **Stop Editing** in the tool bar to complete the setup. This recipe can be performed either on the Dynamics AX role center page or on the enterprise portal.

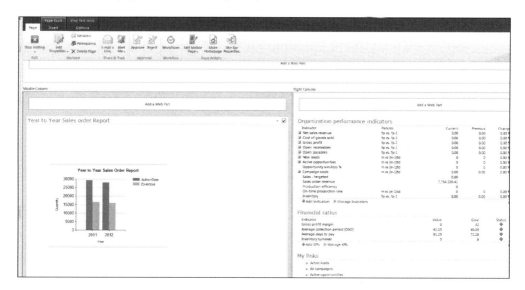

How it works...

The role center modifications can be done by an end user as well as by the administrators. If a report is made visible at the role center, then see that you don't have too many dynamic parameters.

7
Upgrading and Analyzing Reports

This chapter will cover the following recipes:

- ▶ Upgrading a report from its previous version
- ▶ Analyzing and modifying an existing report
- ▶ Implementing validation in reports
- ▶ Surrogate fields in reports
- ▶ Grouping and ordering controls in the report dialog
- ▶ RDP with multiple temporary tables
- ▶ Multi-value lookup
- ▶ Inventory dimensions in reports
- ▶ Financial dimensions in query reports
- ▶ Financial dimensions in RDP reports

Introduction

This chapter will walk you through how to upgrade your reports from previous versions to the new SSRS reporting framework. With this you will also learn how to approach existing reports to identify the components that are a part of it. The next few recipes will discuss how to place validations and structure the report controls in the report dialog. You will also learn how to implement multi-value lookup reports and how to return multiple tables from an RDP. Finally, the most used patterns for reports, such as inventory and financial dimensions will be discussed.

Upgrading a report from its previous version

As discussed earlier, reporting has gone through a major change with the new versions of AX. Though SSRS reports were introduced in AX 2009, there were only a handful of them with limited framework support. AX 2012 uses SSRS as a mainstream report while still supporting the legacy framework. Moving reports from AX 2009 to AX 2012, though termed as an upgrade, is in reality a redevelopment. This recipe will basically discuss how to map the different implementations in an AX 2009 report to the new framework. It assumes that the report in AX 2009 is completely custom developed and not found in AX.

How to do it...

Migrating reports from an older version to a newer one is a multistep process since it is a complete redesign. This process has been broken down into major headings and is described here.

Defining the data source

Designing a report starts with making the choice of the report data source. If the existing report uses only a report query, the ideal choice in 2012 would be to use an AOT Query.

Even if there are simple display methods or computations present in the fetch method, it is fine to use a report query. Choose to go with an RDP only when there is a pure business logic placed in a report. The following are the decisional points that should help you choose the data source:

- Source of the data contained in the report dataset
- Elements of the report that are from the report business logic

▸ Calculated columns based on Microsoft Dynamics AX data

▸ The **Extended Data Types** (**EDTs**) that are used to format data

Mapping the parameters and fields

The next step is based on the data source you choose to work with to create the necessary parameters and decide the fields that are required in the report:

1. **For Query**: If there are parameters from the old report dataset, then add them to the **Ranges** node in the newly created AOT query. This will add them as dialog fields using dynamic filters.

2. **For RDP**:

   1. Identify the data that is needed for the report and create one or more temporary tables based on the business logic. For example, `SalesConfirm` and `ProjInvoice` are reports that use more than one temporary table.

   2. After the temporary table is created, create the RDP class and move the business logic placed inside the `Fetch` method into the RDP. Also to be moved are any computed columns that have been implemented as display methods in AX 2009. The display value is mapped to the field in the temporary table and is filled by RDP.

   3. When creating the RDP, you will identify the parameters that are necessary. Create a contract class with the list of parameters.

Mapping the design

Once the data source decision is complete, the next step is to work on the design. Like AX 2009 has auto design and generated design, AX 2012 has auto design and precision design. The generated design is what maps as precision design in AX 2012, but before plainly moving all the generated design to precision design—and similarly auto design—consider rethinking the strategy. Sometimes, it is possible that what was achieved through generated design in AX 2009 can be achieved with the help of auto design and RDP in AX 2012. Take into account the following points as you do your design mapping:

1. **Choice of control**: SSRS reports have a wider choice of presentation methods, such as charts, matrices, and lists. So consider if you can use an alternate way to display your data.

2. **Segregate display methods**: Display methods must be carefully redesigned. In AX 2009, it was a common practice to write a display method to even fetch a value using the foreign key. Such methods can be eliminated in AX 2012. Here are a few suggestions for the commonly found display methods:

❑ **Find methods**: If a query is the report data source, it allows you to add display methods present in the table as datasource fields. So, directly choose the display method when choosing the fields in the Query selection window in the report designer as shown in the following screenshot:

❑ **Simple computations**: There can be conditional computations, such as `If (PriceDiscTable.Value) then Total = Total + Value`. For such conditional computations, try to use expressions. If expressions prove difficult, then use the business logic in the report design to create a method which then can be referred from the expressions. For more on this, refer to the *Adding data methods in business logic* recipe in *Chapter 3, Report Programming Model*.

 Business logic in C# must be used only for simple mathematical computations. For anything that involves access to AX business logic, the recommended approach would be using an RDP.

❑ **Formatting changes**: For simple formatting purposes such as background color, it is recommended to use expressions.

❑ **Business logic in computations**: If there is business logic in computations, make it a part of the RDP and add a field in the temp.

3. If the company image must be displayed in the report, then it is recommended to use precision design over auto design.

Datasets in AX 2012 R3 vs AX 2009 reports

As compared to the report dataset in AX 2009, the report dataset in AX 2012 has stark differences:

- ▶ Two datasets cannot be related or joined to each other.

- ▶ The dataset is flattened and accessed by the dataset name, unlike in AX 2009, where when there is a **SalesTable** and **SalesLine**, there are two cursors to identify them individually.

- ▶ In AX 2012, use the group by property on the report design to achieve the header line pattern as in AX 2009, where the header fields point to the header table and the lines point to the child table.

 Refer to the *Grouping in Reports* recipe in *Chapter 1, Understanding and Creating Simple SSRS reports*.

- ▶ There are no multiple header/footer/prolog sections in AX 2012. There is only one header and footer for each report.

- ▶ Programmable sections are not present in AX 2012. To display designs conditionally, use expressions for visible properties.

- ▶ This completes the migration of a report.

Developing the controller

If your report also uses the `RunbaseReport` class, then proceed with these steps:

1. If the `RunbaseReport` class chooses the report or design at runtime, then a controller must be created in AX 2012. The controller class can be used to choose the report at runtime.

2. If the ranges in the query are modified based on the caller in the `RunbaseReport` class or in the report, then use the controller class in AX 2012.

Handling UI events

1. **Adding dialog fields**: Simple dialog fields are constructed by the framework from the contract parameters. If any dialog modifications are required, then create a UI controller class.

2. **Reacting to dialog field changes**: Any changes such as lookup modification or dependency fields must be implemented in the UI controller class.

3. **Validations**: Any validations must be placed in the contract class.

4. **Aligning report dialog controls**: Use the `SysOperationAttribute` to order the controls in the contract class. For more complex restructuring, use the Visual Studio parameter nodes to create groups.

Analyzing and modifying an existing report

This recipe aims to guide you on how you can approach the identification of the components involved in an existing report, either for the purpose of upgrading your report or to make customizations. The easiest way would be updating a cross reference, but the chances of having a cross reference updated system are less. Hence, this recipe will help you proceed with an approach where it doesn't require the cross reference to be updated.

How to do it...

1. The first step is to identify the report you need to work on. Here are several instances of your starting point and the corresponding method to find the report name:

   ❑ **Moving from AX 2009**: If you are moving from AX 2009, then use the following links to search for the report name in the current version: `http://technet.microsoft.com/EN-US/library/gg731909.aspx`. If it doesn't exist, check at `http://technet.microsoft.com/EN-US/library/gg731897.aspx`, that it is not deprecated. This will help you identify the report name.

   ❑ **End user tells me the main menu navigation**: If the main menu navigation is known, then go to **AOT | Menu**. Expand the corresponding module and identify the output menu item. If the menu item is connected to a controller class and if the **Linked Permission Type** is **SSRSReport**, then check for the **Linked Permission Object** property for the name of the report. Otherwise, open the controller class and look for the `parmReportName` method to identify the reports that are being used for the controller.

   ❑ **I know the report name but not sure which report layout is used**: Say from the previous step you identify the controller but are still not sure which layout is used, since there are many layouts being referenced. Then you could use this approach. Place the debugger in `\Forms\SrsReportViewer\Methods\init`. When the debugger hits this point, choose `Classes\SrsReportRunController` from the stack trace and look for the variable **reportname** under **this** in the watch window. This will clearly indicate the report name and design. It will also help you identify the controller.

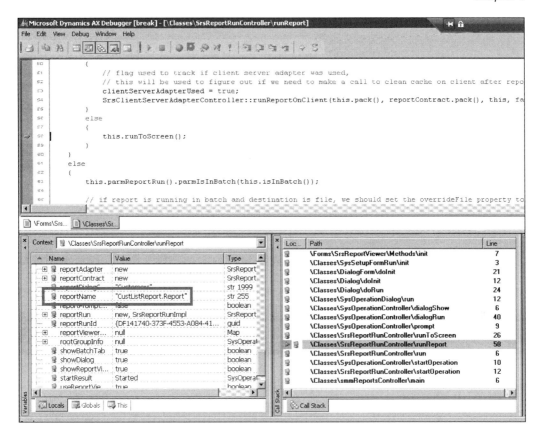

❑ **I'm searching for an example:** If you are looking for an example report
to learn about a certain type of report, then download the Excel sheet
from `http://www.microsoft.com/download/en/details.aspx?id=27877`. This contains the complete list of reports with different
details based on their usage, design, and so on. This can help you choose
the report that might serve you as a good example.

2. To know your report name, the next step is to explore the kind of data sources used in it. To do this, navigate to your report and right-click on it. Go to **Add-ins | Cross reference | Using (Instant View)**.

 This will work even if your cross reference is not updated.

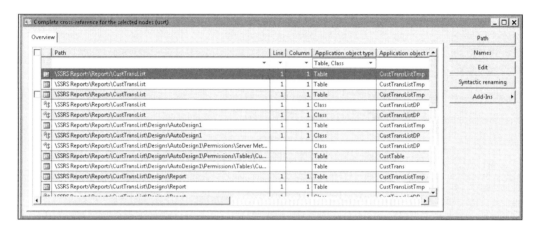

3. This will help you identify the query, temporary table, RDP contract, and any business logic project present as part of the report. What you don't find is the Visual Studio project to which the report belongs.

   ❏ Navigate to the `SRSReportRDLDataContract` and right-click on **Add-ins | Type Hierarchy Browser**. The **Type Hierarchy Browser** shows all the extended classes from where you can shortlist the appropriate RDL contract class. Following these steps can help you identify all the artifacts related to your report.

4. To find the project, there are two options. One is to go by the naming convention. The standard naming convention for a project is `<ReportName>Report` (for example, **CustTransListReport**). In case you don't find it, the alternate way is to visit `http://msdn.microsoft.com/EN-US/library/hh496433.aspx`, where all the reports are listed with the associated project name.

5. In case you identify that the report uses RDP, the next step is to figure out if it has any contract and which UI builder is being used. To identify the contract, navigate to the RDP class, and in the class declaration look for the contract class passed to the `SRSReportParameterAttribute` class. The `SRSReportQueryAttribute` class will help you identify the query it uses.

6. Further, the contract class can optionally be associated with a UI builder. To identify the UI builder, adopt the same approach that was used to identify the contract.

7. The report can have an RDL contract and a UI builder optionally as well. Finding an RDL contract without the cross reference updated is not a straightforward approach. The best approach here would be trying to go by the naming convention. If that is not successful, then use the Type Hierarchy Browser.

8. Modifying your report: There are different approaches that can be adopted to modify a report design, and the choice depends on the level of requirements. Here are a few approaches that you can adopt:

   ❑ **Modify the design**: Use this approach when the number of changes are minimal and are not country/context specific. If too many changes are made, it becomes cumbersome to handle them when the standard report is modified in later releases. This is the simplest of all that is discussed and similarly can be adopted only for minor changes.

   ❑ **Create a new design**: Here, the standard design is duplicated and the design is altered. Use this approach when the report is heavily modified or when implementing it for a specific country, but when the RDP, contract, and UI builder can still be shared. The choice of the design at runtime can be made through the controller class.

   ❑ **Create a new report**: A completely new report can be designed and used instead of the existing report. Adopt this approach when the RDP logic used by the standard report or the UI classes cannot be shared, and the report also requires deeper changes. The reports, however, can share the temptable contract if possible.

9. **Merging changes**: The challenge that arises when modifying a standard report is the manageability in the longer run, when more changes flow in from the SYS level changes from release packs. As of now there are not great tools in AX to merge report changes. There are no references from Microsoft, but there are a few blogs that widely discuss the usage of external code compare tools to do the merge. Though it is not a standard approach, it can work. Please read further at `http://www.k3technical.com/using-code-compare-to-merge-ssrs-reports-in-dynamics-ax-2012/` to understand how you can merge changes between different layers.

How it works...

The steps discussed in the recipe help you to identify all the components involved in a typical reporting project. Create a separate project and add the elements to it; this will make it easier to perform the changes required. Also, apply the design guidelines to see how you can accommodate the changes.

Implementing validation in reports

Validations are important to ensure the integrity of the process. Here, in this recipe, let's see how we can implement validations for reports.

Getting ready

The sample discussed is extending the **InventBatch** report discussed in the *Creating an advanced RDP report* recipe in *Chapter 4, Report Programming Model – RDP*.

How to do it...

1. To make a parameter mandatory, in the report model in Visual Studio, expand and open the parameter that you wish to make mandatory. In the **Properties** node, ensure that the **AllowBlank** property is **False**. Modify it to **True** if the parameter needs to be optional. This property by default is **False**, so any property is mandatory by default. Also, you can set **Default Value** if you want. This is particularly useful for Boolean type parameters where the default value can be **True** in some cases.

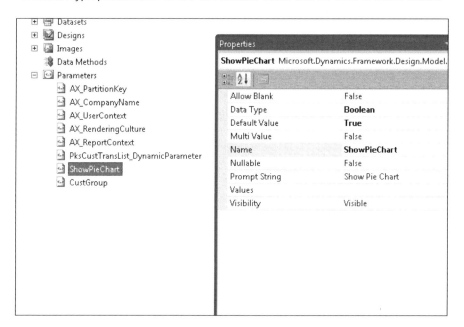

2. Sometimes the validations go beyond verifying mandatory. In that case, the validate operation must be implemented in the contract. As we have seen in previous chapters, there are two kinds of contracts. In the following steps, let's see how to implement validations in each contract.

3. To implement the validation in an RDP contract, the contract must implement the `SysOperationValidatable` interface. Once this interface is implemented, the validate method is automatically triggered by the framework.

4. After implementing the interface, write the validate method. This validate method can be used to place all your validations. Here is an example of how the validation might look:

```
class PktInventBatchTransContract implements
  SysOperationValidatable
{
}
public boolean validate()
{
    boolean isValid;

    if (this.parmProdDate() > today())
    {
        error("Production date must be in the past.");
        isValid = false;
    }
}
```

5. In case of an RDL contract, the approach differs. There is no need to extend the interface since the RDL base class `SSRReportRdlDatacontract` already implements it. Override the validate method from the base class and write your validation as shown here:

```
[
    SrsReportNameAttribute(ssrsReportStr(
      PktRdlCustTransList, CustTransList)),
    SysOperationContractProcessingAttribute(
      classstr(PktRdlCustTransListUIBuilder))
]

class PktRdlCustTransListRdlContract extends
  SrsReportRdlDataContract
{
    Date fromDate, toDate;

    #define.FromDate('FromDate')
    #define.ToDate('ToDate')
}

public boolean validate()
```

```
    {

        boolean isValid = super();

        fromDate = this.getValue(#FromDate);
        toDate = this.getValue(#ToDate);

        if(fromDate && toDate)
        {
            if(fromDate > toDate)
            {
                isValid = checkFailed("@SYS120590");
            }
        }
        return isValid;
    }
```

How it works...

▸ **RDP contract validation**: The RDP contract validation is invoked by verifying if the contract class is implementing the interface. The framework triggers a validate call automatically following the user input. This is because the RDP contract doesn't extend any class, unlike the RDL contract.

▸ **RDL contract validation**: The RDL contract has a base class `SRSReportRDLDataContract` and it is used for all reports. The base class carries out the framework-level validation for the report. To implement a custom validation for a specific report that extends this class and decorate it with the attributes to indicate the report for which it should work. Since the RDL contract stores and retrieves values based on their names, the first line in the validate logic is to retrieve the values followed by the validation logic. Remember not to prevent the super method as it contains validations.

Surrogate fields in reports

The feature of surrogate keys that was introduced with AX 2012 is powerful, but at times creates ambiguity on their usage. A surrogate key is a key whose value has no meaning to people. A large number generated by the system, such as `Recid`, could be a surrogate key. The goal of this recipe is to clarify and showcase examples that use surrogate keys in possible patterns. This recipe is divided into two sections: the first section will discuss the usage of surrogate keys in a query-based report, followed by the section that details their application in RDP-based reports.

How to do it...

1. To implement this recipe, we will use the example of student and student marks tables. Create these tables and relate the student marks table to the student table with the surrogate key. For the student table, add **Student Id** as a replacement key in the table properties.

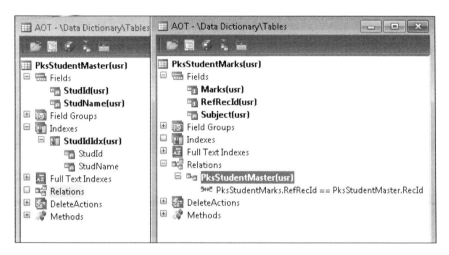

2. Create the surrogate key by creating a new relation in the student marks table and then using the option **New | Foreign Key | Primary Key Based**. In the relations property, make sure **CreateNavigationPropertyMethods** is set to **Yes**.

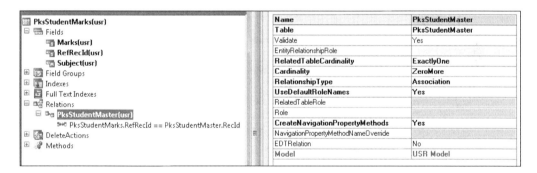

3. Add a method that returns the student ID to the students marks table with the code shown here:

```
public display PktStudId studId()
{
    return this.PktStudentMaster().StudId;
}
```

Surrogate keys in query-based reports

1. Create a query for the student marks table and add the surrogate key to the range.

2. Open Visual Studio, create a new reporting project, and add a new report. Add a new dataset to the report and click on the data source property. In the query prompt window, select the query that was created, and in the fields selection window, you will see the display method that was written for student ID. Check the display method as well. Once you click **OK,** watch it getting added as a dataset field. This is one way to bring the information from related tables through the surrogate key.

 The method described here can also be used for regular computed methods.

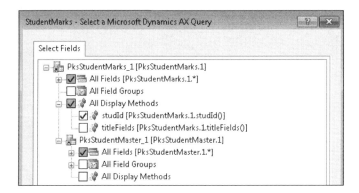

3. Now deploy and run the report in AX. When the report opens up, the range is seen as `Recid`. This may not be a convenient way for the user to make his selection. This approach can be used when the report needs to show the related fields only and no selection is needed.

4. For reports that use the selection field from the parent table, adopt the approach where the parent table is added as a child datasource. Drop all the fields leaving only the relevant field that needs to appear in the selection dialog and in the report. In this case, the student master is added to the child data source and the student ID is added to the range. The rest of the report remains the same. So when a report dialog is shown, the user is able to see the student list instead of `Recid`.

Surrogate keys in RDP

1. In an RDP report, the temporary table that is created can be used to store the replacement values directly. In this example report, the temporary table for student marks will have the student ID field instead of the reference to `Recid`.

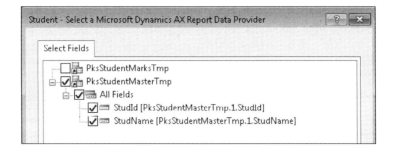

2. Create an RDP for this temporary table. The process report method must be a simple query that fills this temporary table, as shown here:

```
[SysEntryPointAttribute(false)]
public void processReport()
{
    Query                    query;
    QueryRun                 queryRun;
    QueryBuildRange          studIdRange;
    QueryBuildDataSource     qbds;

    PktStudentMarks          studMarks;
    PktStudentMarksContract  studContract;

    studContract = this.parmDataContract() as
      PktStudentMarksContract;

    query = new query();
    qbds = query.addDataSource(tableNum(PktStudentMarks));

    //set the range
    studIdRange = SysQuery::findOrCreateRange(qbds,
      fieldNum(PktStudentMarks,
    RefRecId));

    studIdRange.value(int642str(studContract.parmStudIdSFK()));

    queryRun = new queryRun(query);

    while (queryRun.next())
    {
        studMarks =
          queryRun.get(tableNum(PktStudentMarks));
        this.insertTmpTable(studMarks);
    }
}
```

3. The contract has surrogate key as the parm method since the **StudentMarks** table does not have other values.

```
[
    DataMemberAttribute('StudentId'),
    SysOperationLabelAttribute(literalStr("Student")),
    SysOperationHelpTextAttribute(literalStr("Student
       Details")),
    SysOperationDisplayOrderAttribute('1')
]
public StudISurrogateKey
   parmStudIdSFK(StudISurrogateKey_idSFK = idSFK)
{
    idSFK = _idSFK;

    return idSFK;
}
```

4. Create a report in Visual Studio and add the RDP created as a data source. Preview and deploy the report to AX.

5. When you open the report, you will see that the lookup appears for the replacement key and not the surrogate key. When the user selects the student ID, the appropriate `Recid` is stored in the contract.

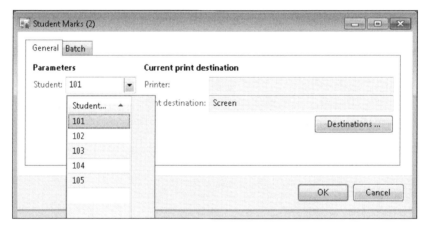

How it works...

Comprehending the approach of surrogate keys in reports:

1. Surrogate keys in query-based reports:

   ❏ If you want the replacement fields only to be displayed in the report, then use the display methods present in the table.

❑   If the replacement values are added as selection fields, then use a multilevel query where the parent table is added as a child data source, and the appropriate replacement keys are retained from the child data source.

2. Surrogate keys in RDP-based reports:

❑   Create new fields in the temporary table for the replacement fields and fill them in the RDP class.

❑   If a contract uses a surrogate key as the parm method, then the lookup is shown appropriately based on the replacement key setup in the table.

Spin-off idea

For the RDP report discussed here, try to increase the replacement key to more than one field and see how the report dialog behaves. In this case, the student name is also added along with the student ID. The resulting dialog box is as seen in the screenshot here:

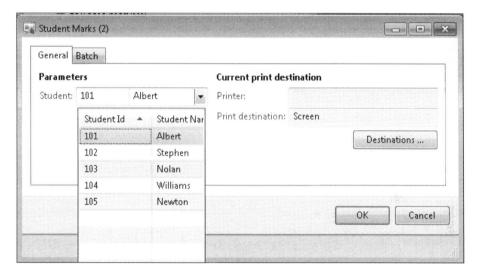

Grouping and ordering controls in the report dialog

The report dialog is constructed automatically by the UI builder in `Sysoperationframework`, but sometimes you may want to influence how the controls are visualized in the dialog. In this recipe, let's see the different options available for grouping and ordering controls in a report. There are multiple options for this. We will start with a simple grouping mechanism and move on to more sophisticated changes.

Getting ready

This recipe will extend the **PktRDLCustTransList** report we built in *Chapter 3, Report Programming Model*, and the **PktInventBatchTrans** report built in *Chapter 4, Report Programming Model – RDP*.

How to do it...

This section will discuss grouping controls at the model level, that is, in the Visual Studio editor, followed by grouping controls at the UI builder and contract level.

Grouping in report model

In the Visual Studio report, expand the **Parameters** node. Right-click and go to **Add | Parameter Group**. Specify the **Date Range** label in the caption property. Drag the **FromDate** and **ToDate** controls into the report:

1. Similarly, add another group called **Options** and specify the label.

2. Create another parameter group and drag both the groups inside this new group. Modify the layout direction to **Horizontal**. This will align all the components within the group horizontally (the default mode is vertical).

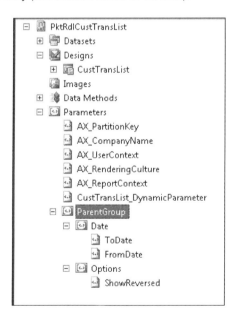

3. Save and deploy the report. The modified report dialog should appear as seen here:

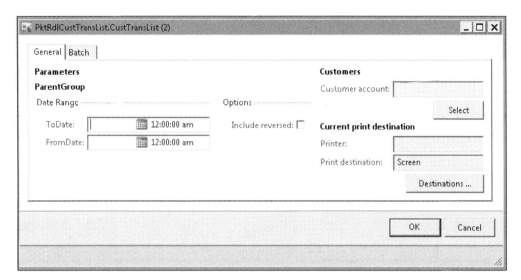

 When creating report parameters that are hidden to the end user, follow the best practice of creating a separate hidden group. This will help easily identify the fields that are part of the report parameters but are not exposed to the user.

Grouping in the UI builder

This grouping mechanism can be applied to both RDP- and query-based reports:

1. The modification here is done completely in the UI builder. Open the UI builder PktRdlCustTransListUIBuilder.

2. Declare a new field in the class declaration for the dialog group as follows:

```
class PktRdlCustTransListUIBuilder extends
  SrsReportDataContractUIBuilder
{
    DialogField dialogFromDate;
    DialogField dialogToDate;
    DialogField dialogReversed;

    DialogGroup dialogDateGroup;

    #define.ShowReversedParam('ShowReversed')
    #define.FromDate('FromDate')
    #define.ToDate('ToDate')
}
```

3. Modify the `addDateFields` method to include a new group. Additionally, we will make this group a checkbox-enabled group. This deactivates the entire group control if the checkbox is deactivated.

 The other important noticeable change here is setting the number of columns to `2`. If this is not set, the groups will get added vertically.

```
private void addDateFields()
{
    dialog                          dialogLocal;
    PktRdlCustTransListRdlContract  transContract;
    SRSReportParameter              reportParameter;
    FormBuildGroupControl           buildGroupControl;

    dialogLocal    = this.dialog();
        buildGroupControl = dialogLocal.curFormGroup();
    buildGroupControl.columns(2);

    transContract  = this.getRdlContractInfo().
dataContractObject()
                          as PktRdlCustTransListRdlContract;

    dialogDateGroup = dialogLocal.addGroup("Date Range");
    dialogDateGroup.frameOptionButton(
      FormFrameOptionButton::Check);
    //enabled by default
    dialogDateGroup.optionValue(1);

    dialogFromDate   = dialogLocal.addFieldValue(
      extendedTypeStr(FromDate),
      DatetimeUtil::date(transContract.getValue(
      #FromDate)), "@SYS5209");
    dialogToDate   = dialogLocal.addFieldValue(
      extendedTypeStr(ToDate),
      DatetimeUtil::date(transContract.getValue(
      #ToDate)), "@SYS14656");
}
```

4. Now, when the report is opened, the report dialog has a new group with a checkbox at the top. The checkbox can be used to enable and disable the controls under this group.

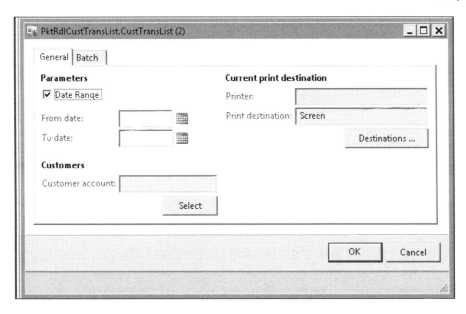

Grouping in contracts

The grouping mechanism described here applies only to RDP-based reports:

1. In the RDP contract of the **PktInventBatchTrans** report, modify the class declaration to add two new groups to the report dialog:

```
[
    DataContractAttribute,
    SysOperationContractProcessingAttribute(
      classStr(PktInventBatchTransUIBuilder),
    SysOperationDataContractProcessingMode::
      CreateUIBuilderForRootContractOnly),
    SysOperationGroupAttribute('BatchGroup', "Batch", '1'),
    SysOperationGroupAttribute('DateGroup', "Date", '2')
]
class PktInventBatchTransContract implements
  SysOperationValidatable
{
    InventDimViewContract       inventDimViewContract;
    InventBatchProdDate         prodDate;
    InventBatchId               batchId;
    boolean                     dummyValue;
}
```

2. Modify the parm methods `BatchId` and `ProdDate` to include the new attributes:

```
[DataMemberAttribute('Batch'),
SysOperationGroupMemberAttribute('BatchGroup'),
SysOperationDisplayOrderAttribute('1')
]
public InventBatchId parmBatchId(InventBatchId
  _batchId = batchId)
{
    batchId = _batchId;

    return batchId;
}


[DataMemberAttribute('ProdDate'),
SysOperationGroupMemberAttribute('DateGroup'),
SysOperationDisplayOrderAttribute('1')
]
public InventBatchProdDate parmProdDate(
  InventBatchProdDate _prodDate = prodDate)
{
    prodDate = _prodDate;

    return prodDate;
}
```

3. Include a new dummy parm attribute to verify the display order:

```
[DataMemberAttribute('Verifydisporder'),
SysOperationGroupMemberAttribute('DateGroup'),
SysOperationDisplayOrderAttribute('2'),
SysOperationLabelAttribute("Dummy Value")
]
public boolean parmDummyValue(boolean _prodDate =
  dummyValue)
{
    dummyValue = _prodDate;

    return dummyValue;
}
```

4. Run the report to see that two new groups, date and batches, are added. The dummy value appears second since its display order attribute was 2.

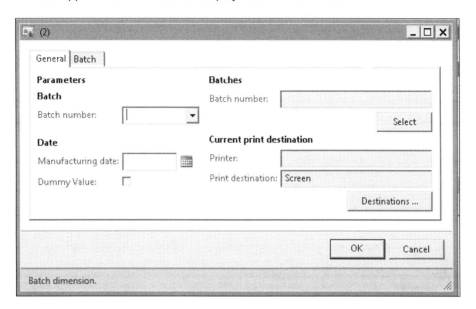

How it works...

In this section, we saw a multitude of short recipes that explain how you can control grouping in reports. The important point to keep in mind is what sort of grouping works for different types of reports. In the case of query-based reports, only the first two models apply, while all three models can be used for RDP.

 In the RDP contract, choose one of the grouping methods—either the RDP contract or use Visual Studio. The Visual Studio grouping overrides the RDP grouping.

RDP with multiple temporary tables

This is another simple recipe that will show you the possibility of using RDP with multiple temporary tables. RDP is a data provider and a single RDP can be used to create different datasets in the report. Walk through this recipe to understand how this can be done.

Getting ready

This recipe requires that you complete the report discussed in the *Surrogate fields in reports* recipe in this chapter.

How to do it...

1. In this recipe, we will use the student table that we used for the *Surrogate fields in reports* recipe. Create two temporary tables: `Student` and `Student Marks`.

2. Create an RDP class that will fill these two tables through the process report method. The difference comes here: generally RDP has a method with the `SRSReportDataSetAttribute` class that is used to return the temporary table. When you have more than one temporary table, create two methods, one for each temporary table, as shown here:

    ```
    [
        SRSReportDataSetAttribute(tableStr(
          PksStudentMasterTmp))
    ]
    public PksStudentMasterTmp getStudentTemp()
    {
        select   studentTmp;
        return   studentTmp;
    }


    [
        SRSReportDataSetAttribute(tableStr(
          PksStudentMarksTmp))
    ]
    public PksStudentMarksTmp getStudentmarksTemp()
    {
        select   studentMarksTmp;
        return   studentMarksTmp;
    }
    ```

3. Open Visual Studio, create a report, and in the new dataset, choose RDP. Click on the **Query** node and select the RDP just created. There will be two datasets that will be returned by the RDP—one for each temporary table. Add the student dataset to the report.

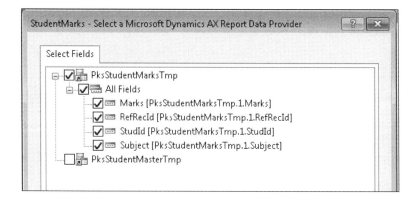

4. Similarly, add another dataset and use the RDP to choose the second temporary table, student marks.

5. The two datasets are not related as in AX and are independent of each other. In this example, we create two multiple data regions, where one lists the students and the other lists their marks.

6. Drag the datasets to create two different data regions, and then run it to see the data being rendered.

How it works...

Standard reports such as **SalesInvoice** and **SalesConfirm** adopt the same approach. In these cases, there is a header table that stores all the header-related information, such as company address, email, and VATnum that is common across all reports, while the other stores the line level information. An RDP class can return any number of temporary tables, not just two.

Multi-value lookup

All the report dialog controls that we have seen so far in this book only store a single value. But there can be cases where you want the users to be able to choose multiple values. This recipe is going to show you how to do it.

Getting ready

This recipe will extend the **PKtInventBatchReport** built in _Chapter 4, Report Programming Model – RDP_.

How to do it...

This recipe will add a multi-value lookup for the batch ID so that the user can select multiple batches to be printed in the report:

1. The first step is to create a parm method in the contract of type list. The parm method should appear as seen here:

```
[
    DataMemberAttribute('MultipleBatch'),
    SysOperationLabelAttribute("Multiple Batch"),
    AifCollectionTypeAttribute('return', Types::String)
]
public List parmMultiBatch(List _multiBatch = multiBatch)
{
    multiBatch = _multiBatch;
    return multiBatch;
}
```

2. Once the parm method is added, the dialog shows a report with a list control, but the lookup has no values in it. To enable and modify the lookup, the UI builder class must be modified. The framework makes it very easy to add lookup for multi-select controls; even the overriding of the event is automatically done. Use the following code to enable multi-batch lookup:

```
class PktInventBatchTransUIBuilder extends
    SysOperationAutomaticUIBuilder
{
    DialogField batchDialog, dateDialog;
    DialogField multiBatchDialog;
}


public void multiBatchLookup()
{
    Query       query;
    QueryBuildData qbds;
    TableId     multiSelectTableNum =
        tableNum(InventBatch);
    container   selectedFields =
        [multiSelectTableNum,
        fieldName2id(multiSelectTableNum,
        fieldStr(InventBatch, InventBatchId))];


    query = new Query();
    qbds = query.addDataSource(tableNum(InventBatch));
```

```
    qbds.addSelectionField(fieldNum(InventBatch,
      InventBatchId));
    qbds.addSelectionField(fieldNum(InventBatch, ItemId));

    SysLookupMultiSelectCtrl::constructWithQuery(
      this.dialog().dialogForm().formRun(),
      multiBatchDialog.control(), query,
      false, selectedFields);
}


public void postRun()
{
    //super();

    this.multiBatchLookup();
}
```

3. We have, so far, added the list control and enabled a multi-lookup. The next step is to use it in the RDP class. To do this, modify the RDP class in the process report method where the list values are enumerated and added to the query range:

```
[
SysEntryPointAttribute(false)
]
public void processReport()
{
    Query                   query;
    QueryRun                queryRun;
    QueryBuildRange         batchRange, dateRange;
    QueryBuildDataSource    qbds;

    InventBatch             inventBatch;
    InventTrans             inventTrans;
    InventDim               inventDim;
    InventTransOrigin       transOrigin;

    InventDimViewContract       viewContract;
    PktInventBatchTransContract batchContract;

    List                    batchList;
    ListEnumerator          listEnumerator;

    batchContract = this.parmDataContract() as
      PktInventBatchTransContract;
```

```
viewContract =
  batchContract.parmInventDimViewContract();

query = this.parmQuery();
qbds = query.dataSourceTable(tableNum(InventBatch));

if (batchContract.parmProdDate())
{
    dateRange = SysQuery::findOrCreateRange(qbds,
      fieldNum(InventBatch, ProdDate));
    dateRange.value(SysQuery::value(
      batchContract.parmProdDate()));
}

batchList = batchContract.parmMultiBatch();
listEnumerator = batchList.getEnumerator();

//copy the range from the list
//to the query
while (listEnumerator.moveNext())
{
    batchRange = qbds.addRange(
      fieldNum(InventBatch, InventBatchId));
    dateRange.value(SysQuery::value(
      listEnumerator.current()));
}

queryRun = new queryRun(query);

while (queryRun.next())
{
    if (queryRun.changed(tablenum(InventBatch)))
    {
        inventBatch =
          queryRun.get(tableNum(InventBatch));
    }

    if (queryRun.changed(tablenum(InventTransOrigin)))
    {
        transOrigin =
          queryRun.get(tableNum(InventTransOrigin));
    }

    inventTrans = queryRun.get(tableNum(InventTrans));
```

```
inventDim     = queryRun.get(tableNum(inventDim));

this.insertTmpTable(inventBatch, transOrigin,
    inventTrans, inventDim);
}
}
```

4. Open the Visual Studio project for the report, expand the dataset, and refresh it by right-clicking and selecting refresh. This will add the new contract parameter to the report. Optionally, set the values to **AllowBlank** and **Nullable**.

5. Run the report and see that the report dialog shows multiple values:

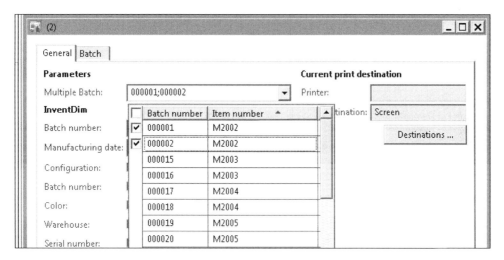

How it works...

Multi-value lookups are easy to build due to the framework support offered in building lookups and maintaining list values. Care must be taken to use the list data returned from multi-select in RDPs appropriately.

Inventory dimensions in reports

An inventory dimension is like a lifeline for trade and logistics, and its presence in reports is indispensable. There is usually a good framework support for the inventory dimension in AX and that continues into the reporting framework. We will explore how to use the standard framework to easily handle inventory dimensions in this recipe. This recipe will also demonstrate nested contracts through this example.

The recipe will add inventory dimensions to the report design and create control parameters that will determine if an inventory dimension is displayed in the report.

Getting ready

This recipe will extend the **PKtInventBatchReport** built in *Chapter 4, Report Programming Model – RDP*.

How to do it...

1. Modify the temporary table of the report to include the dimension field.

2. Open the contract and add a parm method—which will add a Boolean flag for each `inventdim` field—as shown in the following code:

```
[DataMemberAttribute('InventDimViewContract'),
SysOperationControlVisibilityAttribute(false)
]
public InventDimViewContract parmInventDimViewContract(InventDimVi
ewContract _inventDimViewContract = inventDimViewContract)
{
    inventDimViewContract = _inventDimViewContract;

    return inventDimViewContract;
}
```

3. Modify the process report method to fetch the inventory dimension through the **inventrans** and fill the temporary table. The code changes are that simple and they are complete with this step.

4. Open the corresponding Visual Studio report, expand the dataset, and refresh. The new fields will be added to the dataset and the parameters will now show the Boolean dimensions flag for each dimension.

5. Open the precision design and modify the design to include the dimensions from the dataset. The next step is to enable these dimensions based on their corresponding parameters.

6. In the **Row Groups** and **Column Groups** window at the right-hand bottom corner, click on the dropdown and select the **Advanced Mode**. This will make the static control visible in the **Column Groups**.

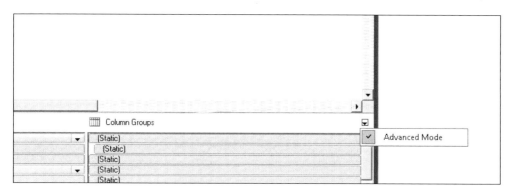

7. Each static control represents one column in the active row. Identify the column count where the inventory dimensions are starting and traverse to the corresponding static control column. The **Properties** window on the left will show the property for each control. Once the static control is selected, choose the **Hidden** property from the properties, open the expression editor, and enter this expression:

```
=Not(Parameters!InventBatchTrans_ViewConfigId.Value)
```

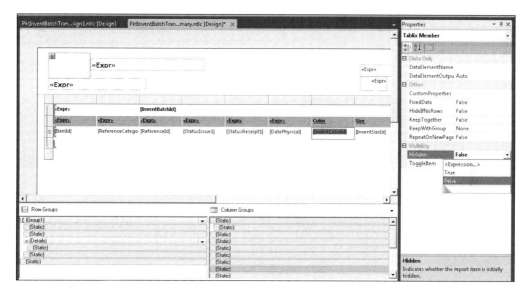

8. Build and deploy the report. The report dialog will show all the inventory dimension parameters, and choosing a specific parameter should print it in the report.

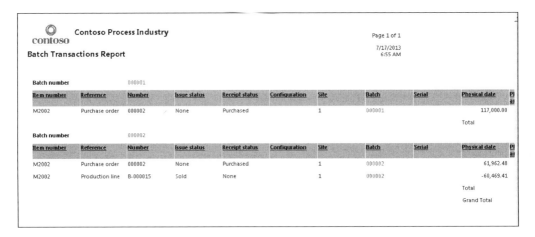

How it works...

A nested data contract is a sort of abstraction where the commonly used parameters can be grouped and used in other contracts. The use of an RDP contract is not much different from other parm methods, except that it returns a class object. The framework automatically creates the parameters in the report design and the dialog by expanding it. The recipe here uses `InventDimViewContract` as a nested contract, thereby avoiding the hassle of rebuilding the entire list of parm methods.

Financial dimensions in query reports

As inventory dimensions influence trade and logistics reports, so do financial dimensions influence financial reports. In this recipe, we will see extensively how financial dimensions can be used in the design of a report, in the report dialog, and more. There are two recipes discussed here: one using financial dimensions in a simple query report and the other in an RDP report.

The following recipe will discuss how to use dimensions in a simple query-based report.

How to do it...

1. Create a new query and add the **LedgerJournalTrans** table to it. Set the **Dynamic field** property to **Yes**.

2. In Visual Studio, create a new project. Create a new report and add a dataset.

3. In the **Query** properties, click the browse button to open the query list. Select the query that was created and check these fields: **journalNum, Txt, LedgerDimension_ String**.

4. Expand the **AXDimensions** node. This shows all the applicable dimensions for this query. Select **CostCenter** and **Department** and click **OK**.

5. Drag the dataset into the auto design node to create the design. Previewing the report shows all the **ledgerjournaltrans** records with the **CostCenter** and **Department** dimensions.

6. To add a filter based on this dimension, create a new parameter under the **Parameters** node of type String. Click on the ellipsis button on the **Values** property. This shows the value window. Here, select the **From Dataset** radio button and set the following field values:

Property	Value
Dataset	LedgerDimension
Value Field	Department
Label Field	Department

7. The previous step will help the user to choose the value that he wants to filter. This filter value must be passed on to the query so that the data is filtered. The easiest way to do this is to create a filter in the table data region.

8. Right-click on the **Filters** node under auto design and click on **Add Filter**. In the new filter, set the following properties:

Property	Value
Expression	=Fields!Department.Value
Name	DepartmentFilter
Operator	Equals
Value	=Parameters!DepartmentParameter.Value

9. The filter region restricts the data that is shown in auto design. So when the report is previewed, it shows only the dimension selected by the user.

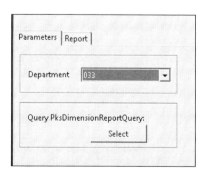

10. Based on the value of the parameter selected by the user, the report is generated.

LedgerDimension					Page 1 of 1
Contoso Retail USA					7/17/2013
LedgerDimension					5:54 PM

Journal batch number	Description	Account	CostCenter	Department
00001		112100--033-5637144576-ANNAPOL-1-000073		033
00007		112100--033-5637144576-ANNAPOL-1-000073		033
00007		112120--033-5637144576-ANNAPOL-1-000073		033
00001		112120--033-5637144576-ANNAPOL-1-000073		033

How it works...

The AX query framework is programmed to automatically bring up the dimensions related to a dimension record. That is the reason why the query shows all the dimensions tables while what was actually added was only `LedgerJournalTrans`.

The lookup set up here works by executing the query and retrieving all the values from the database using the query. This is then exposed in the lookup, and when the user selects the value, it is applied to the auto design filter. It is important to understand that when using filters, the whole query is executed, since filters restrict data only to a specific region.

Financial dimensions in RDP reports

This recipe will extend the simple steps that we learned in the previous recipe to build a more sophisticated report. In this report, the user will be given the option to choose a dimension and a range for it. The report will list all the general journal entries for the selected dimension in the specified range.

How to do it...

1. Since this is an RDP report, start with creating a temporary table, as shown here:

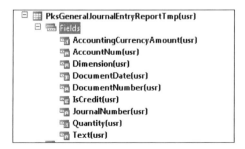

2. Create a new contract with four fields: one for the account, one for the dimension attribute, and the other two for the dimension ranges. Use the following code to create the contract:

```
[
DataContractAttribute,
SysOperationContractProcessingAttribute(
  classStr(PktGeneralJournalReportUIBuilder),
SysOperationDataContractProcessingMode::
  CreateUIBuilderForRootContractOnly)
]
class PktGeneralJournalReportContract
{
    Name             dimensionAttribute;
    MainAccountNum   account;
    DimensionValue   fromDimensionValue;
    DimensionValue   toDimensionValue;
}


[
    DataMemberAttribute('Account'),
    SysOperationLabelAttribute(literalStr("@SYS182387")),
    SysOperationDisplayOrderAttribute('1')
]
public MainAccountNum parmAccount(MainAccountNum _account =
  account)
{
    account = _account;
    return account;
}
[
    DataMemberAttribute('DimensionAttribute'),
    SysOperationLabelAttribute(literalStr("@SYS24410")),
    SysOperationDisplayOrderAttribute('5')
]
public Name parmDimensionAttribute(Name _dimensionAttribute
  = dimensionAttribute)
{
    dimensionAttribute = _dimensionAttribute;
    return dimensionAttribute;
}
[
    DataMemberAttribute('FromDimensionValue'),
    SysOperationLabelAttribute(literalStr("@SYS105870")),
    SysOperationDisplayOrderAttribute('2')
```

```
]
public DimensionValue parmFromDimensionValue(DimensionValue
  _fromDimensionValue = fromDimensionValue)
{
    fromDimensionValue = _fromDimensionValue;
    return fromDimensionValue;
}
[
    DataMemberAttribute('ToDimensionValue'),
    SysOperationLabelAttribute(literalStr("@SYS103530")),
    SysOperationDisplayOrderAttribute('6')
]
public DimensionValue parmToDimensionValue(DimensionValue
  _toDimensionValue = toDimensionValue)
{
    toDimensionValue = _toDimensionValue;
    return toDimensionValue;
}
```

3. The UI builder for the financial dimension plays a crucial role since that is where the dimension and dimension range must be set by the user. The standard comes to our rescue by offering a whole set of logic that can be reused. This ranges from the lookup method to the validate logic. To harness this, the UI builder class must extend the `LedgerAccountReportUIBuilder` class. The UI builder implementation logic is as follows:

```
class PktGeneralJournalReportUIBuilder extends
  LedgerAccountReportUIBuilder
{
    DialogField dialogFieldAccountName;

    Name            dimensionAttribute;

    #define.Columns(2)
    #define.DialogFieldLength(30)
}

public void build()
{
    FormBuildGroupControl    formBuildGroupControl;

    super();

    formBuildGroupControl = this.dialog().curFormGroup();
```

```
            formBUildGroupControl.columns(#Columns);
    }

    public void dimensionAttributeLookup(FormStringControl
       _dimensionAttributeDialogControl)
    {
        super(_dimensionAttributeDialogControl);
    }

    public boolean dimensionAttributeModify(FormStringControl
       _dimensionAttributeDialogControl)
    {
        if (dimensionAttribute != dialogFieldAttribute.value())
        {
            /*If modified "Dimension Attribute" is different
              with previous,set the "From Dimension" and "To
              Dimension" as null*/
            dialogFieldFromDimension.value('');
            dialogFieldToDimension.value('');
            dimensionAttribute = dialogFieldAttribute.value();
        }

        return true;
    }

    public boolean dimensionAttributeValidate(FormStringControl
       _dimensionAttribute)
    {
        boolean ret;

        ret = super(_dimensionAttribute);

        return ret;
    }

    public void dimensionValueLookup(FormStringControl
       _dimensionValueControl)
    {
        super(_dimensionValueControl);
    }
    public boolean dimensionValueValidate(FormStringControl
       _dimensionValue)
    {
        boolean ret;

        ret = super(_dimensionValue);

        return ret;
```

```
}

protected void modifyOverrideMethod()
{
    this.overrideDialogFieldLookup(dialogFieldAttribute,
      methodStr(PktGeneralJournalReportUIBuilder,
      dimensionAttributeLookup));
    this.overrideDialogFieldLookup(
      dialogFieldFromDimension, methodStr(
      PktGeneralJournalReportUIBuilder,
      dimensionValuelookup));
    this.overrideDialogFieldLookup(dialogFieldToDimension,
      methodStr(PktGeneralJournalReportUIBuilder,
      dimensionValuelookup));

    this.overrideDialogFieldMethod(
      dialogFieldAttribute,
      methodStr(FormStringControl, Modified),
      methodStr(PktGeneralJournalReportUIBuilder,
      dimensionAttributeModify));
    this.overrideDialogFieldMethod(
      dialogFieldAttribute,
      methodStr(FormStringControl, Validate),
      methodStr(PktGeneralJournalReportUIBuilder,
      dimensionAttributeValidate));
    this.overrideDialogFieldMethod(
      dialogFieldFromDimension,
      methodStr(FormStringControl, Validate),
      methodStr(PktGeneralJournalReportUIBuilder,
      dimensionValueValidate));
    this.overrideDialogFieldMethod(
      dialogFieldToDimension,
      methodStr(FormStringControl, Validate),
      methodStr(PktGeneralJournalReportUIBuilder,
      dimensionValueValidate));
}

public void postBuild()
{
    SysOperationUIBindInfo binfo = this.bindInfo();
    Object contract = this.dataContractObject();

    dialogFieldAttribute = binfo.getDialogField(
      contract, methodStr(PktGeneralJournalReportContract,
      parmDimensionAttribute));
```

```
    dialogFieldFromDimension = binfo.getDialogField(
      contract, methodStr(PktGeneralJournalReportContract,
      parmFromDimensionValue));
    dialogFieldToDimension  = binfo.getDialogField(
      contract, methodStr(PktGeneralJournalReportContract,
      parmToDimensionValue));
    dialogFieldAccount = binfo.getDialogField(
      contract, methodStr(PktGeneralJournalReportContract,
      parmAccount));

    super();

    dialogFieldAccount.displayLength(#DialogFieldLength);
}
```

4. The next step is to get the RDP class. Create a new RDP class and add the code shown here:

```
[
    SRSReportParameterAttribute(classStr(
      PktGeneralJournalReportContract))
]
class PktGeneralJournalReportDP extends
  SRSReportDataProviderBase
{
    PksGeneralJournalEntryReportTmp reportTmp;
}
[
    SRSReportDataSetAttribute(tableStr(
      PksGeneralJournalEntryReportTmp))
]
public PksGeneralJournalEntryReportTmp getJournalTmp()
{
    select  reportTmp;
    return  reportTmp;
}

private void insertinTmp(
    GeneralJournalAccountEntry            accountEntry,
    GeneralJournalEntry                   journalEntry,
    DimensionAttributeLevelValueView      restrictView,
    DimensionAttributeLevelValueView      accountValue)
{
    ;

    reportTmp.initValue();
```

```
        reportTmp.AccountNum = accountValue.DisplayValue;
        reportTmp.Quantity   = accountEntry.Quantity;
        reportTmp.AccountingCurrencyAmount =
          accountEntry.AccountingCurrencyAmount;
        reportTmp.Text       = accountEntry.Text;
        reportTmp.IsCredit   = accountEntry.IsCredit;
        reportTmp.JournalNumber = journalEntry.JournalNumber;
        reportTmp.DocumentNumber = journalEntry.DocumentNumber;
        reportTmp.DocumentDate = journalEntry.DocumentDate;
        reportTmp.Dimension    = restrictView.DisplayValue;
        reportTmp.insert();
    }


    [
    SysEntryPointAttribute(false)
    ]
    public void processReport()
    {
        GeneralJournalAccountEntry        accountEntry;
        GeneralJournalEntry               journalEntry;
        DimensionAttributeLevelValueView valueView,
          restrictView;
        DimensionAttributeLevelValueView accountValue;

        DimensionAttribute        dimensionAttributeTable;

        PktGeneralJournalReportContract contract;

        Name            dimensionAttribute;
        MainAccountNum  account;
        DimensionValue  fromDimensionValue;
        DimensionValue  toDimensionValue;

        contract = this.parmDataContract();

        dimensionAttribute = contract.parmDimensionAttribute();
        dimensionAttributeTable =
          DimensionAttribute::findByLocalizedName(
          dimensionAttribute, false,
          SystemParameters::find().SystemLanguageId);

        fromDimensionValue = contract.parmFromDimensionValue();
```

```
        toDimensionValue    = contract.parmToDimensionValue();

        account             = contract.parmAccount();

        delete_from reportTmp;

        ttsBegin;

        while select DisplayValue from accountValue
            where   accountValue.DisplayValue == account
            join AccountingCurrencyAmount, Text, quantity from
              accountEntry
            where accountEntry.LedgerDimension ==
              accountValue.ValueCombinationRecId
                join journalNumber, DocumentDate,
                  DocumentNumber from journalEntry
                where journalEntry.RecId ==
                  accountEntry.GeneralJournalEntry
                join restrictView
                where restrictView.ValueCombinationRecId ==
                  accountEntry.LedgerDimension
                &&   restrictView.DimensionAttribute ==
                  dimensionAttributeTable.RecId
                &&   restrictView.DisplayValue  >=
                  fromDimensionValue
                &&   restrictView.DisplayValue  <=
                  toDimensionValue
        {
            this.insertinTmp(accountEntry, journalEntry,
              restrictView, accountValue);
        }

        ttsCommit;

    }
```

5. The process report method is so designed to find all general journal entries for a specific account number in a specified range. A DML is used to retrieve this data.

6. Once the coding changes are complete, create a new report in Visual Studio and link the RDP report that was just created.

7. Create a precision design with a table control as shown in the following image. Choose the fields. For the dimension attribute field in the precision design, enter the following expression:

```
=Parameters!JournalData_DimensionAttribute.Value
```

This will ensure that the label printed is based on the selected dimension. The following image indicates how the report design would look:

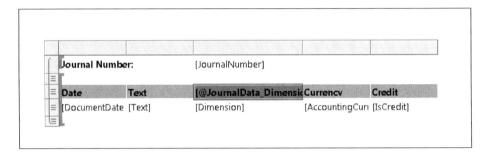

8. Compile and deploy the report. Create a menu item for the report and run the report to see that the report prints only the specified range in the selected dimension.

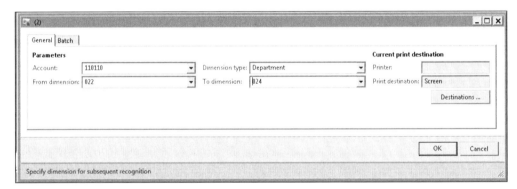

9. Select the parameter on which the report will be printed.

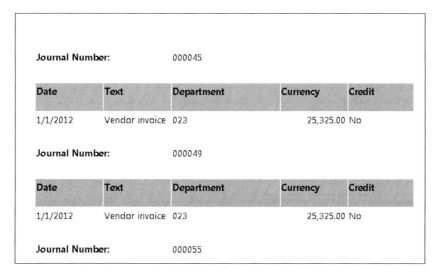

Journal Number:		000045		
Date	**Text**	**Department**	**Currency**	**Credit**
1/1/2012	Vendor invoice	023	25,325.00	No

Journal Number:		000049		
Date	**Text**	**Department**	**Currency**	**Credit**
1/1/2012	Vendor invoice	023	25,325.00	No

| Journal Number: | | 000055 | | |

How it works...

AX makes it really easy to add financial dimensions by standard support for frequently used dimension methods. In this report, the lookup for the dimension attribute and the ranges are derived from the base class.

8
Troubleshooting and Other Advanced Recipes

This chapter will cover the following recipes:

- ▶ Assessing report performance and usage
- ▶ Handling long running reports in AX
- ▶ Troubleshooting reports in AX
- ▶ Auto e-mail, save as file tasks in reports
- ▶ Handling events after report completion
- ▶ Generating and displaying barcodes in reports
- ▶ Hiding controls by context
- ▶ Using AXEnumProvider as the dataset for parameters in reports
- ▶ Adding a new report design to print management
- ▶ Deploying language-specific reports to speed up execution time
- ▶ Improving the functionality of reports

Introduction

The last few chapters should have helped you gain a good command over new SSRS reports in Dynamics AX 2012 R3. This chapter will help handle problems that you might face while executing SSRS reports. It also introduces a few handy recipes that are required time and again in report customization, such as generating barcodes, hiding controls, e-mailing, and so on. This chapter has very useful insights that can aid you in getting the right fundamentals for effective report development.

Assessing report performance and usage

SSRS introduces some interesting capabilities as we have been seeing through the previous chapters. Here is another interesting aspect to add to the list: SSRS report logs. SSRS reports log key usage parameters into the system automatically. The free Report Log Viewer tool can unravel a lot of useful production data that helps to understand which reports are being used, what is consuming a lot of time, and which reports fail. This recipe will throw some light on how to configure and use the log viewer for this purpose.

Getting ready

Download the SSRS report log viewer from `http://www.microsoft.com/en-us/download/details.aspx?id=24774` and install it.

This tool will demonstrate the best way to analyze the Report Server Service Trace Log and Report Server Execution Log, which are useful if you are debugging an application or investigating an issue or event.

How to do it...

1. The Report Log Viewer is installed by default in the following location:

   ```
   Program Files (x86)\Microsoft\Reporting Services LogViewer\
   RSLogViewer.exe.
   ```

   Open the log viewer, select the **Catalog** tab, and click on the **Connect** button.

2. In the prompt dialog, enter the details of the report server, as shown in the following screenshot:

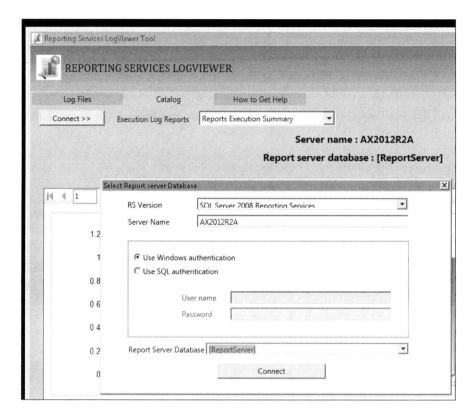

3. In the **Execution Log Reports** field, select **Reports Execution Summary**. This gives a detailed insight into the report's overall performance. Click on **Show Filters** and apply a date range from the different kinds of ranges available.

This report reveals the time for data retrieval, report processing, and report rendering for reports in the selected filter criteria.

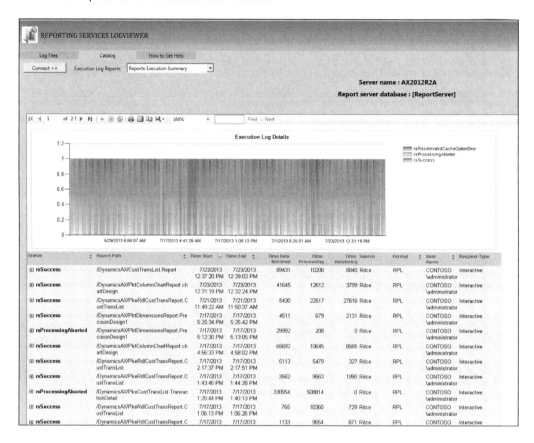

4. The catalog view offers other reports, such as **Reports by User** and **Reports by Month**, as seen in the following screenshot. These offer more beneficial parameters that help in fine tuning the report performance and usage.

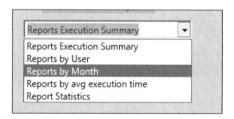

5. Here is another sample report that lists the report usage by month:

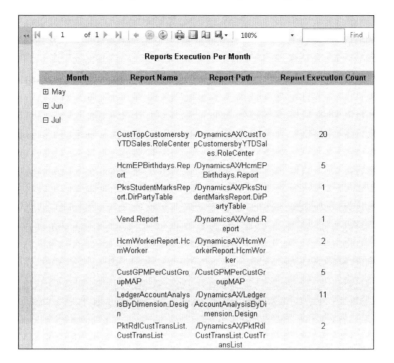

How it works...

The Report Log Viewer connects to the report server database and offers a presentable view of the data from the SQL tables. It also has the capability to analyze the logs that are generated. This is discussed in the *Expression-related issues* section under the *Troubleshooting reports in AX* recipe in this chapter. This is a non-intrusive analysis, so it could be performed even on the production reporting servers without bringing them down.

Some sections in your report may not have data, but the custom header sections might print. In these cases, to make it informative for the user, a "No data available" message might be helpful since the user is then assured that there is no data for that particular data section. Select the `Tablix/List/Matrix` control where you want the message to be available and open the properties window. Find the `NoRowsMessage` property. This property can be filled in with text or with dynamic text using expressions. Type in something like "No data available".

Handling long-running reports in AX

Reports are used to render data from a couple of pages to a larger volume of copies. There can be many cases when a report may not render the data in an acceptable format, which can be identified using tools such as the Report Log Viewer. This recipe will list out the various approaches that can be used to manage performance-related issues in reports.

How to do it...

This section will discuss approaches to resolve long-running reports by adopting best practices at the time of design and at runtime through configuration changes.

Design-based resolution

The following actions can be taken to see if they improve the report performance. The modifications enlisted here are changes to the components involved in a report, and so must not be implemented in a production environment before taking the report through a testing cycle:

1. **Reindex**: If the report uses a query directly or uses one in RDP, see if the indexes have been properly used in the tables.

2. **Restrict the data**: If no index-related issues are found, then see if the following design level changes can be made:

   ❏ Improve the performance by showing only a limited set of data; for example, the first 1000 records.

   ❏ Improve the performance by limiting the data. To do this, add a range to the dialog so that the user can narrow down the data.

3. **Inefficient report parameters**: If the issue is caused by the user not utilizing the ranges and running the report for a broad set of parameters, then consider implementing this change.

   In the controller method for the report, override the `preRunValidate` method and write a code that will warn the user based on the number of records the query might return. When the user executes this report, and if it returns a large number of records, it will throw an error advising the user to use a better range. Use the following code for this purpose:

```
protected container preRunValidate()
{
    /* More than 100,000 rows will take at least 12
       minutes on a warm box with low volume and not
       under load while 1,000 records will take about
       10 seconds, so these are used as the warning
```

```
    and error limits.*/
#Define.ErrorLimit(100000)
#Define.WarningLimit(1000)

/* Using the query from the contract, count up
   to the error limit + 1 since anything over the
   error limit will return the same error*/
container    validateResult;
Query        query = this.getFirstQuery();
int          rowCount =
  queryRun::getQueryRowCount(query, #ErrorLimit + 1);

if (rowCount > #ErrorLimit)
{
    validateResult = [SrsReportPreRunState::Error];
}
else if (rowCount > #WarningLimit)
{
    validateResult = [SrsReportPreRunState::Warning];
}
else
{
    validateResult = super();
}

return validateResult;
}
```

4. **Implement pre-process**: If during design or at a later point you identify that the delay in the report data is caused because of the data insertion into the temporary table in the `processReport` method, then enable pre-processing.

    SSRS uses the **Windows Communication Foundation** (**WCF**) to connect to the **Application Object Server** (**AOS**) for data access. This connection has a threshold limit and it might fail if a report takes a long time to execute. The report server execution waits for the RDP to process the data and return. In the event where the RDP takes a longer time to execute, the reporting service might fail. Pre-process is a strategy to beat through this issue. To understand how to enable pre-process for reports, read the *Pre-processing reports* recipe from *Chapter 4, Report Programming Model – RDP*.

Configuration-based resolution

Report execution time must be always kept at minimum by applying the design time principles and best practices discussed in the preceding section. The following configuration-based methods must be adopted to make sure that the overall reporting experience is smooth.

Data extension-based timeout

This timeout happens when there is a delay for the Reporting Services to fetch data from Dynamics AX. It is to be understood that the AX-specific data extension uses the WCF-based query service to access the data. So, any data-related timeout has to be configured by fine tuning the WCF time out. WCF has two ends: the client and the server; the timeout has to be adjusted at both ends.

Server-side WCF timeout

Following are the steps to adjust the server-side WCF timeout:

1. Locate the `AX32Serv.exe.config` file located in `\Program Files\Microsoft Dynamics AX\ <version>\Server\Microsoft DynamicsAX\Bin`.

2. Open the file for editing (notepad/Visual Studio) and identify the `QueryServiceBinding` element as shown in the following screenshot:

3. Increase the `sendTimeout` property. The default value is set to `10`, which can be changed to a longer time as needed. The range must be decided based on your longest running report.

4. Save the changes.

Client-side WCF timeout

Following are the steps to adjust the client-side WCF timeout:

1. Open the **Run** window and type `AXclicfg` to open the client configuration.

2. Create a new client configuration and give it a name.

3. In the **Connection** tab, click on the **Configure Services** button. A message is displayed as seen in the following screenshot; click **OK** to continue.

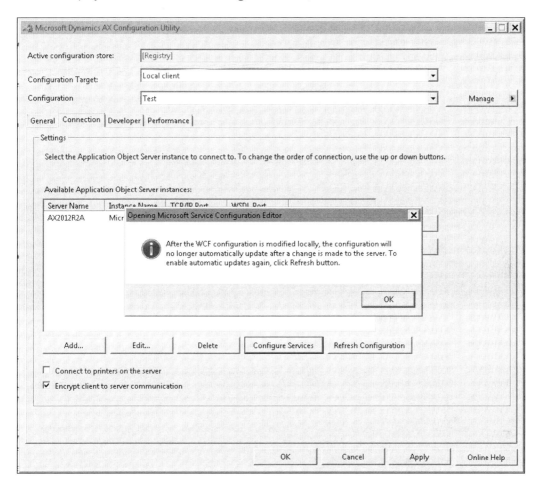

4. In the **Configuration** window that opens up, select the **Bindings** node from the tree node and identify the sibling **QueryServiceEndPoint(netTcpBinding)**.

5. In the adjacent **Binding** tab, locate the **SendTimeOut** property and increase it from the default value of **10** to the desired amount.

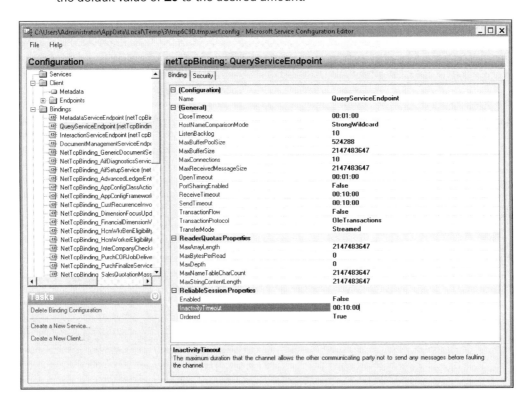

6. Similarly, in the **MaxReceivedMessageSize** property, increase the message size from the default value to the desired value. The maximum value is the int64 limit, since this is an int64 field.

7. Click on **Apply** followed by **OK**.

Report execution timeout

This setting decides how long the report attempts to keep the execution going before it stops the execution through a timeout. The time specified here ideally must be the time taken by the longest report in the application. This can be defined for all reports or a specific report.

Specifying timeouts for all reports

Following are the steps to specify timeouts for all reports:

1. Open the Report Manager with the URL; for example, `http://[SSSRSServerName]:80/Reports`.

2. Click on **Site Settings** to open the property page.

3. In the properties page under **Report Timeout**, specify the number of seconds.

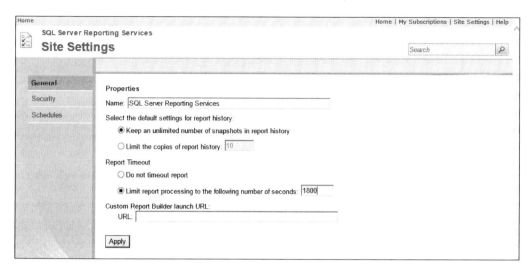

4. Click on **Apply** to save the changes.

Specifying timeouts for a specific report

To specify the timeout for a specific report, select the report and click on the dropdown arrow, and then click on **Manage**. In the Properties page, set the **Report Timeout** that will apply to that specific report.

User session timeout

Though this has nothing to do with performance, it governs the total time a user is allowed to have their session open, untouched. This value must be greater than the report processing timeout:

1. Create a file called `timeout.rss` with the following script and save it to the drive:

```
Public Sub Main()
    Dim props() as [Property]
    props = new [Property] () { new [Property](),
      new [Property]() }

    props(0).Name = "SessionTimeout"
    props(0).Value = timeout

    props(1).Name = "SessionAccessTimeout"
    props(1).Value = timeout

    rs.SetSystemProperties(props)
End Sub
```

2. In the command prompt, run the `rs.exe` command—which can be found in `\` `Program Files\Microsoft SQL Server\110\Tools\Bin`—in the format shown here:

```
$>rs.exe -i C:\timeout.rss -s
  http://[SSSRSServerName]:80/Reports -v timeout="72000" -l 0
```

3. This will set the timeout to 20 hours for both session timeout and session access timeout.

Troubleshooting reports in AX

This recipe will discuss the possible issues that arise during the development of a report, and the approaches that can be taken to identify the cause and resolve these issues. The issues mostly seen in SSRS fall into three broad categories:

▶ Deployment-related

▶ Data-related

▶ Rendering-related

While deployment and rendering are mostly on the SSRS end, data-related issues concern X++ or the programming elements. The recipe will discuss the issues by placing them in these broader categories.

How to do it...

This section is classified into three broad categories: deployment-, data-, and rendering-related issues.

Deployment-related issues

These are issues concerning deploying reports from AX or Visual Studio and getting them updated in AX.

Unable to deploy

1. **Verify SSRS configuration**: The first thing to ensure when you face a deployment issue is the configuration. Ensure that the configuration specified in **System Administration | Setup | Business Intelligence | Reporting Services | Reporting Servers** is accessible and valid. Try opening the SSRS Reporting Services Manager through the browser.

2. **Rebuild Visual Studio project**: Open the Visual Studio project along with the reference assemblies, if any, and rebuild the project.

3. **File lock errors**: On receiving file lock errors, restart the report server.

Unable to refresh

1. **Restore report**: Open the SSRS report node and navigate to your report. Right-click and select **Restore**.

2. **Refresh cache**: Since caching is enabled, there might be cache-related issues. Go to **Tools** | **Caches** and click on **Refresh Elements**.

3. **Redeploy**: Delete the report from the Reporting Services Manager and redeploy the report.

4. **Restart client / reporting server / AOS**: RDL is not parsed every time and is cached in AX. So restart the client / reporting server / AOS to clear the cache and reload the report.

5. **Default values**: For changes in the default values, update the parameters in the report manager. The **Parameters** window can be opened from the dropdown menu under each report and by choosing **Manage** thereafter.

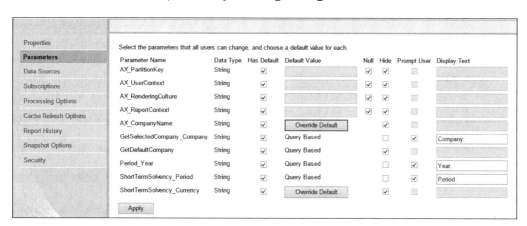

Rendering-related issues

This section will further discuss how issues that arise at the time of report rendering can be handled:

1. **Parameter issues**: If you have issues with the parameters and are unable to identify what parameters are passed to the report, then try to render the parameters in the report design so that they are visible. Navigate to the auto design node and set the **Render Parameters** property to **True**. This will display the parameters in the auto design node window. In the case of precision design, parameters have to be added to the report area manually, as there is no option as in auto design.

> Make sure the **Allow Blank** property is set to **True** for optional parameters, as this can cause a missing report parameters error when running reports from AX.

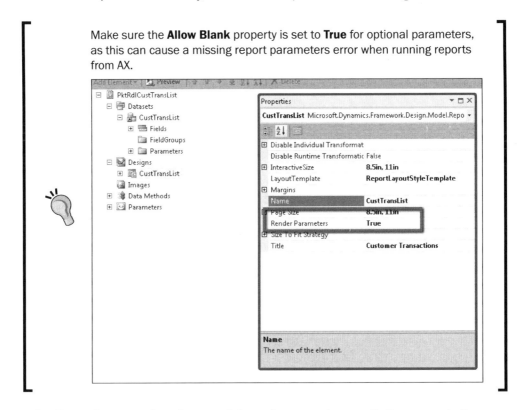

2. **Dynamic parameters**: In case of dynamic parameters, verify the ranges in the query node and whether there is any initialization done in the controller, since ranges for dynamic parameters come from the **Ranges** node under query.

3. **Issues with label/grouping**: Grouping can be implemented at various levels in a report, and it varies based on the report. Make sure to visit the places listed below to identify and resolve issues related to grouping:

    ❑   For a query-based report, visit the `VS Project/UI builder`.

    ❑   For an RDP-based report, visit the `Contract/VS Project/UI builder`.

4. **Initialization and validation issues**: Check the contract / controller classes for issues related to initialization and validation.

5. **Formatting issues**: Use color coding to understand the spacing between controls. This will give you knowledge of the control that is taking up space, based on which you can modify the parameters to fine tune the spacing. Once you are done, you can remove the color coding.

6. **Localization issues**: Use the Visual Studio preview to quickly switch between languages and verify the report rendering in different languages.

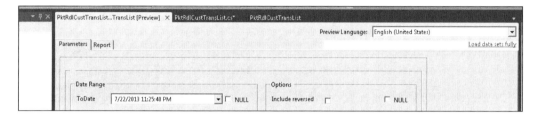

7. **Enum translation issues**: Each Enum field in a query or contract, when added to the dataset, results in two different fields. One holds the label and the other holds the system name. Always use the `Enum.Label` field in report rendering. In the following screenshot, you can see two fields being rendered for the `TransType` field. The name type can be used in programming references and the label type for rendering purposes.

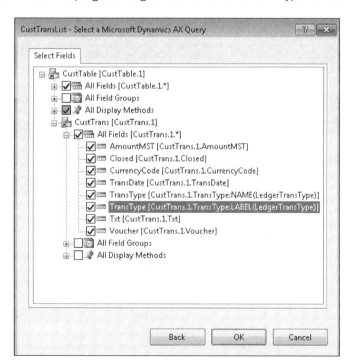

8. **Control visibility issues**: Expressions are mostly used to handle the visibility of controls. Whenever an issue arises, verify the expression attached to the visible property of the control.

9. **Group header issues**: Use the advanced mode to fine tune headers. Refer to the *Inventory dimensions in reports* recipe in *Chapter 7, Upgrading and Analyzing Reports*, to understand how to use Advanced mode.

10. **Expression-related issues**: Try to translate the expression into a data method and do a unit testing. Refer to unit testing business logic in the *Debugging business logic* recipe from *Chapter 3, Report Programming Model*, to identify how to test data methods. Break down the expression into simple pieces in the data method, rather than having one long expression to analyze.

11. **Enable verbose logging**: To enable the log, open the `ReportingServices\ReportServer\bin` folder in the reporting server and identify the `ReportingServicesService.exe.config` file. Open the file and set the value to `4` for the properties `DefaultTraceSwitch` and `Components`. This enables the log to switch to a verbose mode, which creates more detailed logs of the actions in the report server. The log files can be found typically in `%ProgramFiles%\Microsoft SQL Server\MSSQL.x\Reporting Services\LogFiles`.

 Remember to switch the values to `3` after debugging, as this adds load to the report execution.

```
ReportingServicesService.exe.config  ×  PktRdlCustTransList...TransList [Preview]     PktRdlC
    <configuration>
        <configSections>
            <section name="RStrace" type="Microsoft.ReportingServices.Diagno
        </configSections>
        <system.diagnostics>
            <switches>
                <add name="DefaultTraceSwitch" value="4" />
            </switches>
        </system.diagnostics>
        <RStrace>
            <add name="FileName" value="ReportServerService_" />
            <add name="FileSizeLimitMb" value="32" />
            <add name="KeepFilesForDays" value="14" />
            <add name="Prefix" value="appdomain, tid, time" />
            <add name="TraceListeners" value="file" />
            <add name="TraceFileMode" value="unique" />
            <add name="Components" value="all:4" />
        </RStrace>
        <runtime>
            <alwaysFlowImpersonationPolicy enabled="true"/>
            <assemblyBinding xmlns="urn:schemas-microsoft-com:asm.v1">
                <dependentAssembly>
```

12. **Use the Log viewer to read the log**: Though the log file can be opened and read using notepad, it is cumbersome to read in this raw format. Use the Log File Viewer discussed in the *Assessing report performance and usage* recipe in this chapter. Open the Report Log Viewer, and in the **Log Files** tab, navigate to the folder where the log files are located; for example `Microsoft SQL Server\MSRS11.MSSQLSERVER\Reporting Services\LogFiles`. Choose **Current week** in the **Date Range** and **Raw** in the **View Details** text boxes, respectively. This will present the log in a way that is easier to analyze.

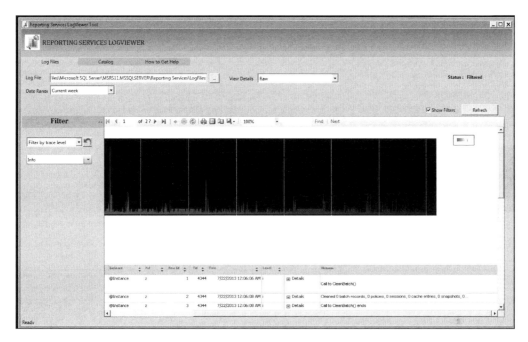

Data-related issues

The first step in a data-related issue is to identify the source of the data. Based on the report data source, you can then decide how best to handle the issue.

Query-based report

To handle issues related to data not showing in a query-based report, use the following approaches:

1. Verify if the user running the report has access to the data in the company.

2. Verify if the query returns data:

    ❏ Write a job to verify the query

    ❏ Add the query to a form and see that the data is returned

    ❏ Use the query service through services like InfoPath to ensure it returns data

3. Queries are cached. Delete data from the **SRSReportQuery** and **SRSReportParameters** tables to clear the cache.

4. If any changes are made to the query/contract, then open the Visual Studio project and refresh the dataset and re-deploy.

5. Ensure that the correct query is used by accessing the query in the controller. You can place the following code in the `preRunModifyContract` method to get the query displayed in the infolog:

```
info(this.getFirstQuery().toString());
```

RDP-based report

To handle issues related to data not showing in an RDP-based report, use the following approaches:

1. Debug by adding the keyword `breakpoint` in the `processreport` method and ensure the flow is smooth.

2. If the RDP uses a query or DML, ensure that it returns the data by running it in a job.

3. Try to invoke the RDP through a job by converting the Temptable instance to a persistent table. Refer to the *Testing the RDP report* recipe in *Chapter 4, Report Programming Model – RDP*.

Controller issues

For runtime design selection issues, look into the controller. Use the `prePromptModifyContract` and `preRunModifyContract` methods in the controller classes for debugging. This is a good entry point.

Auto e-mail, save as file tasks in reports

There are some reports that demand no user interaction and are expected to be directly saved in a file or e-mailed. This recipe will share how the printer settings contract can be used to achieve this in a simple manner.

How to do it...

This recipe has been divided into two sections. The first section details how to save the report to a file, and the second section details how to send it through e-mail.

Saving the report to a file

1. To save a file onto the printer, create a new static method in the controller class or in the class from where the report is invoked.

2. In the method, place the following code to save the report:

```
public static void saveReporttoFile(Args _args)
{
/*if the controller is not overriden for your report
  then use appropriate controller*/
    SrsReportRunController controller = new
      PktRdlCustTransListController();
    SRSPrintDestinationSettings printSettings;

    controller.parmReportName(ssrsReportStr(
      PktRdlCustTransList, CustTransList));

    // get print settings from contract
    printSettings =
      controller.parmReportContract().parmPrintSettings();

    // set print medium
    printSettings.printMediumType(SRSPrintMediumType::File);
    printSettings.fileFormat(SRSReportFileFormat::PDF);
    printSettings.overwriteFile(true);
    printSettings.fileName(@"C:\Temp\CusttransReport.pdf");

    // suppress the parameter dialog
    controller.parmShowDialog(false);

    controller.startOperation();
}
```

Here, the file location is hard coded but you may want to turn it into a parameter or refer a table location.

Sending the report through e-mail

To send the file to an e-mail, the procedure is not much different, except for the need to pass an e-mail contract.

```
public static void mailReport(Args _args)
{
    SrsReportRunController controller = new
      PktRdlCustTransListController();
    SRSPrintDestinationSettings printSettings;
    SrsReportEMailDataContract emailContract;

    // set report name
```

```
        controller.parmReportName(ssrsReportStr(
          PktRdlCustTransList, CustTransList));

        // create email contract
        emailContract = new SrsReportEMailDataContract();

        // fill in the email contract details
        emailContract.parmAttachmentFileFormat(
          SRSReportFileFormat::PDF);
        emailContract.parmSubject("Customer Transaactions");
        emailContract.parmTo("admin@contoso.com");

        printSettings =
          controller.parmReportContract().parmPrintSettings();

        printSettings.printMediumType(
          SRSPrintMediumType::Email);
        printSettings.parmEMailContract(emailContract);
        printSettings.fileFormat(SRSReportFileFormat::PDF);

        // suppress the parameter dialog
        controller.parmShowDialog(false);

        controller.startOperation();
    }
```

How it works...

The print setting is a contract similar to the RDL and RDP contract. The print setting can also be modified inside the controller if it requires manipulation. This must be performed in the preRunModifyContract method in the controller. If the report is required to be opened through code, then all that is needed is to invoke the code given in this recipe. Keeping the printer setting related changes is optional.

Handling events after report completion

To handle events after report completion, the reporting framework in AX gives the ability to hook custom events that will be called after a report is complete. This event can be used to find when the report execution is complete and take the corresponding actions. The recipe here discusses a sample implementation.

How to do it...

1. In this example, let's say that we update the **Printed** field in the table with status **Yes** after the report is printed. The reporting framework has the `renderingCompleted` delegate, which is invoked once a report is complete. So, the first step is to create a method that can be linked to this delegate.

2. The method's signature must match the delegate, while the rest such as the name, instance method, or static method doesn't matter.

```
public static void renderingComplete(SrsReportRunController _
sender, SrsRenderingCompletedEventArgs _eventArgs)
{
    Query               query;
    QueryRun            queryRun;

    InventBatchId       batchNum;
    PktBatchPrintStatus batchStatus;

    SRSReportExecutionInfo executionInfo;

    executionInfo = _eventArgs.parmReportExecutionInfo();

    if(executionInfo && executionInfo.parmIsSuccessful())
    {
        // Get the report's query
        query = _sender.getFirstQuery();

        // Mark all the records as printed
        queryRun = new QueryRun(query);

        ttsbegin;
        while(queryRun.next())
        {
            batchNum =
              queryRun.get(tableNum(InventBatch)).(
              fieldNum(InventBatch, inventBatchId));
            update_recordset batchStatus
                setting Printed        = NoYes::Yes,
                        PrintDateTime =
                        executionInfo.
                        parmExecutionDateTime();
```

```
                        where batchStatus.inventBatchId ==
                            batchNum;
            }
            ttscommit;
        }
    }
```

3. The next step is to hook the event to the delegate. This can be done anywhere before the `preRunModifyContract` event, but the standard recommendation is to write it inside the `preRunModifyContract` method as shown in the following code:

    ```
    protected void preRunModifyContract()
    {
        this.renderingCompleted += eventhandler(PktInventBatchTransCon
    troller::renderingComplete);
    }
    ```

4. When the report execution is complete, the method will be invoked and the records fetched through the query will be updated.

How it works...

Since SSRS report execution is asynchronous, as it connects to the AOS via the WCF service, the rendering complete will be the best approach to hook events after the report is complete. Though the method attached to the delegate here is a static method, instance methods can also be used. The arguments controller gives complete access to the report that is executed. The `SRSRenderingCompletedEventArgs` has access to the `SRSReportExecutionInfo` object. The execution info carries information pertaining to the report that was just executed, such as the number of pages, whether the print was successful, layout, execution time, and much more.

Make sure the event is hooked in `preRunModifyContract` to ensure it gets called during both the batch and interactive modes.

There can be cases where you want a contract in the attribute but do not want the UI builder to expose it to the user. The reporting framework in AX provides a very easy way to incorporate this. Open the `parm` method in the contract that you don't want to expose. Add the following attribute along with other attributes:

`SysOperationControlVisibilityAttribute(False)`

This attribute, when found in the `parm` method, will automatically prevent the UI builder from adding this to the dialog.

Generating and displaying barcodes in reports

Shop floor and warehouse reports require barcodes to be printed to handle goods. Many other reports also demand barcode strings to be printed in the report. This recipe is focused on building barcodes in SSRS. Here, we will attempt to print the barcode of the inventory batch table.

How to do it...

1. Create a simple query. Add the `InventBatch` table as the data source. Keep the fields selective only with `InventBatch` and `ItemId`.

2. This will be an RDP-based report, so create a temporary table with the fields shown in the screenshot. The fields Barcode and `BarcodeHR` will store encoded values and so must extend the EDT **BarcodeString**.

3. Create a contract class where the barcode setup field in the contract is used to choose the format of the barcode, such as `Code39/EAN` and so on:

```
[
    DataContractAttribute,
    SysOperationGroupAttribute('BatchGroup', "Batch", '1')
]
class PktInventBatchBarCodeContract
{
    InventBatchId           batchId;
```

```
        BarcodeSetupId              barcodeSetupId;
        FontSize                    batchFontSize;
        FontName                    barcodeFontName;
}


[DataMemberAttribute('Batch'),
SysOperationGroupMemberAttribute('BatchGroup'),
SysOperationDisplayOrderAttribute('1')]
public InventBatchId parmBatchId(
  InventBatchId _batchId = batchId)
{
    batchId = _batchId;
    return batchId;
}
[
    DataMemberAttribute('BarcodeSetupId'),
    SysOperationGroupMemberAttribute('BatchGroup'),
    SysOperationHelpTextAttribute(literalStr("@SYS102646")),
    SysOperationDisplayOrderAttribute('2')
]
public BarcodeSetupId parmBarcodeSetupId(BarcodeSetupId
  _barcodeSetupId = barcodeSetupId)
{
    barcodeSetupId  =   _barcodeSetupId;

    return barcodeSetupId;
}


[
    DataMemberAttribute('BarcodeFontName'),
    SysOperationGroupMemberAttribute('BatchGroup'),
    SysOperationDisplayOrderAttribute('3')
]
public FontName parmBarcodeFontName(FontName
  _barcodeFontName = barcodeFontName)
{
    barcodeFontName    =   _barcodeFontName;

    return barcodeFontName;
}
```

4. Create an RDP class—which will apply the selected barcode setup chosen by the user in the report dialog to encode the batch number to the barcode—using the code here:

```
[
    //bind query - shows in the report dialog
    SRSReportQueryAttribute(queryStr(
      PktinventBatchBarCode)),
    //bind the contract
    SRSReportParameterAttribute(classStr(
      PktInventBatchBarCodeContract))
]
class PktInventBatchBarCodeDp Extends
  SRSReportDataProviderBase
{
    BarcodeSetupId  barcodeSetupId;
    FontName        barcodeFontName;
    FontSize        barcodeFontSize;

    PktInventBarCodeTmp  barCodeTmp;
}


[SysEntryPointAttribute(false)]
public void processReport()
{
    QueryRun                       queryRun;
    PktInventBatchBarCodeContract  contract;
    BarcodeSetup                   barcodeSetup;
    Barcode                        barcode;
    QueryBuildRange                batchRange;



    contract = this.parmDataContract() as
      PktInventBatchBarCodeContract;

    barcodeSetup    =
      BarcodeSetup::find(contract.parmBarcodeSetupId());
    barcode         = barcodeSetup.barcode();



    batchRange  = this.parmQuery().dataSourceTable(
      tableNum(InventBatch)).addRange(fieldNum(
      InventBatch,InventBatchId));
```

```
        batchRange.value(contract.parmBatchId());

        queryRun = new QueryRun(this.parmQuery());

        while (queryRun.next())
        {
            this.insertBarCodeTmpTable(queryRun.get(tableNum(
              InventBatch)) as InventBatch,
              barcodeSetup, barcode);
        }
    }

    protected void insertBarCodeTmpTable(
            InventBatch        _inventBatch
          , BarcodeSetup       _barcodeSetup,
            Barcode            _barcode)
    {
        int                    currentInfologLine;
        SysInfologEnumerator   infoEnumerator;

        // encode barcodes
        barCodeTmp.clear();

        if(_barcodeSetup)
        {
            currentInfologLine = infologLine();

            if (_barcodeSetup.validateBarcode(_inventBatch.
inventBatchId))
            {
                _barcode.string(true,
                _inventBatch.inventBatchId);

                if (_barcodeSetup.FontName)
                {
                    barCodeTmp.Barcode = _barcode.barcodeStr();
                }

                barCodeTmp.BarcodeHR = _barcode.barcodeStrHR();
                barCodeTmp.InventBatchId =
                  _inventBatch.inventBatchId;
                barCodeTmp.insert();
            }
            else
```

```
        {
            infoEnumerator =
              SysInfologEnumerator::newData(infolog.copy(
              currentInfologLine + 1, infologLine()));
            return;
        }
    }
}

[SRSReportDataSetAttribute(tableStr(PktInventBarCodeTmp))]
public PktInventBarCodeTmp getBarCodeTmp()
{
    select  barCodeTmp;
    return  barCodeTmp;
}
```

5. Create a controller class as shown in the following code. The controller class will find the barcode setup and set the `FontName` and `FontSize` accordingly. This makes it possible to dynamically change the barcode type at runtime.

```
public class PktInventBatchBarCodeController extends
SrsReportRunController
{
}

public static void main(Args _args)
{
    PktInventBatchBarCodeController  controller =
      new PktInventBatchBarCodeController();

    controller.parmReportName(ssrsReportStr(
      PktInventBatchBarCode, InventBatchBarCode));
    controller.parmArgs(_args);
    controller.startOperation();
}

public void preRunModifyContract()
{
    BarcodeSetup                          barcodeSetup;
    PktInventBatchBarCodeContract    contract =
      this.parmReportContract().parmRdpContract() as
        PktInventBatchBarCodeContract;

    barcodeSetup =
      BarcodeSetup::find(contract.parmBarcodeSetupId());

    if (barcodeSetup)
    {
```

```
            contract.parmBarcodeFontName(
              barcodeSetup.FontName);
            contract.parmBatchFontSize(barcodeSetup.FontSize);
        }
        else
        {
            contract.parmBarcodeFontName('');
            contract.parmBatchFontSize(0);
        }
    }

    public void prePromptModifyContract()
    {
        BarcodeSetup                    barcodeSetup;
        PktInventBatchBarCodeContract    contract;
        Query                           query;
        InventBatch                     inventBatch;
        QueryBuildDataSource            queryBuildDataSource;
        QueryBuildRange                 qbrInventBatchId;

        contract = this.parmReportContract().parmRdpContract()
          as PktInventBatchBarCodeContract;

        if (!contract.parmBarcodeSetupId())
        {
            select firstonly barcodeSetup
                where barcodeSetup.BarcodeType ==
                  BarcodeType::Code39;

            if (barcodeSetup)
            {
                contract.parmBarcodeSetupId(
                  barcodeSetup.BarcodeSetupId);
            }
        }

        query                   = this.getFirstQuery();
        queryBuildDataSource    =
          SysQuery::findOrCreateDataSource(query,
          tableNum(inventBatch));

        if (this.parmArgs()
```

```
        && this.parmArgs().record() is InventBatch
        && this.parmArgs().record().isFormDataSource())
    {
        inventBatch = this.parmArgs().record() as
            InventBatch;
        qbrInventBatchId =
            SysQuery::findOrCreateRange(
            queryBuildDataSource, fieldNum(
            InventBatch, InventBatchId));
        qbrInventBatchId.value(queryValue(
            inventBatch.inventBatchId));
    }
}
```

6. Create a report and attach the RDP class as a data source.

7. Create a new precision design and add a table control.

8. In the table control, delete all the columns except the first column and select the **InventBatchId** field in the first column.

9. Insert three columns at the bottom and select the barcode, `barcodehr`, and barcode fields sequentially.

10. Select the text boxes for the barcode field. In the font toolbar, modify the font to **BC C39 3 to 1 HD Wide**, set the size to **48pt**, and set the alignment to **Center**. This is a static way of specifying the barcode setup.

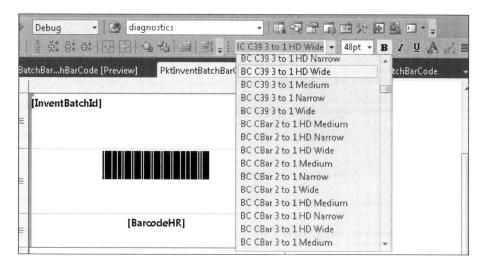

11. Select the last barcode box at the bottom and in the **Properties** window, set the **WritingMode** property to **Vertical**. This will print the barcode in a vertical direction.

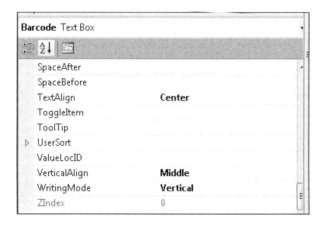

12. Select the barcode and in the property window, set the following expression for font family.

```
=iif(IsNothing(Parameters!BarcodeFontName.Value),"Tahoma",
    Parameters!BarcodeFontName.Value)
```

This will make the font dynamic so that it can be chosen at runtime.

13. Resize the barcode text box to fit the barcode when printed.

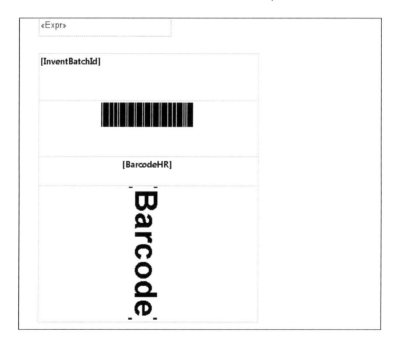

14. Run the report to see the barcode being printed in both horizontal and vertical directions.

How it works...

Dynamics AX has inbuilt classes that support encoding for most types of barcodes, and more can be added easily by extending the `Barcode` class.

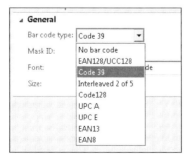

The report here flexibly allows the user to choose the encoding mechanism at runtime. The report picks up the available barcode from **Organization administration | Setup | Barcode**.

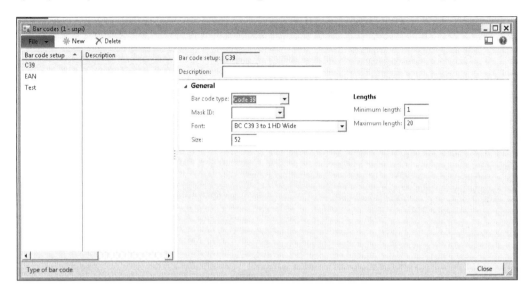

The RDP receives this setup parameter through the contract and instantiates the appropriate `Barcode` class. This helps in building more dynamic and generic solutions, since the barcode report can run for any kind of barcode without changing the font for each format. Also of note is the ease with which barcodes can be printed vertically in comparison to AX 2009, where the only feasible solution was to save it as a vertical image and print it in the report.

Sometimes you may want to create interactive text in the report but still use the standard labels as part of the message; for example, Page 1 of 10 where the string "Page" and "of" are plain strings. In the case of pages, the value comes from the global variable, but you may also want to use labels to construct such texts. In that case, use the String format option. Open the report control properties and in the **Value** property, select the Expression option and place your text in the format seen here:

```
=System.String.Format("This is a label id converted
at run time {0}", Lables!@SYS1560);
```

Hiding controls by context

Among the customizations done in a report, one of the most common is to disable certain report controls by context. This recipe will showcase how to hide a report control in the report design using the context.

How to do it...

1. Create a new report in Visual Studio with the **CustTable** query as the data source.

2. Add an auto design and drag the data source to the design.

3. In the Parameters node, add a new parameter of type Boolean and call it **HiddenParm**. Set its properties as follows:

Property	Value
Nullable	True
AllowBlank	True
Default Value	False

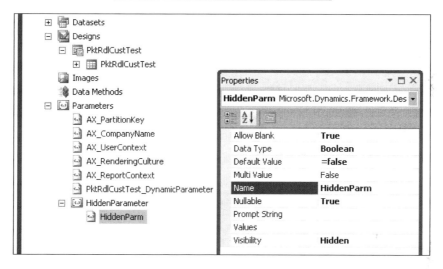

4. In the **Designs** node, navigate to the control which must be toggled based on the flag. In the **Properties** window, set the visible property through expression to point to the newly added parameter using the following expression:

```
=Not(!Parameter.HiddenParm.Value)
```

5. The next step is to set this flag from the controller based on the context. To do this, navigate to the controller class and in the `preRunModifyContract` method, access the contract and set the value as shown here:

```
class PktRdlCustTransListController extends
  SrsReportRunController
{
}
protected void preRunModifyContract()
```

```
    {
        #ISOCountryRegionCodes
        SrsReportRdlDataContract     contract =
          this.parmReportContract().parmRdlContract();

        if(SysCountryRegionCode::
          isLegalEntityInCountryRegion([#isoIN]))
        {
            contract.setValue("HiddenParm", true);
        }
    }
    public static void main(Args args)
    {
        PktRdlCustTransListController controller;

        controller = new PktRdlCustTransListController();
        controller.parmReportName(ssrsReportStr(
          PktRdlCustTransList, CustTransList));
        controller.parmArgs(args);
        controller.startOperation();
    }
```

6. Re-deploy the report and run it to see the field getting disabled or enabled based on the context.

How it works...

This recipe, in spite of its simplicity, will be immensely applicable as an idea in report development to toggle report controls. The best practice to keep in mind is to add the hidden parameter by creating a separate group under the parameters node. This will help in understanding and extending at a later point.

Using AXEnumProvider as the dataset for parameters in reports

When you use Enum as a parameter in reports, it works well within the AX client. However, to deploy it to the **Enterprise Portal** (**EP**), the parameter lookup must be built through the AX Enum provider. This recipe will discuss how an Enum provider can be added to a report and used in parameters.

Getting ready

To verify the recipe output, you may require the enterprise portal configured for your Dynamics AX installation.

How to do it...

1. In the report, identify the Enum field that must be added to the parameters. Drag it to the **Parameters** node to create a new parameter.

2. Create a new dataset and set the **Data Source Type** to **AX Enum Provider**. Click on the ellipsis button (...) on the **Query** property.

3. In the application explorer, click on **DataDictionary | Tables** and select the table that has the enumerator, then go to **Fields** and select the **Enum** field and identify the Enum that it uses. Type the value in the **Query** property in the dataset.

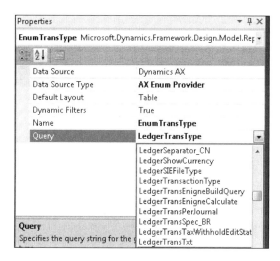

4. This will add a dataset with the fields **Name**, **Value**, and **Label**.

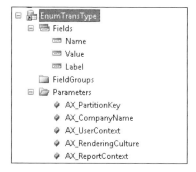

5. Go to the Enum parameter that was added in the **Parameters** node and click on the ellipsis button (...). In the **Select values**, set these properties:

Field	Value
Dataset	Enum provider dataset that was added
Value field	Value
Label field	Label

6. This completes the process. Once this is done, you are good to deploy the report. The system will automatically take care of filling the Enum values at runtime and will display it in the lookup, both in EP and the rich client.

Adding a new report design to print management

Print management allows end users to specify the print format and type (print/e-mail) of reports based on hierarchical relations, such as modules, accounts (customer/vendor), and transactions (picking/packing). The goal of this recipe is to explain how you can make a new report design for one of the existing document types as an option for users to choose in the print management setup.

How to do it...

This recipe assumes that a new design ready for one of the document types supported by print management, say `SalesInvoice`, is available:

1. Open the **PrintMgmtReportFormat** table and add a new record, as shown in the following screenshot. If the report must be applied to a specific country, then fill in the country name.

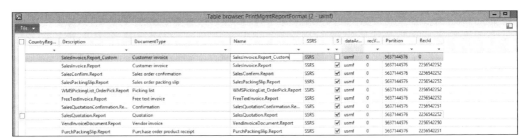

2. If it is required to make this the default report in print management, then in the `PrintMgmtDocType` class, modify the `getDefaultReportFormat` method to replace the report name with the document type. If the report layout is country-specific, then apply the appropriate condition.

```
if (SysCountryRegionCode::isLegalEntityInCountryRegion([#isoIN]))
        {
                return ssrsReportStr(SalesInvoice, Report_Custom);
        }
```

3. Navigate to **Accounts Receivable | Setup | Forms | Forms Setup**. Click on the **Print Management** button.

4. In **Print management setup**, navigate to the **Customer Invoice** record and drop down the **Report Format** field to see the new report that was added.

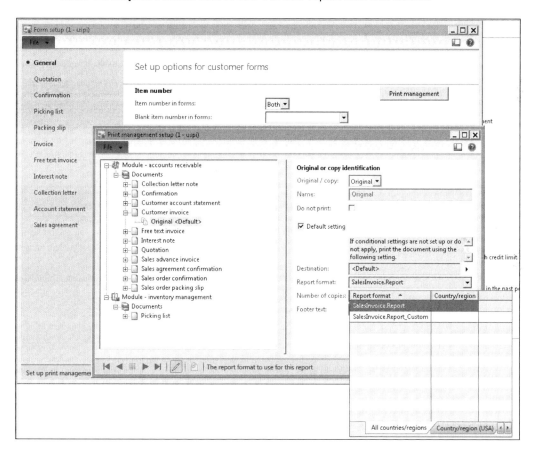

Though AX SSRS is an extension of SSRS, it still does stop a few SSRS features from being directly used, such as resetting page numbers after a group change, using Maps in reports, and a few chart types such as Spark line.

Deploying language-specific reports to speed up execution time

Generally, when a report is deployed to the report server, it is deployed once and is rendered per language. However, large-scale transactional reports such as Sales Invoice, which run in batch operations, can harness this option to speed up processing. Walk through this recipe to see how this can be done.

How to do it...

1. Navigate to **SystemAdministration |Setup | Business Intelligence | Reporting services | Report Deployment** settings.

2. In the **Report Deployment** settings, create a new record for the report and activate **Use static report design**.

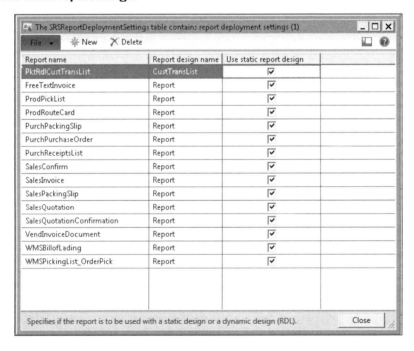

Report name	Report design name	Use static report design
PktRdlCustTransList	CustTransList	☑
FreeTextInvoice	Report	☑
ProdPickList	Report	☑
ProdRouteCard	Report	☑
PurchPackingSlip	Report	☑
PurchPurchaseOrder	Report	☑
PurchReceiptsList	Report	☑
SalesConfirm	Report	☑
SalesInvoice	Report	☑
SalesPackingSlip	Report	☑
SalesQuotation	Report	☑
SalesQuotationConfirmation	Report	☑
VendInvoiceDocument	Report	☑
WMSBillofLading	Report	☑
WMSPickingList_OrderPick	Report	☑

Specifies if the report is to be used with a static design or a dynamic design (RDL).   Close

3. Re-deploy the report to the report server.

How it works...

Enabling the static report design speeds up the report as it uses what is called static RDL. Static RDL is different from dynamic RDL because the labels are pre-rendered. This works by creating a language-specific version in the report server for each language, making the processing of the report faster. However, keep in mind that changing a label means that the report must be deployed again. When redesigning any report in this list, make sure to uncheck **Use static report design**.

Improving the functionality of reports

Designing a report and making it function better relies on getting it fundamentally right. This recipe will cover some simple steps, which when implemented, can help design a better, faster, and more reliable report.

How to do it...

1. **Use query**: Opt to use a query-based report over an RDP-based report wherever possible, and use RDP only if there is a compulsion to use business logic for the query.

2. **Use SSRS for totals**: Use the totals functions in SSRS to run totals, and don't calculate them in the RDP logic.

3. **Use relations in RDP**: Create relations in an RDP table to get automatic drill through in reports.

4. **Make parameters optional**: Remember to set **Allow blank** to **True** and **Nullable** to **True** for optional report parameters.

5. **Use Run on property for menu item**: In the menu item that invokes a report, make sure the property is set to **Called from**, otherwise it may not be invoked from a batch process.

6. **Use SSRSReportStr:** When specifying the design in reports, avoid strings and use the inbuilt function `SSRSReportStr(ReportName, DesignName)`. This validates the design at compile time.

7. **Concentrate on computation in RDP**: Complete all computations in the RDP and don't spread logical computations to the report through data methods.

8. **Limit C# data methods**: Use C# based data methods to make formatting-related changes, and avoid using it to invoke AX service for querying and so on.

9. **Limit Display methods form Query node**: Though you are allowed to choose display methods using the query data source, always limit the number of methods and consider if they are really needed in the report. When there are a lot of display methods or a performance delay is noticed, create a view. This can bring in a significant difference to the performance of the report.

10. **Use query ranges**: Strive to place select conditions as much possible as ranges on the query rather using the Filter option in the report design or by adding if conditions in the RDP.

11. **Use set-based processing RDP**: Evaluation of an RDP requires a query to collect user inputs. If not, try to use set-based operations, such as insert_recordset and update_recordset to process records in bulk to the temporary table used in RDP. These operations are exponentially faster.

12. **Resize images**: The AOS service has a limit of 1 GB for streaming data to the reporting service. Using reports that contain images and a large number of transactions can cause choking or slowing down. Avoid using the BMP file format; use compressed image formats, such as JPG or PNG instead.

9

Developing Reports with Complex Databases

The following recipes will be covered in this title:

- ▶ Creating reports by fetching the data using complex queries
- ▶ Creating reports by fetching the data using views
- ▶ Creating reports by fetching the data using maps

Introduction

In the earlier chapters, we designed simple SSRS reports using queries or database tables. However, sometimes businesses need more analytical reports with a complex logic that would not be possible through queries or database tables. We need to use other AOT objects to develop such reports. In this chapter, we will develop the SSRS reports in Dynamics AX R3 using complex queries, views, and maps to fulfill business requirements. Using queries, maps, and views will help fetch the data in a faster and easier way.

Creating reports by fetching the data using complex queries

In this recipe, we will develop an SSRS report in Dynamics AX R3 using complex queries. This will help to fetch the complex data and show it in the report. In this recipe, we will create three queries and get the data from these queries in a single SSRS report.

Getting ready

In this recipe, we will create three queries which will be further used in the next recipe for fetching data. These three queries will be based on the sales order, purchase order, and transfer order.

How to do it...

1. Go to **AOT | Queries**, right-click on **New Query**, and create a new query named PKTCustInvoiceTrans.

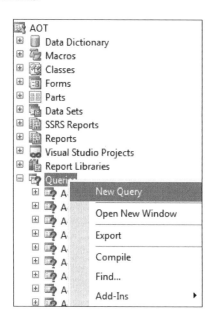

2. This query is used to fetch the data related to post sales orders. By using this query we can fetch related customer details and tax information corresponding to the posted sales order.

- PKTCustInvoiceTrans(ussr)
  - ⊞ Methods
  - ⊟ Data Sources
    - ⊟ CustInvoiceTrans(CustInvoiceTrans)
      - ⊞ Fields
      - ⊞ Ranges
      - ⊟ Data Sources
        - ⊟ InventTable(InventTable)
          - ☐ Fields
          - ☐ Ranges
          - ⊟ Data Sources
            - ⊟ EcoResProductTranslation(EcoResProductTranslation)
              - ⊟ Fields
                - Name
                - LanguageId
              - ⊞ Ranges
              - ⊞ Data Sources
              - ⊞ Relations
          - ⊞ Relations
        - ⊟ TaxTrans(TaxTrans)
          - ⊟ Fields
            - SourceRecId
            - SourceTableId
          - ⊞ Ranges
          - ⊟ Data Sources
            - ⊟ TaxTrans_IN(TaxTrans_IN)
              - ⊟ Fields
                - Source
              - ⊞ Ranges
              - ☐ Data Sources
              - ⊞ Relations
          - ⊞ Relations
        - ⊟ InventDim(InventDim)
          - ⊟ Fields
            - inventBatchId
          - ⊞ Ranges
          - ☐ Data Sources
          - ⊞ Relations
        - ⊟ CustInvoiceTrans_IN(CustInvoiceTrans_IN)
          - ⊟ Fields
            - ExciseType_IN
            - ExciseRecordType_IN
            - AssessableValue_IN
          - ⊞ Ranges
          - ⊟ Data Sources
            - ⊟ TaxInformation(TaxInformation_IN)
              - ⊟ Fields
                - Commissionarate
                - Division
                - Range
              - ⊞ Ranges
              - ⊟ Data Sources
                - ⊟ TaxRegistrationNumbers(TaxRegistrationNumbers_IN)
                  - ⊟ Fields
                    - RegistrationNumber
                  - ☐ Ranges
                  - ☐ Data Sources
                  - ⊞ Relations
              - ⊞ Relations
            - ⊟ ExciseTariffCodes(ExciseTariffCodes_IN)
              - ⊟ Fields
                - TariffCode
              - ⊞ Ranges
              - ☐ Data Sources
              - ⊞ Relations
          - ⊞ Relations
    - ⊟ CustInvoiceJour(CustInvoiceJour)
      - ⊞ Fields
      - ⊞ Ranges
      - ⊟ Data Sources
        - ⊟ CustTable(CustTable)
          - ☐ Fields
          - ⊞ Ranges
          - ⊟ Data Sources
            - ⊟ DirPartyTable(DirPartyTable)
              - ⊟ Fields
                - Name
              - ⊞ Ranges
              - ⊟ Data Sources
                - ⊟ DirPartyPostalAddressView(DirPartyPostalAddressView)
                  - ⊟ Fields
                    - Address
                  - ⊞ Ranges
                  - ☐ Data Sources
                  - ⊞ Relations
              - ⊟ Relations
                - DirPartyTable_FK
          - ⊞ Relations
      - ⊞ Relations
  - ⊞ Group By
  - ⊞ Having
  - ⊞ Order By
  - ⊞ Dependent Objects
  - ⊞ Composite Query

3. Similarly, we will create a query based on the purchase order and name it as `PKTVendinvoiceTrans`. This will help to fetch the data related to the vendor and tax information corresponding to the invoiced purchase order.

4. In the same way, we will create another query named `PKTInventTransferJourLine` which will fetch all the data related to the transfer order.

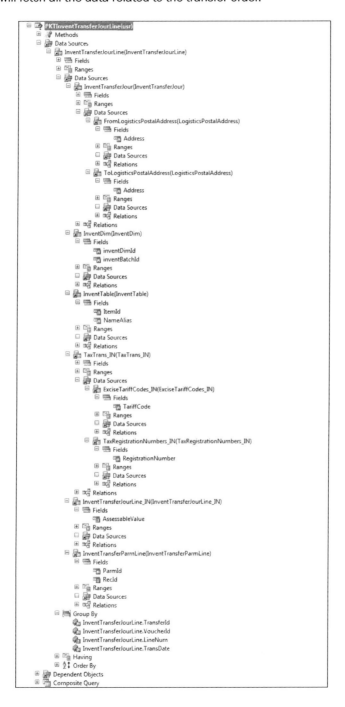

Creating reports by fetching the data using views

In this recipe, we will create views which will be used further on the maps to fetch the data in the RDP class for creating the SSRS report in Dynamics AX R3. Views are the virtual tables that contain the fields specified in the query as the data source of the view. Views store the data, made by joining the multiple data sources, as a table and can be reused in other X++ SQL statements.

Getting ready

This recipe is a continuation of the previously developed report in the recipe *Creating reports by fetching the data using complex queries* in this chapter.

How to do it...

1. Right click on the **AOT | Data Dictionary | Views** node and select **New View**.

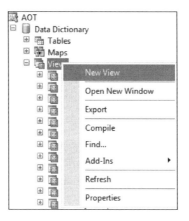

2. Create a new view named `PKTCustInvoiceTrans` and add a data source as query created in previous recipe `PKTCustInvoiceTrans`.

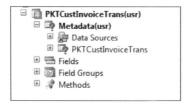

3. Now we will add the fields in the view.

4. In a similar way, we will create another view named `PKTVendInvoiceTrans` for fetching the data related to posted purchase order. In this view, we use the above created query `PKTVendInvoiceTrans` as the datasource.

5. Now we will add the fields in the view.

6. The next step is to create a last view named `PKTInventTransferJourLine` by adding the query created in previous recipe `PKTInventTransferJourLine` as the datasource.

7. The last step is to add the fields in the above view.

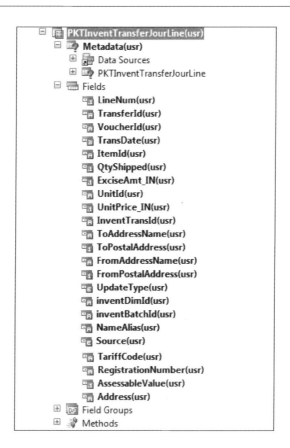

Creating reports by fetching the data using maps

Maps unify access to similar columns and methods that are present in multiple tables and views. Maps enable the use of the same field name to access fields with different names in different tables. We will map all the three view fields created in the previous recipe with the map fields.

Getting ready

To work through this recipe, you will need to have AX 2012 R2 or AX 2012 R3 rich clients with developer permission.

How to do it...

1. Firstly, go to **AOT | Data Dictionary | Maps**, right-click the node and create a new map named `PKTSalesPurchTransferMap`.

2. Add the fields in the map created in the previous step.

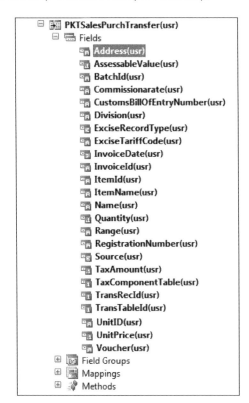

3. Now, we will add all the above created three views in the mapping node of the map and map the fields of view with the fields of maps.

4. After mapping the fields, we will add a method in the map to insert the data into a temporary table.

```
public static void insertTableTmp(
    PKTTmpTable              _pKTTmpTable,
    PKTSalesPurchTransfer    _pKTSalesPurchTransfer)
{

    insert_recordset _pKTTmpTable(InvoiceNumber,
        AssessableValueMST, ItemId,
        DescriptionOfGoods, ExciseTariffCode,
        InvoiceDate, TotalDutyAmountMST)
    select InvoiceId, AssessableValue, ItemId, ItemName,
        ExciseTariffCode, InvoiceDate, sum(TaxAmount) from
        _pKTSalesPurchTransfer;
}
```

5. The last step is to use this method in the process report of the RDP class to fetch the data using the map. We can give the view name as the parameter of the map method and fetch the data from the map using the view name.

```
[SysEntryPointAttribute(false)]
public void processReport()
{
    PKTCustInvoiceTrans          pKTCustInvoiceTrans;
    PKTVendInvoiceTrans          pKTVendInvoiceTrans;
    PKTInventTransferJourLine    pKTInventTransferJourLine;
    PKTTmpTable                  pKTTmpTable;

    PKTSalesPurchTransfer::insertTableTmp(pKTTmpTable,
        pKTCustInvoiceTrans);
    PKTSalesPurchTransfer::insertTableTmp(pKTTmpTable,
        pKTVendInvoiceTrans);
    PKTSalesPurchTransfer::insertTableTmp(pKTTmpTable,
        pKTInventTransferJourLine);
}
```

 For more details on MAP, see the following link:
https://msdn.microsoft.com/en-us/library/bb278211.aspx.

10
Unit Test Class and Best Practices Used for Reports

We will cover the following recipes in this chapter:

- ▶ Creating a unit test class for a contract class
- ▶ Creating a unit test class for a controller class
- ▶ Creating a unit test class for an RDP class
- ▶ Best practices for AX 2012 report development

Introduction

In earlier chapters, we have discussed the process of developing simple and advanced SSRS reports in Microsoft Dynamics AX R3. In this last chapter, we will discuss unit test classes and the best practices used while developing SSRS reports. Unit test framework is integrated into MorphX IDE in Microsoft Dynamics AX R3. Unit test classes are classes that are used to test the feature logic. These unit test classes are written along the business feature logic to test the feature logic. We can add test methods to test each requirement of feature code. Unit test classes have some of their own methods, such as `assertTrue`, which checks whether two values are equal and whether a condition is true; `assertFalse`, which checks whether a condition is not true; and `assertNotEqual`, which checks whether two values are not equal.

Creating a unit test class for a contract class

To write the unit test class of a contract class, first of all we need to create a new contract class and then test the logic of that contract class using the unit test class. In this recipe, we will use an existing contract class; we will write the unit test class of that existing contract class. As explained in earlier chapters, a contract class consists of parm methods which are used to set or get the variables. A unit test class extends the **SysTestCase** class.

We can also check the code coverage of business logic in Microsoft Dynamics AX R3 using a unit test parameter.

Getting ready

To work through this recipe, you will require AX 2012 R2 or AX 2012 R3 rich client with developer permission. You need a contract class for the unit test class. We will use the existing contract class, VendInvoiceContract.

How to do it...

We will first set some parameters of unit test in Dynamics AX R3 to measure the code coverage of business logic, as follows:

1. Go to **Tools | Unit test | Parameters** as shown in the following screenshot:

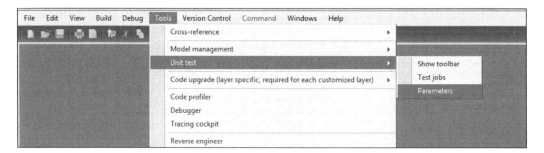

2. This opens the unit test parameter form. Check the Record code coverage option.

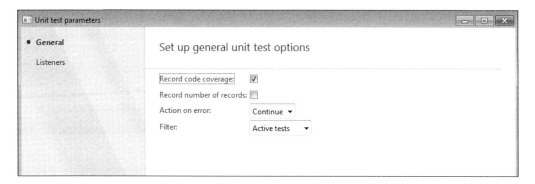

3. The `VendInvoiceContract` class consists of eight methods. So we will write the unit test methods of every method in the contract class. As per standard practice, the code coverage of the whole class should be 100%.

4. As per best practices, the naming convention of the unit test class should start with the class name suffix with test and the naming convention of unit test method should start with test suffix then method name.

5. Firstly, we will create a new class named `PktVendInvoiceContractTest` and extend the class with the `SysTestCase` class:

```
class PKTVendInvoiceContractTest extends SysTestCase
{
    #define.DimensionFocus('DimensionFocus')
}
```

6. Now, we will add the `testParmFromDate` method, which will be the test method of the `parmFromDate` method of the `VendInvoiceContract` class:

```
public void testParmFromDate()
{
    VendInvoiceContract contract =
      VendInvoiceContract::construct();

    this.assertEquals(dateNull(), contract.parmFromDate());

    contract.parmFromDate(2\2\2020);
    this.assertEquals(2\2\2020, contract.parmFromDate());
}
```

In this method, the `assertEqual` method, which checks whether two values are equal, is used to test the code of `parmFromDate`.

7. Similarly, we can write the test method of another method of the `VendInvoiceContract` class:

```
public void testParmInvoiceType()
{
    VendInvoiceContract contract =
      VendInvoiceContract::construct();

this.assertEquals(OpenPaidBoth::Open,
  contract.parmInvoiceType());

    contract.parmInvoiceType(OpenPaidBoth::Both);
    this.assertEquals(OpenPaidBoth::Both,
      contract.parmInvoiceType());
}

public void testParmToDate()
{
    VendInvoiceContract contract =
      VendInvoiceContract::construct();

    this.assertEquals(dateNull(), contract.parmToDate());

    contract.parmToDate(1\1\2010);
    this.assertEquals(1\1\2010, contract.parmToDate());
}
public void testParmWithTransactionText()
{
    VendInvoiceContract contract =
      VendInvoiceContract::construct();

    this.assertFalse(contract.parmWithTransactionText());

    contract.parmWithTransactionText(true);
    this.assertTrue(contract.parmWithTransactionText());
}
public void testInitialize()
{
    VendInvoiceContract contract =
      VendInvoiceContract::construct();

    contract.parmInvoiceType(OpenPaidBoth::Paid);

    contract.initialize();
    this.assertEquals(OpenPaidBoth::Open, contract.
parmInvoiceType());
```

```
    }
    public void testValidateDateRange()
    {
        VendInvoiceContract contract =
          VendInvoiceContract::construct();

        contract.parmDimensionFocus("");
        contract.parmFromDate(dateNull());
        contract.parmToDate(dateNull());
        this.assertFalse(contract.validate(),
          'validate must return false when
          either from date or to date are null.');

        contract.parmFromDate(1\1\2001);
        contract.parmToDate(dateNull());
        this.assertFalse(contract.validate(),
          'validate must return false when
          either from date or to date are null.');

        contract.parmFromDate(dateNull());
        contract.parmToDate(2\2\2020);
        this.assertFalse(contract.validate(),
          'validate must return false when
          either from date or to date are null.');

        contract.parmFromDate(1\1\2001);
        contract.parmToDate(1\1\1982);
        this.assertFalse(contract.validate(),
          'validate must return false when FromDate >
          ToDate, all other contract values are valid.');

        contract.parmFromDate(1\1\2001);
        contract.parmToDate(2\2\2020);
        this.assertTrue(contract.validate(),
          'validate must return true when FromDate <
          ToDate, all other contract values are valid.');
    }
```

Creating a unit test class for a controller class

In the previous recipe, you learned how to write a unit test class for a contract class. In this recipe, you will learn how to create unit test classes for a controller class. A controller class is used for report execution as well as processing of report data. For the unit test class, first we will create a new controller class and then test the business logic inside that controller class in AX R3.

Getting ready

To work with this recipe, we need to create a controller class named `PKTVendInvoiceController` that extends `SRSReportRunController`.

How to do it...

1. The first step is to add a `PKTVendInvoiceController` class which extends `SRSReportRunController`:

    ```
    public class PKTVendInvoiceController extends
      SrsReportRunController
    {
    }
    public void execute(Args _args)
    {
        this.parmReportName(ssrsReportStr(PKTVendInvoice,
          Report));
        this.parmArgs(_args);
        this.startOperation();
    }

    public static PKTVendInvoiceController construct()
    {
        return new PKTVendInvoiceController();
    }

    public static void main(Args _args)
    {
        PKTVendInvoiceController::construct().execute(_args);
    }
    ```

2. Now, add a unit test class called `PKTVendInvoiceControllerTest`, which extends the `SysTestCase` class:

    ```
    public void PKTVendInoviceControllerTest extends
    SysTestCase ()
    {

    }
    ```

3. Next, write the unit test method for the construct method named `testConstruct`, which will return the instance of the `PKTVendInvoiceController` class:

    ```
    public void testConstruct()
    ```

```
{
    this.assertTrue(PKTVendInvoiceController::construct() is
PKTVendInvoiceController);
}
```

4. Finally, write the unit test method for the execute method. The execute method tells us which report should be printed. So, in the unit test method, we will equate the report design using the `assertEqual` method:

```
public void testExecute()
{
    Args    args;
    PKTVendInvoiceController pktVendInvoiceController;
    pktVendInvoiceController .execute(args);
    this.assertEquals(ssrsReportStr(PKTVendInvoice,
        Report), pktVendInvoiceController .parmReportName());
}
```

Creating a unit test class for an RDP class

Report data provider is the most important class while creating and designing an SSRS report in Dynamics AX R3. In an RDP class, all the business logic has been written in this class. In earlier chapters, we discussed the creation of SSRS reports using the RDP class. So in this recipe, we will use the existing RDP class VendInvoiceDP and we will write the unit test class for this RDP class.

Getting ready

To work with this recipe, we will create `PKTVendInvoiceDPTest` class which will extend the `SysTestCase` class.

How to do it...

1. In an RDP class, all the business logic is written in the `processReport()` method. So we will write the unit test method for the `processReport()` method. First, create the `PKTVendInvoiceDPTest` class:

```
class PKTVendInvoiceDPTest extends SysTestCase
{
    RecId mainAccount_11005;
    RecId accountStructureId;
    #define.inv1('inv1')
    #define.DimHier_BalSht('DimHier_BalSht')
    #define.p1('p1')
```

```
            #define.v1('v')
            #define.test1('test1')
            #define.vend1('vend1')
            #define.vend2('vend2')
            #define.vend3('vend3')
            #define.vend4('vend4')
            #define.vend5('vend5')
            #define.Currency1_NT('Currency1_NT')
            #define.Currency2_NT('Currency2_NT')
            #define.Currency3_NT('Currency3_NT')
            #define.Currency4_NT('Currency4_NT')
            #define.Currency5_NT('Currency5_NT')
            #define.DimFocus_DeptCostCenter('DeptCostCenter')

            #define.inv2('inv2')
            #define.p2('p2')
            #define.v2('v2')
            #define.test2('test2')

            #define.inv3('inv3')
            #define.p3('p3')
            #define.v3('v3')
            #define.test3('test3')

            #define.inv4('inv4')
            #define.p4('p4')
            #define.v4('v4')
            #define.test4('test4')

            #define.inv5('inv5')
            #define.p5('p5')
            #define.v5('v5')
            #define.test5('test5')
    }
```

2. To write the unit test class, we first have to insert the hardcode data into tables through which data is being fetched for reports. So, override the `setUpData()` method and insert the hardcode data into the tables:

```
public void setUpData()
{
    DimensionHierarchy dimensionHierarchy;
    GeneralJournalEntry generalJournalEntry;
```

```
GeneralJournalAccountEntry generalJournalAccountEntry;
LedgerEntry ledgerEntry;
MainAccount mainAccount;
SubledgerVoucherGeneralJournalEntry
   subledgerVoucherGeneralJournalEntry;
VendTrans vendTrans;
VendTransOpen vendTransOpen;

mainAccount.initValue();
mainAccount.MainAccountId = 'MainAccountId';
mainAccount.Name = 'Test';
mainAccount.Type =
   DimensionLedgerAccountType::BalanceSheet;
mainAccount.LedgerChartOfAccounts =
   LedgerChartOfAccounts::current();
mainAccount.doInsert();

mainAccount_11005 = mainAccount.RecId;

select firstonly RecId, Name from dimensionHierarchy
where dimensionHierarchy.Name == #DimHier_BalSht;

accountStructureId = dimensionHierarchy.RecId;

//------------------------ Vendor transaction # 1 -----------
-------------
vendTrans.AccountNum = #vend1;
vendTrans.Invoice = #inv1;
vendTrans.PaymMode = #p1;
vendTrans.AmountCur = 3;
vendTrans.AmountMST = 5;
vendTrans.TransType = LedgerTransType::Purch;
vendTrans.Approved = NoYes::Yes;
vendTrans.CurrencyCode = #Currency1_NT;
vendTrans.DueDate = mkdate(21,01,2000);
vendTrans.TransDate = mkdate(01,01,2001);
vendTrans.Voucher = #v1;
vendTrans.Txt = #test1;
vendTrans.Approved = NoYes::Yes;
vendTrans.doInsert();

generalJournalEntry.JournalNumber = #v1;
generalJournalEntry.AccountingDate =
   vendTrans.TransDate;
```

```
generalJournalEntry.Ledger = Ledger::current();
generalJournalEntry.doInsert();

subledgerVoucherGeneralJournalEntry.GeneralJournalEntry
  = generalJournalEntry.RecId;
subledgerVoucherGeneralJournalEntry.Voucher = #v1;
subledgerVoucherGeneralJournalEntry.VoucherDataAreaId
  = curext();
subledgerVoucherGeneralJournalEntry.AccountingDate
  = generalJournalEntry.AccountingDate;
subledgerVoucherGeneralJournalEntry.doInsert();

generalJournalAccountEntry.PostingType
  = LedgerPostingType::VendBalance;
generalJournalAccountEntry.LedgerDimension
  = DimensionDefaultingEngine::
  getLedgerDimensionFromAccountAndDim(
  mainAccount_11005, accountStructureId);
generalJournalAccountEntry.GeneralJournalEntry
  = generalJournalEntry.RecId;
generalJournalAccountEntry.doInsert();

ledgerEntry.GeneralJournalAccountEntry
  = generalJournalAccountEntry.RecId;
ledgerEntry.doInsert();

//----------------------- Vendor transaction # 2 -----------
-------------
vendTrans.AccountNum = #vend2;
vendTrans.Invoice = #inv2;
vendTrans.PaymMode = #p2;
vendTrans.AmountCur = 6;
vendTrans.AmountMST = 9;
vendTrans.TransType = LedgerTransType::Payment;
vendTrans.Approved = NoYes::Yes;
vendTrans.DueDate = mkdate(21,01,2001);
vendTrans.TransDate = mkdate(02,02,2002);
vendTrans.CurrencyCode = #Currency2_NT;
vendTrans.Voucher = #v2;
vendTrans.Txt = #test2;
vendTrans.doInsert();

generalJournalEntry.JournalNumber = #v2;
```

```
generalJournalEntry.AccountingDate =
  vendTrans.TransDate;
generalJournalEntry.Ledger = Ledger::current();
generalJournalEntry.doInsert();

subledgerVoucherGeneralJournalEntry.GeneralJournalEntry
  = generalJournalEntry.RecId;
subledgerVoucherGeneralJournalEntry.Voucher = #v2;
subledgerVoucherGeneralJournalEntry.VoucherDataAreaId
  = curext();
subledgerVoucherGeneralJournalEntry.AccountingDate
  = generalJournalEntry.AccountingDate;
subledgerVoucherGeneralJournalEntry.doInsert();

generalJournalAccountEntry.PostingType
  = LedgerPostingType::VendBalance;
generalJournalAccountEntry.LedgerDimension
  = DimensionDefaultingEngine::
  getLedgerDimensionFromAccountAndDim(
  mainAccount_11005, accountStructureId);
generalJournalAccountEntry.GeneralJournalEntry
  = generalJournalEntry.RecId;
generalJournalAccountEntry.doInsert();

ledgerEntry.GeneralJournalAccountEntry
  = generalJournalAccountEntry.RecId;
ledgerEntry.doInsert();

vendTransOpen.AccountNum = #vend2;
vendTransOpen.AmountCur = 3;
vendTransOpen.AmountMST = 4.5;
vendTransOpen.PossibleCashDisc = 1;
vendTransOpen.DueDate = mkdate(21,01,2001);
vendTransOpen.CashDiscDate = mkdate(21,01,2001);
vendTransOpen.RefRecId = vendTrans.RecId;
vendTransOpen.doInsert();

vendTransOpen.AccountNum = #vend2;
vendTransOpen.AmountCur = 3;
vendTransOpen.AmountMST = 4.5;
vendTransOpen.PossibleCashDisc = 1;
vendTransOpen.DueDate = mkdate(31,01,2001);
vendTransOpen.CashDiscDate = mkdate(31,01,2001);
```

```
vendTransOpen.RefRecId = vendTrans.RecId;
vendTransOpen.doInsert();

//----------------------- Vendor transaction # 3 -----------
-------------
vendTrans.AccountNum = #vend3;
vendTrans.Invoice = #inv3;
vendTrans.PaymMode = #p3;
vendTrans.AmountCur = 48;
vendTrans.AmountMST = 35;
vendTrans.TransType = LedgerTransType::Settlement;
vendTrans.Approved = NoYes::Yes;
vendTrans.DueDate = mkdate(21,01,2003);
vendTrans.TransDate = mkdate(03,03,2003);
vendTrans.CurrencyCode = #Currency3_NT;
vendTrans.Voucher = #v3;
vendTrans.Txt = #test3;
vendTrans.doInsert();

generalJournalEntry.JournalNumber = #v3;
generalJournalEntry.AccountingDate
  = vendTrans.TransDate;
generalJournalEntry.Ledger = Ledger::current();
generalJournalEntry.doInsert();

subledgerVoucherGeneralJournalEntry.GeneralJournalEntry
  = generalJournalEntry.RecId;
subledgerVoucherGeneralJournalEntry.Voucher
  = #v3;
subledgerVoucherGeneralJournalEntry.VoucherDataAreaId
  = curext();
subledgerVoucherGeneralJournalEntry.AccountingDate
  = generalJournalEntry.AccountingDate;
subledgerVoucherGeneralJournalEntry.doInsert();

generalJournalAccountEntry.PostingType
  = LedgerPostingType::VendBalance;
generalJournalAccountEntry.LedgerDimension
  = DimensionDefaultingEngine::
  getLedgerDimensionFromAccountAndDim(
  mainAccount_11005, accountStructureId);
generalJournalAccountEntry.GeneralJournalEntry
  = generalJournalEntry.RecId;
```

```
generalJournalAccountEntry.doInsert();

ledgerEntry.GeneralJournalAccountEntry
  = generalJournalAccountEntry.RecId;
ledgerEntry.doInsert();

vendTransOpen.AccountNum = #vend3;
vendTransOpen.AmountCur = 13;
vendTransOpen.AmountMST = 23;
vendTransOpen.PossibleCashDisc = 2;
vendTransOpen.DueDate = mkdate(23,02,2003);
vendTransOpen.CashDiscDate = mkdate(24,02,2003);
vendTransOpen.RefRecId = vendTrans.RecId;
vendTransOpen.doInsert();

vendTransOpen.AccountNum = #vend3;
vendTransOpen.AmountCur = 35;
vendTransOpen.AmountMST = 12;
vendTransOpen.PossibleCashDisc = 2;
vendTransOpen.DueDate = mkdate(23 ,02,2003);
vendTransOpen.CashDiscDate = mkdate(24 ,02,2003);
vendTransOpen.RefRecId = vendTrans.RecId;
vendTransOpen.doInsert();

//----------------------- Vendor transaction # 4 -----------
-------------
vendTrans.AccountNum = #vend4;
vendTrans.Invoice = #inv4;
vendTrans.PaymMode = #p4;
vendTrans.AmountCur = 500;
vendTrans.AmountMST = 260;
vendTrans.TransType = LedgerTransType::Transfer;
vendTrans.Approved = NoYes::Yes;
vendTrans.Txt = #test4;
vendTrans.DueDate = mkdate(21,01,2005);
vendTrans.TransDate = mkdate(04,04,2004);
vendTrans.CurrencyCode = #Currency4_NT;
vendTrans.Voucher = #v4;
vendTrans.doInsert();

generalJournalEntry.JournalNumber = #v4;
generalJournalEntry.AccountingDate
  = vendTrans.TransDate;
```

```
generalJournalEntry.Ledger = Ledger::current();
generalJournalEntry.doInsert();

subledgerVoucherGeneralJournalEntry.GeneralJournalEntry
  = generalJournalEntry.RecId;
subledgerVoucherGeneralJournalEntry.Voucher = #v4;
subledgerVoucherGeneralJournalEntry.VoucherDataAreaId
  = curext();
subledgerVoucherGeneralJournalEntry.AccountingDate
  = generalJournalEntry.AccountingDate;
subledgerVoucherGeneralJournalEntry.doInsert();

generalJournalAccountEntry.PostingType
  = LedgerPostingType::VendBalance;
generalJournalAccountEntry.LedgerDimension
  = DimensionDefaultingEngine::
  getLedgerDimensionFromAccountAndDim(
  mainAccount_11005, accountStructureId);
generalJournalAccountEntry.GeneralJournalEntry
  = generalJournalEntry.RecId;
generalJournalAccountEntry.doInsert();

ledgerEntry.GeneralJournalAccountEntry
  = generalJournalAccountEntry.RecId;
ledgerEntry.doInsert();

vendTransOpen.AccountNum = #vend4;
vendTransOpen.AmountCur = 280;
vendTransOpen.AmountMST = 130;
vendTransOpen.PossibleCashDisc = 18;
vendTransOpen.DueDate = mkdate(23,02,2005);
vendTransOpen.CashDiscDate = mkdate(23,02,2005);
vendTransOpen.RefRecId = vendTrans.RecId;
vendTransOpen.doInsert();

vendTransOpen.AccountNum = #vend4;
vendTransOpen.AmountCur = 100;
vendTransOpen.AmountMST = 20;
vendTransOpen.PossibleCashDisc = 20;
vendTransOpen.DueDate = mkdate(24,02,2005);
vendTransOpen.CashDiscDate = mkdate(24,02,2005);
vendTransOpen.RefRecId = vendTrans.RecId;
vendTransOpen.doInsert();

vendTransOpen.AccountNum = #vend4;
```

```
    vendTransOpen.AmountCur = 120;
    vendTransOpen.AmountMST = 110;
    vendTransOpen.PossibleCashDisc = 12;
    vendTransOpen.DueDate = mkdate(25,02,2005);
    vendTransOpen.CashDiscDate = mkdate(25,02,2005);
    vendTransOpen.RefRecId = vendTrans.RecId;
    vendTransOpen.doInsert();


    //----------------------- Vendor transaction # 5 -----------
    -------------
    vendTrans.AccountNum = #vend5;
    vendTrans.Invoice = #inv5;
    vendTrans.PaymMode = #p5;
    vendTrans.AmountCur = -1;
    vendTrans.AmountMST = 2.5;
    vendTrans.TransType = LedgerTransType::Transfer;
    vendTrans.Approved = NoYes::Yes;
    vendTrans.Txt = #test5;
    vendTrans.DueDate = mkdate(21,01,2006);
    vendTrans.TransDate = mkdate(05,05,2005);
    vendTrans.CurrencyCode = #Currency5_NT;
    vendTrans.Voucher = #v5;
    vendTrans.doInsert();


    generalJournalEntry.JournalNumber = #v5;
    generalJournalEntry.AccountingDate = vendTrans.TransDate;
    generalJournalEntry.Ledger = Ledger::current();
    generalJournalEntry.doInsert();


    subledgerVoucherGeneralJournalEntry.GeneralJournalEntry
      = generalJournalEntry.RecId;
    subledgerVoucherGeneralJournalEntry.Voucher = #v5;
    subledgerVoucherGeneralJournalEntry.VoucherDataAreaId
      = curext();
    subledgerVoucherGeneralJournalEntry.AccountingDate
      = generalJournalEntry.AccountingDate;
    subledgerVoucherGeneralJournalEntry.doInsert();


    generalJournalAccountEntry.PostingType
      = LedgerPostingType::VendBalance;
    generalJournalAccountEntry.LedgerDimension
      = DimensionDefaultingEngine::
      getLedgerDimensionFromAccountAndDim(
      mainAccount_11005, accountStructureId);
```

```
        generalJournalAccountEntry.GeneralJournalEntry
           = generalJournalEntry.RecId;
        generalJournalAccountEntry.doInsert();

        ledgerEntry.GeneralJournalAccountEntry
           = generalJournalAccountEntry.RecId;
        ledgerEntry.doInsert();
    }
```

3. Now, create another method which returns the instance of the
   `VendinvoiceDP` class:

```
private VendInvoiceDP constructDataProvider(
    Name _dimensionFocus,
    FromDate _fromDate,
    ToDate _toDate,
    OpenPaidBoth _invoiceType,
    NoYes _withTransactionText)
{
    VendInvoiceContract contract;
    VendInvoiceDP vendInvoiceDP;

    contract = VendInvoiceContract::construct();
    contract.parmDimensionFocus(_dimensionFocus);
    contract.parmFromDate(_fromDate);
    contract.parmToDate(_toDate);
    contract.parmInvoiceType(_invoiceType);
    contract.parmWithTransactionText(_withTransactionText);

    vendInvoiceDP = new VendInvoiceDP();
    vendInvoiceDP.parmDataContract(contract);

    return vendInvoiceDP;
}
```

4. Finally, write the unit test method of `processReport` and equate the two
   values using the `assertsEqual()` method to test the business logic:

```
public void testProcessReport()
{
    VendInvoiceDP vendInvoiceDP;
    VendInvoiceTmp vendInvoiceTmp;

    ttsBegin;
    this.setUpData();
    vendInvoiceDP = this.constructDataProvider(
        #DimFocus_DeptCostCenter, mkdate(1, 1, 2000),
        mkdate(31, 12, 2005), OpenPaidBoth::Both, true);
```

```
    vendInvoiceDP.processReport();
    vendInvoiceTmp = vendInvoiceDP.getVendInvoiceTmp();

    this.assertEquals(#p1  , vendInvoiceTmp.PaymModeVendTrans);
    this.assertEquals(#v1                  , vendInvoiceTmp.
Voucher);
    this.assertEquals(mkdate(01,01,2001)   , vendInvoiceTmp.
TransDate);
    this.assertEquals(#inv1                , vendInvoiceTmp.
Invoice);
    this.assertEquals(#test1               , vendInvoiceTmp.Txt);
    this.assertEquals(5.00                 , vendInvoiceTmp.
AmountMST);
    this.assertEquals(3.00                 , vendInvoiceTmp.
AmountCur);
    this.assertEquals(5.00                 , vendInvoiceTmp.
RemainAmountMST);
    this.assertEquals(3.00                 , vendInvoiceTmp.
RemainAmountCur);
    this.assertEquals(NoYes::Yes           , vendInvoiceTmp.
Approved);
    ttsAbort;
}
```

Best practices for AX 2012 report development

The upcoming sections will discuss the best practices for report development:

Report design

The following points must be kept in mind while developing reports:

- ▶ Use templates to design reports to provide a consistent report presentation across the system
- ▶ Use labels in caption and description properties for report controls
- ▶ Use auto design for all simple reports
- ▶ Use a proper report name so that it can be easily referred back to in AOT
- ▶ Use auto design for form-based reports, such as Invoice or Confirmation reports, where a field's position is set to a value instead of auto
- ▶ Include a report design in the report which is not used

AOT queries

Keep these points in mind while developing reports:

- ▶ Provide a field list while creating a query so that only required field values are selected

- ▶ Use a Query directly in a report which has multiple joins and grouping instead of using the RDP class

Data source table

The following best practices must be kept in mind while developing SSRS reports in Dynamics AX 2012 R3:

- ▶ Use the **Regular** table to insert data in the reporting table while using the `srsReportDataProviderPreProcess` class as RDP, and use **TempDB** tables when dealing with a high volume of data. Also, set the **CreatedTransactionId** property to **Yes**.

- ▶ Use **Extended Data Types** (**EDT**) for the table fields to handle labels and other properties automatically.

- ▶ Provide table relations to the foreign key fields to enable auto links to the report. It helps to drill through to the master form.

RDP class

Follow these best practices while working with the RDP class:

- ▶ Use the RDP class to insert data into the temp table while dealing with a complex query which involves multiple joins.

- ▶ In the `SrsReportDataProviderPreProcess` class, use a user connection in the beginning of `processReport()` method. The use of this class is best while dealing with a large volume of data.

- ▶ Use client-based operations such as printing information, warnings, or errors.

Contract class

When using contract classes, keep these points in mind while developing reports:

- ▶ If you need to add any parameter in a report, use the contract class to add a simple dialog to get the user input as a parameter. Perform a validation to check if all parameters have correct values, or to check the mandate parameters.

- ▶ Use proper EDTs and labels in your syntax.

Controller class

The following best practices must be kept in mind while developing reports:

> ► While dealing with multiple report designs, use the controller class to modify contracts.

> ► Process business logic in the controller class and send the dataset to the RDP class.

UI Builder class

When using the UI Builder class, follow these best practices:

> ► Use the UI Builder class when a specific UI is required to be rendered before report generation

> ► Use the build method to add all dialog fields to the report dialog

> ► Use the postRun() method to override dialog fields' behavior; for example, providing lookups and modified events on the basis of other selected parameters

General best practices

The following table provides additional general best practices to develop Microsoft Dynamics AX reports:

Best practice	Advantages
Use query-based reports, whenever possible, for best performance.	A query to access data has the following advantages: ► A query with a display method has no code that needs to run. ► You can query for data directly from a table. ► The filter of data occurs in SQL, which is faster. ► There are no X++ classes to develop. ► You define a query in the AOT.
Return a TempDB based temporary table when appropriate.	In-Memory, tables are not an SQL-based concept, so the performance is slower than when you return a TmpDB temporary table. This is especially true for large datasets.
Use a view wrapped in a query for calculated fields.	Views provide the ability to add calculations. For more information, see View Overview.
Keep business logic as close to the data as possible.	This promotes reuse of business logic. When the business logic filters data, less data is moved through the system, and it demands fewer resources.

Best practice	Advantages
Use precision design for all reports.	Auto design is a good start point to create precision design for a report. Auto design will not create medium or complex reports. For more information, see *Creating a simple precision design* recipe, in *Chapter 4, Report Programming Model – RDP* and *Creating auto designs from datasets* recipe, in *Chapter 1, Understanding and Creating Simple SSRS Reports*.
Do not define a sort or a group in a Microsoft Dynamics AX query.	The dataset returned to SQL Server Reporting Services will be flattened. Use sort and group in the Reporting Services report definition.
Use RDP class based reports when calculated fields in a view perform poorly.	In reports where there is reuse of one or more expensive calculated fields, performance might improve when you use temporary tables to cache data.
Avoid using RDP classes when the data for the report is in a table and the report dataset can use the table.	RDP classes provide extra flexibility but also introduce complexity and potential performance degradation. Use an RDP class when the report data needs to be calculated and complex business logic is required to define the data for a report. When the report data is accessible in Microsoft Dynamics AX tables, then use a query and display methods or use a view.

 For more details, you may visit `http://technet.microsoft.com/EN-US/library/dn280817.aspx`.

Index

A

Adventure Works database
  URL 141
aggregation
  in reports 36-38
AOT queries
  best practices 318
Application Object Tree (AOT) 3
auto design
  chart reports 192, 193
  creating, from datasets 8-11
  image, adding 40
  sub-report, creating 170-173
AX
  long running reports, handling in 254
  VS, connecting to 7
AX 2009
  URL 210
AX 2012 R3 datasets
  vs. AX 2009 reports 209
AX 2012 report development, best practices
  AOT queries 318
  contract class 318
  controller class 319
  data source table 318
  general 319, 320
  RDP class 318
  report design 317
  UI Builder class 319
  URL 320
AXEnumProvider
  using as dataset for parameters,
    in reports 282-284

B

barcodes
  displaying, in reports 271-280
  generating, in reports 271-280
business logic
  about 141
  data methods, adding 82-84
  debugging 86
  unit testing 87, 88
  used, for adding datasource 130-133
  used, for building parameter lookup 136-141

C

caller
  UI, modifying by 72, 73
chart data region
  creating 27-29
chart reports
  in auto design 192, 193
charts
  creating, in reports 24-27
column chart report
  creating 186-189
company images
  displaying 122, 123
complex queries
  used, for fetching data for reports 290-293
configuration-based resolution,
    long running reports
  about 256
  client-side WCF timeout 256-258
  data extension-based timeout 256
  report execution timeout 258

T

TempDB tables
  URL 96
templates 11
temporary tables
  existing temp table, using in RDP 123-127
ternary operator (?)
  URL 56
troubleshooting, reports
  about 260
  data-related issues 265
  deployment-related issues 260
  rendering-related issues 262

U

UI
  modifying, by caller 72, 73
UI Builder class
  best practices 319
  connecting, contract class used 65
  grouping 223, 224
    used, for adding lookup on
        report dialog 62-64
  used, for creating reports 58-93
unbound parameters
  to query, ranges adding from 66-70
unit test class
  creating, for contract class 302-304
  creating, for controller class 305-307

  creating, for RDP class 307-316
URL drill
  adding, through action in reports 84, 85
user defined parameters
  bounded parameters 43
  unbounded parameters 43

V

validation
  implementing, in reports 214-216
views
  about 54
  used, for fetching data for reports 294-296
Visual Studio Tools
  URL 2
VS
  connecting, to AX 7

W

WCF
  in SSRS reports. URL 128

X

XML feed
  Spin-off recipes 136
  URL 133, 137
  using, as datasource 133-136

Thank you for buying
Microsoft Dynamics AX 2012 R3 Reporting Cookbook

About Packt Publishing

Packt, pronounced 'packed', published its first book, *Mastering phpMyAdmin for Effective MySQL Management*, in April 2004, and subsequently continued to specialize in publishing highly focused books on specific technologies and solutions.

Our books and publications share the experiences of your fellow IT professionals in adapting and customizing today's systems, applications, and frameworks. Our solution-based books give you the knowledge and power to customize the software and technologies you're using to get the job done. Packt books are more specific and less general than the IT books you have seen in the past. Our unique business model allows us to bring you more focused information, giving you more of what you need to know, and less of what you don't.

Packt is a modern yet unique publishing company that focuses on producing quality, cutting-edge books for communities of developers, administrators, and newbies alike. For more information, please visit our website at www.PacktPub.com.

About Packt Enterprise

In 2010, Packt launched two new brands, Packt Enterprise and Packt Open Source, in order to continue its focus on specialization. This book is part of the Packt Enterprise brand, home to books published on enterprise software – software created by major vendors, including (but not limited to) IBM, Microsoft, and Oracle, often for use in other corporations. Its titles will offer information relevant to a range of users of this software, including administrators, developers, architects, and end users.

Writing for Packt

We welcome all inquiries from people who are interested in authoring. Book proposals should be sent to author@packtpub.com. If your book idea is still at an early stage and you would like to discuss it first before writing a formal book proposal, then please contact us; one of our commissioning editors will get in touch with you.

We're not just looking for published authors; if you have strong technical skills but no writing experience, our experienced editors can help you develop a writing career, or simply get some additional reward for your expertise.

Microsoft Dynamics AX 2012 R2 Services

ISBN: 978-1-78217-672-5   Paperback: 264 pages

Harness the power of Microsoft Dynamics AX 2012 R2 to create and use your own services effectively

1. Learn about the Dynamics AX 2012 service architecture.

2. Create your own services using wizards or X++ code.

3. Deploy your services in a variety of ways using High Availability.

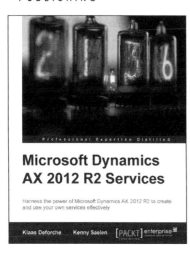

Microsoft Dynamics AX 2012 Development Cookbook

ISBN: 978-1-84968-464-4   Paperback: 372 pages

Solve real-world Microsoft Dynamics AX development problems with over 80 practical recipes

1. Develop powerful, successful Dynamics AX projects with efficient X++ code with this book and eBook.

2. Proven recipes that can be reused in numerous successful Dynamics AX projects.

3. Covers general ledger, accounts payable, accounts receivable, project modules and general functionality of Dynamics AX.

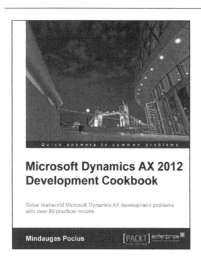

Please check **www.PacktPub.com** for information on our titles

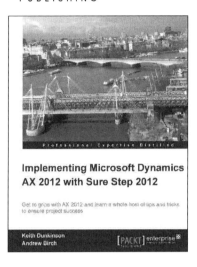

Implementing Microsoft Dynamics
AX 2012 with Sure Step 2012

Get to grips with AX 2012 and learn a whole host of tips and tricks
to ensure project success

Keith Dunkinson
Andrew Birch

Implementing Microsoft Dynamics AX 2012 with Sure Step 2012

ISBN: 978-1-84968-704-1   Paperback: 234 pages

Get the grips with AX 2012 and learn a whole host of
tips and tricks to ensure project success

1. Get the confidence to implement AX 2012 projects
   effectively using the Sure Step 2012 Methodology.

2. Packed with practical real-world examples
   as well as helpful diagrams and images that
   make learning easier for you.

3. Dive deep into AX 2012 to learn key technical
   concepts to implement and manage a project.

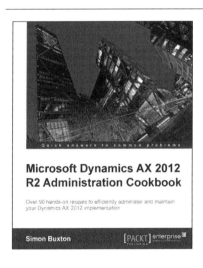

Microsoft Dynamics AX 2012
R2 Administration Cookbook

Over 90 hands-on recipes to efficiently administer and maintain
your Dynamics AX 2012 implementation

Simon Buxton

Microsoft Dynamics AX 2012 R2 Administration Cookbook

ISBN: 978-1-84968-806-2   Paperback: 378 pages

Over 90 hands-on recipes to efficiently administer and
maintain your Dynamics AX 2012 implementation

1. Task-based examples for application and
   third-party interactions through the AIF.

2. Step-by-step instructions for performing user
   and security management operations.

3. Detailed instructions for performance and
   troubleshooting AX 2012.

Please check **www.PacktPub.com** for information on our titles

22938874R00197

Made in the USA
Middletown, DE
12 August 2015